A Good Hot Argument:
the Life and Times of Bud Lucas

H.L. Owens

Copyright © 2023 by H.L. Owens

All rights reserved.
No part of this publication may be reproduced, stored in a retrieval system, or transmitted, in any form or by any means, electronic, mechanical, photocopying, recording, or otherwise, without prior permission of the author.

Registered with U.S. Copyright Office

Published by Maggy's PB Press
MaggysPBPress@outlook.com

ISBN-979-8-9878488-0-7

Edited by Michael C. Livingston

Grateful acknowledgement is made to the following for kind permission to quote material in copyright:

Nigel Stephen Lewis: excerpt from *The Cover Plan Conspiracy: the British and Exercise Tiger 1944 - Part III* by Nigel Lewis. Kindle edition published by Nigel Lewis, 2017.

Open Road Integrated Media: excerpts from *The Fifties* by David Halberstam. Kindle edition published by Open Road Integrated Media, 2012.

Oxford University Press: excerpts from *Wartime: Understanding and Behavior in the Second World War* by Paul Fussell. Published by Oxford University Press, 1989.

Simon & Schuster, Inc.: excerpt from *Exercise Tiger: The Dramatic True Story of a Hidden Tragedy of World War II* by Nigel Lewis. Published by Prentice-Hall Press, 1990.

Twin Oaks Community, Inc.: excerpts from *A Walden Two Experiment, The First Five Years of Twin Oaks Community* by Kathleen Kinkade. Published by William Morrow & Co., 1974.

and to:

the St. Augustine Lighthouse & Maritime Museum for permission to use an image from its digital collection published at staugustinelighthouse.org.

for Eliza

Figure 1: Ruth and Buddy

Preface

The purpose of this book is to present the life of Bud Lucas as much as possible on his own terms. It relies mainly on his letters and other papers collected during his lifetime, historical information that is publicly available, and interviews and correspondence with living relatives. Original documents are quoted *verbatim* except for minor variances in punctuation. The decision to quote *verbatim* necessitated the rather frequent use of "*sic*" to confirm that the text appears as in the original, and was not the result of typographical error. To enhance readability, errors in compounding (e.g. week end, alot, our selves) are not noted and words misspelled consistently (e.g., arguement, chior, suppried, plesant, maby, good by, definate, equiptment) are noted solely on first appearance.

Bud was born into a fairly large family. His mother was a Smith from Surry County, North Carolina.

Z.T. Smith m. Mary Susan Jackson

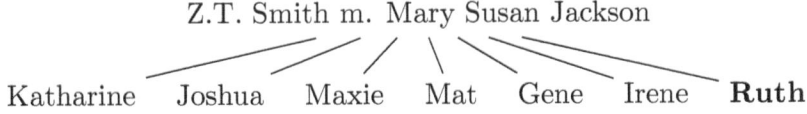

Katharine Joshua Maxie Mat Gene Irene **Ruth**

His father's people were from Montgomery County, Virginia.

Davis Kaywood Lucas m. Josephine Deforest

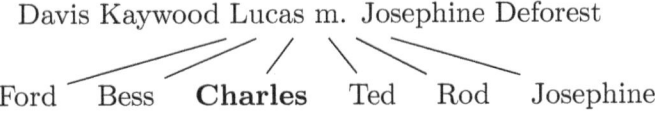

Ford Bess **Charles** Ted Rod Josephine

Figure 2: Irene, Bud, Mary Jo

Chapter titles were borrowed from *A Shropshire Lad* by A. E. Housman (1, 9, 10, 11, 12, 13), *The Vicar of Wakefield* by Oliver Goldsmith (3), "Love and Black Magic" by Robert Graves (4), a Navy recruiting poster c. 1941 (5), "A Skeleton in Armor" by Henry Wadsworth Longfellow (6, 16), "Corporal Stare" by Robert Graves (7), a *Time* magazine headline from the 29 October 1945 edition (8), and "Marigolds" by Robert Graves (15).

Contents

1	The land of lost content	1
2	Newcomers	5
3	The equal dealings of providence	10
4	A soldier is the lad for me	17
5	Choose now while you can	26
6	Tales of the stormy sea	37
7	We bawled church anthems in choro	52
8	Rush to the fireside	83
9	Come you home a hero	114
10	May I squire you round the meads	137
11	My love is true and all for you	153
12	Why must true lovers sigh?	178
13	Leave your home behind you	201
14	Stranger in a strange land	239
15	New beginnings and new shoots	257

16 Thus the tale ended   268

17 Looking backward   271

Appendix   276

> Into my heart an air that kills
> From yon far country blows:
> What are those blue remembered hills,
> What spires, what farms are those?
>
> That is the land of lost content,
> I see it shining plain,
> The happy highways where I went
> And cannot come again.
>
> A.E. Housman
> *A Shropshire Lad* XL

Chapter 1

The land of lost content

Uncle Bud was born in Charlottesville, Virginia in 1925, about a month before John Thomas Scopes, a substitute teacher in math and science, was put on trial by the state of Tennessee for violating the Butler Act, which prohibited the teaching of evolution in any state-funded school. By the time I got to know Bud, he was rather old, and wearing thick tortoise-shell glasses that magnified his eyeballs in a way that was distracting. He would invariably ask me whether I had heard of Charles Darwin, hoping to start an argument. He did this with everyone.

Bud was the second of his parents' five children. In 1934, his family moved to Charlotte, where he sang in the boys' choir at St. Peter's Episcopal Church with Dickie Baxter and Jack Spong, who would one day become the Bishop of Newark, New Jersey and a fierce advocate of ecclesiastical modernization. As "going to church" was something just about everyone in Charlotte did, mentioning Darwin or evolution had good potential for sparking an argument, and Bud did love a good, hot argument. And just like Clarence Darrow, who had helped defend Scopes, he enjoyed calling people yokels and morons (but not to their faces).

Bud was named for his father Charles, who came from a farming community near Christiansburg, Virginia, about two hours north of Mount Airy, North Carolina, where Bud's mother Ruth was born. The two are believed to have met after Charles got a teaching job in Mount Airy in 1921, the year they married.

Charles affectionately called Ruth "Boonie", but not because Mount Airy, with its granite quarry and tobacco and furniture factories, was any more podunk than tiny Christiansburg.

Bud was well-educated and well-read. When he was 15, his mother sent him off to a small prep school (just 135 boys) in Bell Buckle, Tennessee. One story is that Ruth did not know what else to do with him. Charles had died the year before, and Bud was supposedly misbehaving, or "acting out" as one might say today—picking fights and blowing things up more than usual (experimenting with homemade munitions was a favorite pastime). But, the fact that Ruth's parents had sent her and all her siblings off to prep school at the same age seems reason enough for her to have sent Bud. The choice of Webb School was perhaps informed by Paul Sanger, a surgeon and colleague of Charles who was himself a graduate of Webb.

In 1943, Ruth asked Bud about sending the two youngest children to Charlotte Country Day, a new private school that advertised itself as providing boarding-school-quality education

> As for Suzie [Susannah] + Martin going to the Country Day School [Bud wrote to his mother], I think that the convenience of transportation should be the major factor because it doesn't make too much difference which one they go to, although my greatest trouble in the grammar grades was mearly [sic] the idea of getting used to it. I never have + probably never [will] get used to being away from home against my will for any length of time. Therefore the school that is easier to get accostomed [sic] to is best in my opinion. If you think this idea an illusion on my part maybe it's because I changed schools so many times that I have a phobia for strangeness in schools. I remember in the 4th grade I was moved to 4 different places + had 4 different teachers [1]

Charles was in medical school at the University of Virginia when Bud was born. Clinical training and a fellowship at Memorial Hospital for the Treatment of Cancer and Allied Diseases (now Memorial Sloan Kettering Cancer Center) followed. By the time Bud

The land of lost content

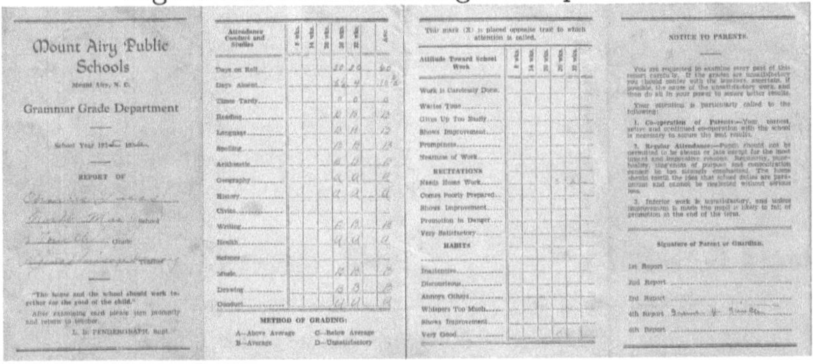

Figure 1.1: Bud's fourth grade report card

was in the fourth grade, he had lived in Charlottesville, Boston, Roanoke, New York, Mount Airy, and Charlotte.

Irene Smith, who signed Bud's fourth grade report card (Fig. 1.1), was Ruth's sister. The sixth of seven children, Ruth being the youngest, Irene never married. She lived with her father, a widower, in the house she had grown up in, at 129 Arch Street in Mount Airy, along with their servant Minnie and her daughter Lydia. Ruth always came home to have her babies (Martin, the last, was born in April 1936, when Bud was in the fourth grade). All the children felt at home in Mount Airy, and looked forward to visits with their Aunt Irene and grandfather, Z. T. Smith, who gave them peppermint candies that tasted of tobacco.

Zachary Taylor Smith was born in Patrick County, Virginia on February 19, 1847. His father moved the family to Stokes County, North Carolina in 1848. In April 1864, he volunteered to serve in the Army of the Confederacy and became a private in Company C, Fourth Battalion, North Carolina Junior Reserves, known after the war as the 72nd Regiment. In December 1864, he was taken prisoner in the siege of Fort Fisher, carried to the federal prison at Point Lookout, Maryland, and paroled the following June. In 1867, he was sent to Winston to a boys school. He spent two years working in Iowa and Nebraska, taking up land on the Republican River that he sold before returning to North Carolina and going into business for himself in Mount Airy. In 1879, he married Mary

Susan Jackson of Mount Airy. They had seven children, four girls and three boys. The oldest boy, Joshua, died at the age of five. He had been named for Z. T.'s only brother, who had died at the age of 23 from wounds received as a sergeant in Company G of the 7th Texas Regiment. Z. T. was 51 and Mary Susan 43 when Ruth was born. Ruth was often heard to say she was raised by her brothers, Matt and Gene. The Smiths sent Ruth and all her siblings to school and to college.

After Irene died in 1965, the Arch Street house was bulldozed to make way for a supermarket. When Bud visited Mount Airy in 1978, he felt overwhelmed with sadness as "old memories of Irene, Lidia, Minny + being molded by my 1st grade experiences all flooded my mind."

> But wherein was the sadness? The nurture and love which Irene, Lidia and Minny gave to me I can not give back now; and this explains the sadness, in part. Bu[t] I know that I can pass it on to others, which I would not be able to do if I had not received love from them. So I am now both sad + glad, both feelings brought tears to my eyes today, I guess.[2]

The other part of his sadness had to have been the breakup of his second marriage, and the prospect of separation from his two-year-old daughter, about which more anon.

Chapter 2

Newcomers

Charles and Ruth's reasons for wanting to settle in Charlotte may be guessed at. In addition to its proximity to Christiansburg and Mount Airy, Charlotte was a strong manufacturing (textiles in particular), banking and distribution center with proven potential for growth. That the family was in Charlotte in time for the General Textile Strike in September of 1934 is known from an item in the "Junior" version of the local newspaper noting there were two new girls at Alexander Graham School, one of whom was Bud's older sister Mary Jo, "from New York." As soon as they arrived, Charles was busy giving medical society talks on various cancerous conditions and treatments, setting up his practice, and persuading the City of Charlotte to open a tumor clinic for those who could not otherwise afford treatment. He reportedly refused to accept admitting privileges from local hospitals that would not offer the same to Jewish colleagues. (Charlotte hospitals would not desegregate until forced in 1965.) The family lived initially in a rental house on Queens Road in Myers Park, a development designed by John Nolen for posh white-collar residents of the rapidly segregating city.[1] In March 1935, they bought the McLaughlins' 162-acre farm "on the Monroe Road" in Matthews, where over the next few years they would build a new house, garage, servants' quarters, laundry, smokehouse, grist mill and mill pond, all made affordable by Depression-era labor costs. They paid $2,000 and gave the McLaughlins a $4,000 mortgage for the balance. In

1937, their servants consisted of a nursemaid, a cook, a gardener, a laundry lady and two farm laborers. Theirs was a vision of a farm household as self-sufficient as practicable, which is to say that they never intended to raise crops or livestock commercially, or depend entirely upon the farm for their living. "General farming" of this type had been the norm in the Piedmont before the Civil War, in large part because of limits on transportation, the rivers in the Piedmont running not to the sea, but into South Carolina.

The Charlotte Tumor Clinic opened under Charles's direction in the fall of 1936, just as Bud was entering fifth grade. Bud's passion for the radio and guns was by this time firmly established, and he was hoping his father would give him a .22 for Christmas (he did). Charles on the other hand collected police "wanted" notices, which he papered on the walls of the grist mill. Regrettably, this odd wallpaper was destroyed in May 1966, when a couple of juveniles deliberately set fire to the mill and burned it to the ground.

The mill was built to generate electricity for the house. Campbell Creek on the west side of the Lucas homestead was and is a shallow affair without sufficient flow for a mill. A mill pond was needed to collect water to where the flow over the gate would be enough to turn the wheel. The Lucas mill could operate for only a few hours before the process had to be repeated. Susannah often recalled how Bud and his younger brother David would complain when sent down to the mill to open the gate on dark winter nights. If that sounds a cruel chore by today's standards, the suffering appears to have had no lasting effect. As David was to recall of those years,

> I had a good sense of personal safety and was tolerated by older persons going about their chores and work. I felt very secure in all situations and expected older people to act the same as my parents. I can not recall ever being disappointed.[2]

The year after the tumor clinic opened, Charles was diagnosed with lymphoma-sarcoma (pharynx), now generally accepted to have been the result of ionizing radiation exposure, the dangers of which were not well understood in the 1930s. Bud had just started the seventh grade. Charles returned to Memorial Hospital in New York for treatment, staying with his friend and colleague Al Hocker and his wife Margaret at their apartment on 90th Street. Both Charles and Al had trained at Memorial, specialized in cancer treatment, and established tumor clinics in their hometowns. Given Al's surgical training in otolaryngology and his continuing study of radioactive isotopes in the treatment of thyroid cancer, it was probably to him that Charles and Ruth had turned for diagnosis and treatment. It was during this difficult and no doubt dark time that the red-brown pencil portrait of Charles that hung over the mantle in the library was made. Al took a series of photographs of Charles in a striped dressing gown around that same time. There were two of him looking at the portrait, one intently, the other with amusement. Another of him lying casually on his bed reading, with horrified expression, "The Doctor Looks at Murder." Another laughing self-consciously as he closes the book, another of him looking calmly into the camera.

The years in New York left Ruth with many happy memories. A "boonie" she might have been, but she enjoyed the ready access to transportation and shopping, croquet in Central Park, evenings spent with friends at restaurants and the theater. She was comfortable with Al and Margaret, she trusted Al's judgment, and after Charles's death, she would take the train to New York several times to seek his advice (as in 1945 when Mary Jo had a suspicious-looking mole) and to visit. And when Al died, she returned for his funeral.

"Grandpa", Ruth's father, died the summer of 1938. Charles died at home nine months later. Susannah, who was probably in Mount Airy at the time, was to recall (often) that no one told her that her father had died. His death made the front page of the *Charlotte Observer*, whose editors opined the day of his funeral, "A generous, self sacrificing, humanitarian and brilliant servant of the common good and friend of man, he was the soul of all that is worthy and honorable and noble and inspiring."

Figure 2.1: Charles

> Few people in Charlotte knew Dr. Lucas. He plunged into his work as soon as he landed [in the city], and was lost to everything but his talented and charming family and a few selected kindred friends and spirits in his obsession to serve humanity through his genius. But those who did know him knew him for a prince in the household of the cultured and distinguished and the humane.[3]

The funeral was at the home, with Rev. Mr. Willis G. Clark of St. Peter's Episcopal Church and Dr. Z. V. Roberson of Roanoke, Virginia, officiating, accompanied by St. Peter's boys' choir. Dr. Roberson had, while pastor of Mount Airy's Presbyterian church, officiated at Ruth and Charles's wedding. For Ruth to have tracked him down and arranged his participation was characteristic, as was her choice of pallbearers: Dr. Elias Faison ("'Lias", attended the family), Dr. O.D. Baxter ("Dick", Dickie's father, a radiologist, attended Charles in his last days), Dr. Paul Sanger (the Webb School alum), John Rowold (Bud's godfather), Harry Whitner (Dr. Hamilton McKay's brother-in-law and family

Newcomers

friend), Dr. E. K. McLean ("Mac", also attended the family), Dr. Walter Summerville (Mecklenburg County Coroner), and Dr. Preston Nowlin ("Pres", at the University of Virginia with Charles, Chief of Medical Staff at Presbyterian Hospital). With the exception of Dr. Summerville, who was busy playing golf, every one of these men would, over the coming years, continue to support Ruth through frequent visits, letters (during the war), and courtesy medical consultations.

Chapter 3

The equal dealings of providence

Faced with raising five children without a husband, Ruth at least did not have to worry too much about money. Her elder sister Katharine had married tobacco magnate R. J. Reynolds, who left her a wealthy woman when he died in 1918. Katharine had set up trusts for Ruth and Charles (and probably the rest of her siblings and their spouses as well) in 1923, the year before she died. While living, they had the income from the trust principal. This infusion of wealth is generally believed to have been a great good fortune, but one can't help thinking that, but for Katharine's assistance, Charles might have—probably would have—remained in teaching. Or that, had he managed to put himself through medical school, he might have had to settle for a practice in Roanoke (he opened a medical office there in January 1930, attending his father for several years before he died at age 57). Anything other than specialize in cutting-edge treatments for cancer such as radiotherapy, with all its hidden dangers. So, although one might agree with Bud, who told a family court counselor in 1981 that "his mother's family had considerable wealth, and, as a result, his father attended school most of his life", to that should be added: "and died young."

The securities held in trust for Charles, valued in 1939 at

$17,822 (or about $354,630 in 2021 dollars) all went to Ruth (though she had to sue the bank to get them). It is doubtful that she then sold any shares (more than half were in the R.J. Reynolds Tobacco Co., which she held out of family loyalty until the $26.4 billion leveraged buyout in 1989 by those LBO specialist bastards Kohlberg Kravis Roberts & Co.). The monthly mortgage payment on the farm would have been $100 plus interest at 6% (around $2,000 in 2021). The income from Ruth's trust plus the securities from Charles's trust would have been about $4,000/yr (about $75,000/yr in 2021), a bit more if she did not reinvest the dividends from Charles's securities. For reference, the national median household income in 2019 was about $70,000.

Ruth had other income as well, e.g., from the sale of timber and her share of her father's estate (about $5,000, $4,000 of which she used to buy Bud 90 acres on her northern boundary). David wrote in 2000 that "My family was well off. My Father, to some discomfort of my Mother, caused, arranged... [sic] for us to live in physical circumstances considerably below our means." If, by "physical circumstances considerably below our means", he meant living on a farm as opposed to in town, having to trek down to the mill in the cold and dark, milk the cow, slop the pigs, feed the chickens, bale hay and pick vegetables, etc., it should be noted that Ruth made no effort to alter those circumstances after Charles died. But, without doubt, Ruth had enjoyed living in New York.

Ruth took an apartment in town for the 1942-1943 school year while Bud and David were off at Webb and Mary Jo was working in the artillery shell plant and attending night school, but that was because of the gas shortage. To make it work, Ruth had to relocate or kill some of the livestock, and return to the farm on weekends and holidays. Much of the winter she spent nursing first Susannah, then Martin, then Mary Jo through mumps, followed by chickenpox. The next year, she asked the bank's permission to buy a small house in town, rather than pay rent, but the bank said no, so she sent "the children" (which was how she referred to Martin and Susannah) to the nearby Country Day School, which had conveniently relocated from downtown to a house on Sardis Road.

(Hence Bud's advice to make "the convenience of transportation" the primary consideration in deciding where the children should go to school.)

To help care for the children, Ruth regularly turned to a local elementary school teacher, Ailsie Mayo Cross, whom Charles had hired to assist with bookkeeping. Ailsie loved to bake cookies and fudge with the children, who found her endlessly bright but vacuous chatter somehow comforting. Ailsie lived in a small apartment in town with her sister Lois. Their mother Minnie Hampton (1861-1934), Ailsie was sure to let you know, was a distant relative of General Wade Hampton (the soldier, slaveholder and two-term South Carolina Representative to Congress who died in 1835). Webb School was made possible for Bud and David with help from Irene. The two were both serious students and did well there. Years after them, Martin would attend Webb, but Martin was never a serious student. Bud's freshman year (1940-1941), he was allowed to bring his .22, but not his "radios, chemicals & stuf[f]", which he informed his mother he "sure miss[ed]." In January, he wrote to David wanting to know,

> Has the saltpeter come yet. Have you ex-pearmented [*sic*] with any more bombs yet. I am about to get my first distinction in Latin. Don't forget to give me a sample of the gun powder.[1]

In addition to Latin, Bud studied English, algebra, geometry, physics, history and science. His best grades were in math and science. For recreation he went camping, shooting and fishing, and played football. Reports home commended him for working hard and declared him a "good boy" with "a fine record for conduct." Bud's letters from this period demonstrate enthusiasm for his experience and for the future, notwithstanding the coming war. "Dear Mother," he would begin, for that is what he always called her.

> I have just finished going to a fire. It was the house of the principal of the city school. I was in my room at the dormitory studying when I heard the sirine [*sic*]. Boys

came piling out of the dormitory and the school hose was rolling out. Some boys hooked it (the school hose) on [the] back of a car so they could get to the house quicker. When we get there the flames were bursting out of the windows like everything. The city hose was late getting there and the house was all ablaze including the sides. The fire was finally put out and a lot of the furniture saved. This makes the second fire I have seen in Bell Buckle.

Have all my things been moved down to the mill? I hope they have. I've only got 108 more days till school is out. I've already made tons of plans for fighting the poachers, so tell David to make sure they are plentiful when I get back. Which do you think would be better, to run a telephone line down to the mill or a telegraph line. A telephone would be cheaper if I could use the old/ones we had in the house. But I would learn more on the telegraph I beleave [sic]. You only have to have one line for the telegraph and 2 lines for the telephone. Let me know how things are getting along. Much love to all, Bud [2]

Mr. Webb knew how to keep the boys interested in their school work and physically fit.

Dear Mother

Just think it's only 24 more days till school is out. You just can't imagine how much I have learned this year here. For English I have to memorize 60 lines of poetry. I am going to memorize most of my lines from the Skeleton in Armor by Poe [i.e., Longfellow]. Last week I went on the camping trip in the smokeys [sic]. We walked 30 miles in two days, carrying about 20 to 35 lbs. of supplies, and climbing mountains at 45° angles. For my first time I sleped [sic] out of doors all knight [sic] for 2 knights. We met some mountiners [sic], one of them was carrying a luger, but they were friendly, & suspicous [sic] of us. They asked us if the government furnished any equipment. I found the first knight out a 5 gallon can with a little corn in the bottom. The spring where we stayed the second night was a place where a still had been. The mash box was still there. The place where I slept the first night was below a heigh [sic] ledge where some boys slept on. About day brake [sic] the guys that slept on the ledge woke me up by rolling rocks down on me. If one had hit me, I am afraid that I would be ten ft under. One of the rocks that they rolled down was about 3 ft in diameter and it just missed a boy sleeping about 3 ft. The minute we entered the mountains every one around there knew it. They kept on swearing that they were mighty fine people around here. On the second day we met two mountineers [sic] on horse back. The one with the luger cursed up a storm but he was very friendly, carried our packs and stuff. I believe that I will take four years of latin because Mrs. Webb said that a chemistry professor said that the boys who do superior work in chemistry have taken latin. 4 years of it.

I beleave [sic] that David will have to take first latin here, I'm almost positive. What do you think about the foreign situation? Do you think that we ought to convoy English merchant ships? I Do? Even at the chance of getting us directly into the war, like it did in the last one. Love to all,
Bud[3]

An April survey by the American Institute of Public Opinion had found that a majority of voters interviewed opposed using the U.S. Navy to convoy vessels carrying war materials to Britain, unless Britain's defeat appeared certain without it.[4] Virtually everyone, for and against, understood the decision to convoy meant war.

Though it did improve over the years, Bud's spelling was always a challenge. This would have hurt his grades in language courses, which he would later say he "hated."[5] In the fall of his junior year (1942-1943), Bud wrote to his mother,

> My English class is very poor this year, so I am going to try to take "trig." if Mr. Webb thinks best.[6]

To which she replied,

> I hardly know what to say about your dropping English. Isn't trig a one term course? Couldn't you continue your English to the half-year exams and then take up trig. the next term? Do what ever you and Mr. Webb agree on, as best—not over looking the fact that you will want to go back to school when you can.[7]

The equal dealings of providence 15

Figure 3.1: Bud with "the T"

"When you can" meaning here, "after the war", because they both expected he would be drafted at the end of the school year. Irene advised,

> Why not drop Spanish instead of English if you have to drop anything. If you are related to the Smiths you do not learn English well in your old age.[8]

He ended up dropping neither course, taking a B+ in English and a B in Spanish for the semester.

By junior year, getting back and forth to Bell Buckle was by means of "the T", his father's old Ford that Bud had fixed up. Its use would have been very limited, with tires in short supply and rationed along with gas. No touring or weekend trips home, and no dating, not that either Bud or David had the slightest interest in the opposite sex at this time. After the war, "the T" would get the boys to and from college.

Chapter 4

A soldier is the lad for me

The war brought thousands of servicemen to Charlotte with the opening of Morris Field, Camp Sutton outside Monroe, and the naval ordnance plant where Mary Jo would work. Area families were asked to welcome these servicemen into their homes for Sunday dinners and Saturday night parties, and the Lucas farm, which Ruth had named "Deverill", was a favorite gathering place. Mary Jo was one of several young women trained to supervise inspectors at the munitions plant in order to free male ensigns for other duty. Bud thought the job would be too dangerous. The plant was, in fact, an extremely dangerous place to work. She took the job anyway.

>Dear Bud—
>Well—I'm a working girl now—started Friday. And the first thing we were impressed with was that we were not to talk about our work! It's all very secret and confidential because naturally if we're Inspectors we'll have to know about it. So I can't tell you anything much. You'd be surprised how much your dumb sister has learned about explosives and mechanical stuff in the past few days of concentrated study. In fact, I think I know more about explosives right now than you do. Shells are very complicated you know.
>The routine day is up at 6:30 AM and it's dark for an-

other hour and a half—wait on the corner for my ride at 7:30—then out to the plant. We show our pass books (we wear badges all the time) and enter after a careful inspection to see that we haven't any cameras, guns, bombs, etc. Then we go to the Administration Bldg. where we study all day. There is a very sweet young Naval ensign who teaches us—he is one of the best teachers I've ever had and it isn't his profession either. We knock off every once and a while though for a smoke and a Coke and chat with the other ensigns and lieutenants. The work is really intensely interesting and I do not regret working there for a minute in spite of the long hours (48 hours a week) and many other inconveniences. We eat at 12 (maybe) in the cafeteria. Every body eats there until the others open up. I am getting very self-conscious from being stared at so much. The minute we enter any place—specially the cafeteria the whole room concentrates on us. It seems that we are novelties from two angles—first—we are about the only ones, except for two other secretaries, who are "society dames" to put it in the lingo. In the second place—we are the first group of women Inspectors in this kind of work. We are guinea pigs—the nine of us. If we do O.K. the other plants will probably start using women and place the men in other duties. It is ridiculous the way people will stick their heads in the doors—just look at us and walk on—or maybe some strange men stop and talk. Every one—maids, janitors, ensigns, TNT handlers, Miliken [sic] Co. big shots, gang fore men—will come by and just look! Now I know how a gold fish feels. I won't see very much of you all during Christmas I'm afraid. I come home and just about fall into bed—specially school nights. And I'll be working Christmas day too. May be they'll let us off early—but then again they may not.

Have you thought about joining the Navy—I was just thinking that if you were you'd better enlist before you turn 18—since they passed that new bill saying you can't enlist. On the other hand there is more chance for advancement in the Army I think. Anyway I'll talk it over with you Christmas.

We just gave Mister [Martin] a bubble bath. He walked in this morning when I was lying in mine and was so fascinated he wouldn't leave 'til I promised him one to night. It was a struggle to get the luxurious little devil out of it.

> But worst of all—he expects Santa to leave him a large jar under the Christmas Tree! Affectionately,
> Mary Jo[1]

Mary Jo, named for her grandmothers Mary Susan Smith and Josephine Deforest Lucas, was indeed a "society dame", at least by Charlotte standards. Having made her debut the previous year along with dozens of girls like her across the state, Mary Jo was always in demand. Young officers with cars and the wherewithal to keep her in champagne and cigarettes tended to fare best. Mary Jo was not ambitious—two years of college would be quite enough–but of all Ruth's children, she was the most status conscious. After leaving business school at Queens and the job at the shell plant, Mary Jo dabbled at working, mostly unpaid positions with the local radio station (gofer), the Office of Price Administration ("snooper"), Red Cross (canteen hostess) and Mercy Hospital (Nurse's Aide).[2] Her connection to the local radio station was through her best friend Pat Stoyle, who worked there.

> I've been loafing around WBT a lot. Everybody is beginning to think I'm a permanent fixture and I'm always being sent on errands. They figure I may as well work. It's a lot of fun and I'm on quite friendly terms with such clebraties [sic] as the Briar Hoppers and the Rangers' Quartet. A job I could really do well, though, is writing a gossip column—only I'd probably have to leave town under guard.[3]

For a while, Mary Jo thought WBT might hire her to be Grady Cole's secretary. "He's a skirt chaser + an old goat but after 9 months at the plant, I can handle him", Mary Jo told Bud, but it was not to be.[4] Being a "snooper" for the OPA was

> right up my alley after being a Navy inspector. I had my first assignment Tuesday—investigating beer in the Piedmont grill. I ordered some and the waitress said they didn't have anything but quarts. So I had to down a whole quart of the stuff—right after lunch too.[5]

After qualifying as a Nurse's Aide in December, Mary Jo moved to Raleigh for a six-week drafting course at North Carolina State. Irene felt the training "suits her talents and she is happier."[6] Her improved outlook may have had as much to do with her social life as anything else. "My work is going fine—also having a good time with the Ensigns and Army on the side", she wrote to Bud. One Army captain (infantry) in particular had her interest: "Floyd [Saunders] was here last Friday", she told Bud, "he is the one!"[7]

Mary Jo's work at N.C. State was good enough to get her an offer from the Pratt Whitney Company "(airplanes)" for nine months additional training "at State pay, all expenses, and $25.00 per month extra", and an assistant engineering position in Hartford, Connecticut for a minimum of one year. Ruth advised her not to accept; "I told her I thought she had best stick to what she had just finished training for—draughting in a ship yard."[8] As restless as she was to get away from home, Mary Jo turned the offer down, telling Bud,

> I do not know what will happen to me except that I will go to the beach before I do anything else. I want to go to Florida and get a job. Moma, of course, does not like the idea. But there is one thing that I am very sure of, and that is that I can't stay here—because the minute I get home I want to go somewhere else.[9]

Later that summer, Mary Jo was visiting her Aunt Maxie in Winston-Salem when she learned that her Army captain had been killed. Ruth wrote Bud that evening:

> Mary jo had very bad news today—Floyd died in France of wounds received on July 5th. She is still over visiting Maxie so I had to phone her. I called again tonight to see how she was + I suppose she will not try to come home until Monday—her birthday. I'm so sorry for her but I'm afraid it will be a long time before she is happy again.[10]

Floyd's death intensified the need to try and nudge Mary Jo into some kind of meaningful occupation.

> Have not made up my mind about fashion school [she explained to Bud] because I should not want to go to New York while you are expected home and it's a very important descision [sic] and should take more than a couple of weeks thought... I have thought of Medical technician work but some how in spite of all the talks I give myself I cannot be enthusiastic about blood and germs. And because people interest me I have thought of social work but I have come to the conclusion that it is because people amaze me and not because I have an overwhelming love of humanity. I reflected on some of my shell plant workers and realized that I had rather uplift the lower classes from a distance rather than from personal contact... Also thought of journalism but the kind of gossip column I would write would bring in too many libel suits.[11]

Among Mary Jo's many diversions in 1944 had been young Ensign Potter "from out at the plant." "He's quite a nice Harvard man from Boston", Mary Jo had told Bud, "but I have an irresistible impulse to call him Pottsy—he just looks that way. He has a car and good whiskey which is wasted on me since I don't know the difference in any of it."[12] Bud did not especially like what he was hearing about "Pottsie."

> I know you don't like Pottsie [Mary Jo wrote to Bud in September] but he asked me to the Coast Guard v. Air Corp football game Saturday and I could not resist. Besides I am trying to sway him to [Republican Party presidential candidate Thomas E.] Dewey because he has not made up his mind. That makes three prospective votes I'm working on. Honestly I am getting so sick of him. But I cannot say to him, "Pottsie, I will tell you the truth. I had just as soon let you take me to dances, dinner, and the foot ball games—and even the movies—but I'll be damned if I want to marry you." It is likely to hurt his feelings and besides he wouldn't use his gas to take me the above mentioned places. Are you not shocked to find your dear sister so mercenary? But he is the only one who has a car and it is that or never go any where. One of the Air Corp looies [lieutenants] has a car but I date his pal which is inconvenient. But do not get cynical about women just from me telling you about how two faced I am...

> I am sitting on the floor typing this on a suit case. My room is one ungodly mess from the fall closet going over. I just can't bear to give away my old clothes and that is the main reason for the confusion I drag out a dress re-solving to give it to charity and I think about how I wore it to the Deb Ball or Led the Conga line at the Club in it or I got it because Floyd liked me in black and I just can't give it away. It's kinda like throwing away every momento [sic] of every good time I ever had. That's unreasonably sentimental. So I just think I'll pack these away until I get more hard boiled or the moths get them.
>
> I didn't finish telling you about Pottise though. He's a Jay Gee [lieutenant junior grade] now and when I told him I couldn't go to his wetting down party he checked by Kuester's [a favorite restaurant in town] to see if I had told him the truth about having to attend moma's dinner party. And he won't take me to the Officers Club Since I went off with the Air Corp one night and he has a regular Gestapo system which amuses us no end. He's even accused me of just going out with him to be going out! Isn't that amazing![13]

Bud felt somewhat better when Mary Jo let him know she and Hutch Sullivan were going out.

> Yes, we see quite a bit of Hutch. I've got a date with him tomorrow and he comes out just about every weekend. I'm glad you like him—I'm very fond of him too and I think the family is. I do not think that Hutch makes friends easily but the ones he does make are fast friends and he enjoys their company rather than companionship of new acquaintances. In other words he concentrates on a few old friends rather than numerous people that he only knows slightly. I'm rather that way myself
>
> Mother and David are going to a talk on the advantages the Navy offers to 17 year olds at Central tomorrow night. Hutch and I are going to take care of the kids until they get out. I don't know what we'll do with them since there won't be time for a movie—probably take them to the Bamboo Room [of the Barringer Hotel] and let them drink Cocs [Coca Colas] while we drink beer or wine.[14]

Hutch was one of several lonely young men who had adopted the family during the war. A cotton broker and recent graduate of the University of the South (Sewanee), Hutch was the only child of Claude H. Sullivan, a physician, and Marjorie Peak (whom everyone called "Honeybun"). The Sullivans had moved to Charlotte from Georgia in the 1930s, and begun attending St. Martin's Episcopal Church, a mission of St. Peter's on East 7th Street, St. Peter's being on West 7th Street. It seems probable that the families met either through this or the medical connection and that Ruth knew Hutch's parents were spending the war at Camp Dix, New Jersey, where Dr. Sullivan was serving. Hutch, like Ruth's nephew Gene, Jr., felt somewhat guilty for staying home (neither met draft standards for eyesight), but Ruth enjoyed Hutch's mordant sense of humor and literary bent (to say nothing of his accordion playing). Nor did she mind having his food ration cards.

Hutch never married. Some have said he asked Mary Jo and she turned him down, but she turned down so many it would be easy to lose track. Mary Jo, a week older than Hutch, appreciated his good manners and deferential attitude and the two remained lifelong friends, bound by their mutual love of gossip over drinks and what one might call an offhandedly cynical, tending-to-bitter outlook. Hutch and Mary Jo's politics landed consistently to the right of Bud's, if not Ruth's. The divergence was not so obvious during the war, but became so afterwards, amid rising concerns about labor unrest and the menace of communism. "We don't always agree of course", Ruth wrote to Bud,

> I think I must be a "middle of the roader" between her [Mary Jo's] Toryism [conservatism] and your socialistic tendancies [sic]—There are more theories which sound plausible and promise to benefit mankind which simply do not work out that way. Human nature—its tendancy to abuse power and to confuse values must always be considered.[15]

Mary Jo did try to warn Bud against what she saw as youthful credulity.

> I can see you've been reading philosophers who scorn the material things of life etc. With few exceptions, however, those idealistic philosophers never starved—and quite a few of them got rich. Maybe I'm earthly (as Mary Denny says) but a man with a wife and babies to be fed, clothed, and sheltered can't spend too much time contemplating about whether he is "above all being true to himself". It takes a man in comfortable circumstances to think that one up—or maybe I'm wrong. We can talk about that when you get back—but you can be ambitious, practical + also have a heart of gold—witness Aunt Irene.[16]

Mary Rebecca Denny of Red Springs, North Carolina, was a professor of English at Queens College and a lifelong friend of the family. Mary Jo stayed with her for a couple of weeks during the war, while Mary Denny (the family always used both names) was at Duke getting her master's. Mary Denny sent Bud fruitcake and wrote to him about English and American literature (Van Wyck Brooks), her students (feeding them pancakes) and Ruth and the children. In May 1945, Mary Denny told Mary Jo she thought Mary Jo might be able to get work as a Nurse's Aide at the hospital at Camp Butner, which was then housing German POWs. ("I'm going to try about July I think. Want to get to the beach with Anne [Smith] + Irene first."[17]) As for Mary Jo's advice not to "spend too much time contemplating about whether he is 'above all being true to himself'", Bud's response was simply, "Boy! Would I like to argue on a few points of philosophy with you!"[18] That summer, Morris Field was deactivated. "[C]an't the Army find the darndest words", Mary Jo told Bud.

> I'm exhausted after two weeks of saying fare well and there's no one left now. So us Charlotte girls will settle down to a manless existence. Incidentally I am now a member of the Spinsters' Club—a purely social organization of younger old maids.[19]

Over the coming years, Bud and Mary Jo would grow further apart philosophically and politically, but, despite their differing attitudes and Mary Jo's growing tendency to adopt what Sinclair

A soldier is the lad for me 25

Lewis referred to as a "derisive gaiety" (see *Dodsworth*), the bond of affection would remain strong.

Figure 4.1: Martin, Mary Jo, David, Susannah, Bud

Chapter 5

Choose now while you can

The Selective Training and Service Act of 1940, which set the minimum draft age at 21, was meant to limit the number entering military service so that no more than 900,000 would be in training at any one time. After Pearl Harbor, 18-year olds were required to register. The bill that Mary Jo referred to in her "working girl" letter passed in November 1942, lowered the minimum draft age to 18 and cut off enlistments after December 5, 1942. It was still possible, however, to "volunteer for induction" and thereby hope to get some say as to one's service branch, the alternative being just to wait for the draft board letter with an assignment to whatever branch was most in need, usually Army infantry, with the Marines getting more later.

Bud volunteered to be inducted into the Coast Guard, which had been transferred in 1941 from the Treasury Department to the Department of the Navy. His eldest daughter Eliza was to recall his saying that he chose the Coast Guard because he wanted to defend the country against invasion. (He may have heard about the young coast guard who discovered a German agent off the coast of New York.[1]) Some have said they believe Ruth "pulled strings" to get Bud the Coast Guard assignment, but there is simply nothing to indicate it was anything other than Bud's choice. Besides, one would expect anyone for whom strings had been pulled to have been given a place in an advanced training school (the three to six months vocational training needed to acquire a rating, also known as "A-school"). Certainly that was something Ruth very much hoped for. Bud, however, was assigned directly to a ship. That is not to say Ruth would not have pulled strings if she could have, but she did not have the connections. Among the many papers she saved ("How I long for an attic!...I'd never have room enough to store things however much I had—being such a collector of junk"[2]) was Bud's original "Application for Appointment as Aviation Cadet" including three signed, original recommendation letters, suggesting it was never submitted. When David was disappointed to learn in 1945 that the program was closed, Ruth wrote to Bud, "I must admit I'm not sorry. It is certainly one of the most dangerous branches of the service."[3] It was no accident that, during the war, ads invariably featured handsome Air Corps officers with beautiful women on their arms. Even the training was dangerous, killing more than 15,000 U.S. aircrewmen. Bud was not even out of boot camp before witnessing the danger firsthand. On "Navy Day" 1943 he wrote his mother,

> There were 3 companies in the parade today ours was the 2nd. We marched down to the parade grounds in our whites. The navy planes were zooming low over us. Wacks [sic], horse petroll [sic] men, marines and we were in the show. We marched down King Street before the reviewing stand. There was a big cheering crowd there. We only had one misshap [sic] + that was the mid-air colision [sic] of two planes. One got by o.k. the other managed to turn his plane around to avoid crashing down main St. only to crash into the bay. He was killed.[4]

Maybe Bud changed his mind about applying to be an aviation cadet. Or maybe he asked Ruth to mail in the application after the recommendation letters arrived, and she just "forgot." He certainly did not lose interest in flying. After a year at sea,

> I've still got that crazy idea of building my own airplane. The last time I had that idea I thought I could make one

> fly now I [*sic*] positive I can. Even though I've had very little actual exp. with the real thing, the things I've learned from boats + the experience I get from my "T" Ford + etc. ought to suffice the actual experience. I read about this Englishman who was making a flight from New Zealand to Australia by way of two islands + while landing in the bay of one of them he nosed over + damaged the wings (wooden) + messed up the engine with salt water. With a book of instructions + the aid of some of the natives he fixed it up + completed his hop. I guess it was reading that book that inspired me on the subject again. But if I don't build it when I'm young I will when I'm old + want a diversion.[5]

A year after he wrote that, Bud and David started writing to each other about buying a plane and constructing runways and hangars.[6] Thoughts of flying resurfaced in 1953, when he considered taking flying lessons and tried unsuccessfully to get an engineering job with Cessna. In 1966, he took those lessons and wrote to Ruth about wanting to "build a nice terft [*sic*] of pasture grass good for landing an airplane"[7] so he could fly home whenever he wanted. Ruth did not share his enthusiasm.

After registering (6'1", 160 lbs) with the Mecklenburg County draft board, Bud spent the summer of 1943 taking a couple of math courses at Davidson College with his former choir buddy, Dickie Baxter, whose parents had a farm in Matthews. Dickie, a Porter Military Academy graduate, would spend most of the war at Camp Croft in South Carolina before ending up with the occupying forces in the Pacific, a lieutenant in Army Air Force Intelligence. On September 18, 1943, Bud left home for the U.S. Coast Guard Training Station in St. Augustine. He had signed on as a Regular Reservist (as had all those who joined the Coast Guard after the start of the war) thereby obligating himself to serve "the duration plus six" months. He started out as a nonrate, bottom-rung Apprentice Seaman assigned to Company B2, billeted in the Hotel Ponce de Leon.

> ...As soon as I left the train station (there wasn't any band) I got in a handsome [*sic*] or carriage or something

and the driver gave us a seris [*sic*] lecture on the beauties of the city. We arrived at Pons [*sic*] De Leon Hotel—it's a classy joint—and got enrolled, had chow, and half finished the physical exam. They drained a 1/2 pint again for the Wasermen [*sic*] [syphilis antibody test]. I'm in Company B2 and I won't start training till it's formed—100 men.

Most of the fellows here are good fellows, some real good and some not worth a damn. You get tex [*sic*] books—just like school and study simafor [*sic*], international code, roap nots [*sic*], splicing and etc.

You get blisters on your hands from rowing and there's right much marching. I expect to get my shots tomorrow. Seven of them.

I haven't got my uniforms yet, but when I do I'll send you my picture. The training will probably last 7 weeks then I'll be shipped to places unknown probably I'll run one of those landing barges or some small boat...[8]

The heavy training schedule and almost daily exchange of letters between Bud and his mother and the correspondents she conscripted to keep his mail rolling in helped the weeks pass quickly. Bud stopped smoking (it is not known when he started) and joined the training station "chior" (a word that appears often in his letters and invariably spelled this way). In addition to semaphore, he learned to wash his clothes in cold water, shoulder arms, march, row a lifeboat, pack a seabag and tie knots. He earned the nickname "Junior", "because I don't smoke, chew + and am not 'full of rash oaths'", and "the first money I ever made in my life", a total of $21, he sent home with the instruction, "Just buy War Bonds or something with it." For jumping a hedge, adjusting his cover while at attention, allowing his eyes to wander while marching, and forgetting to muster for watch (twice) he earned extra duty in the galley and another nickname, "K.P. Kid." Ruth counseled perseverance and continued to hope he would be sent to "school." "I hope spelling doesn't count on your tests," she wrote. "If so it will be too bad."

Despite adequate test scores, Ruth and Bud's early hope of a place for him in radio or gunnery school slowly faded away. If Bud was discouraged or homesick during these weeks, he mostly kept his feelings out of his letters, which were consistently upbeat, detailed descriptions of his surroundings, training activities, shipmates, and the company commander, Mr. Briggs, whom Bud described as "a regular fellow with a sense of humor", and "no more street smart than is necessary to be" with "a reasonable amount of patience", and it seems, humility.

> Because we have come in last at the boat rows every time, Mr. Briggs decided to take the crew out himself. We got in the boat, pushed off + backwatered at Brigg's command. He had the tiller a little to one side so when the water hit it, the handle threw him off balance + he flopped right over the side. He managed to grab the gunwhale [sic]+ we [d]ragged him in. We thought it very funny but didn't laugh till he made a comment on what a fine show he had made. We all agreed that he did.[9]

For the avoidance of doubt about the effect of the military censors on the tone and content of letters sent from overseas (the only letters subject to censorship), the concern was to prevent the transmission of information that could be useful to the enemy, such as military installations, transportation facilities, ports, time en route, war incidents occurring en route, ship movements, etc.[10] If there was any "requirement" to maintain a cheerful tone (and there probably was) it was self-imposed.

After graduating from boot camp in November, Bud was sent to New River, North Carolina, for expedited landing barge training. The Allied invasion of Normandy was just over six months away, and Bud would be there, running a landing barge, just as he had predicted. Those raised in post "shock and awe" America may not realize how dangerously unprepared the U.S. was to enter the war. Although the Allies had long (pre-Pearl Harbor) had the possibility of some form of cross-Channel attack under consideration, there simply were not the resources, landing craft in particular, considered necessary to the task in 1942 or 1943, and even 1944 would be a stretch. So, when the Red Army's 1943 summer offensive finally put the Germans on their heels, the Allies gave serious consideration to the "strategy of throwing everything into the immediate battle in the Mediterranean" in hope of obviating the need for a cross-Channel invasion. But in November, while Bud was at Camp Lejeune, Marshal Stalin was in Tehran letting it be known he wanted "no diversion whatsoever" from the planned cross-Channel operation known as Overlord.[11] *That* is when the Allies began Overlord planning in earnest. Hence the need for expedited landing barge training.

In January 1944, the Allies extended the planned invasion front from 25 miles on the east coast of the Cotentin peninsula to 40, and added two divisions to the assault forces. The extended front would include the beaches known to Americans as Utah and Omaha. The flagship of the Utah beach assault force (Task Force U) would be the newly commissioned attack transport U.S.S. *Bayfield*, Captain Lyndon Spencer, U.S.C.G., commanding. Bud joined *Bayfield's* crew in Norfolk, Virginia in early December 1943 as a Seaman 2/C, just in time for its shakedown cruise.

> ...One of the Ens. told us today that we had to be ready for our shakedown cruise in about 3 weeks but it's very indefinite + we might stay twice that long.
> The Ensign who lectures on the ship to shore movement invaided [sic] Sicily in a A.P.A. named the Leonard Wood. He said that no nation in the world could protect her whole coast line. The best she could do would be to scatter a small force of watchmen along the beach + hold her large reserve in the rear. That's the reason you can't tell wheather [sic] an invasion is a success 'till 2 or 3 days after. The reserves are brought up by the enemy + we have to suppily [sic] the men that we've landed [(]which by the way have little opposition) with reinforcements. In the invasion of Sicily 5 landing barge men were wounded but 2 did it to them selves [sic]. The guys that have it tough are the fellows we put ashore.
> When we land on a beach, we have to ride a wave in then to back off we hold tightly to the wheel so that the rudder won't turn + break as we back off. I happiliy [sic] learned today that we don't stand on the poop deck anymore like they used to do. We stand on the lower deck and look out the side. If I work hard + am recommended by my officer

> I'll make a coxwain [sic] an [sic] have a boat of my own. I think of you all often + wish to be—I was with you. Love, Bud.[12]

"I think of you all often + wish to be—I was with you" would be the closest Bud would come to saying he was feeling lonesome. Even after eighteen months at sea, he would say only,

> Here at the end of an attempt to write I always want to say something about how I feel. The last words are always hardest to write. I'll just say that I wish I was home.[13]

It may be hard to imagine the interminable boredom and loneliness of military service in the pre-electronic age, or the importance of letters, as evidenced in part by Bud's refusal to throw any of his away. "I can't imagine why you brought all my letters home", Ruth wrote in 1945, "was greatly tempted to put them in with the bundles of salvage paper but put them in your drawer." And of course she also kept all that he had written. Ruth clearly understood the importance of maintaining connection, and did not hesitate to enlist support. "Dear Bud", Mary Jo would write from Raleigh in 1944,

> Called up moma last night and, as usual, she cussed me out for not writing you. You should have gotten you a few girl friends before you left—to keep your mail coming in. Not meaning to be pushing you along but it might not be such a bad idea. Sorry that you are missing your cornbread. Seems that they would feed it to you occassionally [sic].[14]

In his book *Wartime*, Paul Fussell quotes Captain Douglas G. Aitken,

> I never realized before what a lot the post could mean and must write to *everyone I ever knew* in the hope that they will write back. (Emphasis Fussell's.)[15]

Perhaps to a lesser extent, the feeling was the same in boarding schools. "I got a letter from Bobby Gilliland [at Webb] today", Bud wrote his mother from boot camp, "He told me all about the football throws [plays]. I would be playing right end on the Senior team if I were there—dammit!" David's letters from Webb covered a wider range.

>Dear Buddy,
>There is nothing much that I can write you, but I bet you have plenty to say. There is only one new teacher up here and he knows his stuff. He teaches me G[e]ometry; Miss Miles Spanish; Mr. Williams English and Mr. Morgan Chemistry. It is a crypt [sic] course. I never have to study at night, and all the subjects are interesting.
>I'm doing a lot of reading about the Civil War. If you get into an argument about it write me...
>The food up here is remarkebly [sic] good in every thing but meat. I even eat liver when they have. The meat we have most is fried. Catfish, tasty? Ugh.
>There is an English refugee boy here. He is about 12 years old. His table manners are horrid. He eats like a starved lumberjack. H[is] table conservation [sic] is as follows "Give me the bread" he takes 6 biscuits "You SOB, pass the beans" We don't, so he puts his knee on the table and grabs the beans in his hands. I don't mean that he takes the plate. He just plunges his hands in them and dumps them on his plate. He cusses a blue streak.
>Their [sic] are a lot of other freaks up here. I will tell you about them later.
>By now,*
>David
>*War bonds and stamps[16]

>Dere Bub!
>I got in my first fight this year the other day, here's how. You know that English Bird I told you about? Well, a boy told him to go mess up my room, so he did. I went up to the boy and asked if he did it (Do you remember how Pop always said, "hit first and talk afterwards"?[)] he said yes, so I clipped him on the chin and broke his tooth. He didn't do anything, but tell Mr. Webb. Mr. Webb is a right old guy so he said to the boy "Ha, Ha, served you right" and that was the end of the matter.
>Tell me what you're doing. Why don't you learn navigation?

We've been having sling battles down on the bridge. You wouldn't believe it, but at 200 yds. I can make a boy have to dodge every time. I've made me a super sling about 2' long. and you can't see the rocks coming to you. The other boys can't shoot worth a damn. I can stand at the dormitory and hit the fire hoses all the time.

What are you interested in now? Tell me more about the coast guard. You say you'll be transfe[r]red in 3 weeks. Where to? Why?

¿Sabes tu ma Señorita?
Escribe me una carta español.
Buena noches.
Señor David[17]

Dear Buddy,

I'm a bad, bad boy. Monday morning my roommate and myself immitated [sic] the fire sirens. A lot of boys grab[b]ed the fire wagon and dragged it all the way down town. The teachers haven't said anything about it. (yet) It's cold as ____ up here.

We had a little snow this morning. We had a holiday Saturday so Mort, Weisse and myself went to Hoover Gap 16 miles from Bell Buckle walking. We the[n] hitched a ride to Beach Grove and then to Bell Buckle.

I've made a tracing of an Army map I've found. I'll mark where we've been on it.

That one punch system really works. I've slugged two guys since the last frisco. They didn't do a thing but cry. If you do it, be sure it is with all your might. Hit them on the Adams apple, chin, or nose. It'll take the fight out of anybody. Most of the last year's Juniors are still here. The Junior, Senior foot ball games are very close 6-0, 0-0, 12-6 and so forth. [Bobby] Gilliland is the star (and dose [sic] he know it) Ellis and Mole are also on the team.

I've been procrastinating a lot so I'm signing off!
Love David[18]

Ruth's attitude toward her sons' sometimes violent behavior tended toward resignation. She wrote to Bud that she was "sorry to hear that David has been fighting. I hope there was sufficient reason for it—He got a B on conduct—that probably accounts for it." Susannah was to recall that Bud and David used to order her and Martin to lie in a ditch, then shell them with walnuts. Once a walnut landed on her head and "Mama just told me to go bleed over the bathtub." Martin was apparently able to garner more sympathy; besides being the baby, he had asthma and allergies and missed a lot of school. David described him as being "a very bad boy with a lot of ideas on how to procrastinate and goldbrick."

> When mother wakes him up in the morning "Maaaaaa Maaaaawww Ha-choo Cough-cough—brrr—brr." "Martin! How do you feel." "O, O, O, O, O" "You had better stay home today." Every afternoon when I get home he is up and well. (I do it every now and then myself, but Mother is rather cold blooded to me) I fell down the steps the other day and Mother said "Don't do that, it worries me" (I'll swear she did).[19]

Ruth was not unaware. Writing to Bud at Webb that Martin, then age 7, was "well and looks fat + fine", but was "so mean we can hardly live with him. Ask Mr. Webb if he will take him next year—I'm about serious. He won't study + talks in school and thinks it's all a joke. I'm afraid he won't be promoted."[20] Martin shared a room with Susannah until she was 11 and Martin 9. Susannah, David felt, was "meaner than a snake." David wrote that the two of them "come to blows quite frequently now and Mother sides first with one and then the other. When I fight them, just guess who Mother sides with. ...Thanks for the valentine. I sure wish you were home so I could have some one to fight with without Mother taking my opponent's side."[21]

While Bud was in training, Ruth was occupied with farm and housework, tending to the children's needs (parents were not yet expected to play with their children) and doing her part to entertain local troops. She also volunteered as a nurse's aide at Mercy Hospital and chaired the YWCA's interracial committee. (The "Y" would maintain separate and unequal facilities until 1964.) She was also trying to learn to drive. She had not needed to drive in Charlottesville, Boston or New York, but now she really was a boonie. What with gas rationing, Mary Jo's becoming more independent, Bud in the service and David away at school, having someone to drive her and the children was becoming an issue. Cars were not yet equipped with automatic transmissions, so driving meant shifting gears manually, and gears, Ruth wrote Bud in October of 1943, "are my Waterloo." Driving from the house to the road was not too difficult, but the highway... Mary Jo confided to Bud,

> Moma's driving lessons are continuing though I wouldn't know if they were exactly progressing. She still clips off several inches of hedge at the turn of the driveway and she is always so relieved to get on our little country road [now Margaret Wallace Road] that she starts lickety split for home and I have to tell <u>Moma</u> to slow down. If she ever catches on to which gear does what she might learn to drive.[22]

The transportation issue probably influenced Ruth's decision to allow David to leave Webb at the end of 1943 and finish his junior year at Central High, which made him available to drive the children to and from school. "It is very nice to be home and on the farm since I'm the only one who can drive", David wrote Bud. "I keep Mother from running all over town. He sho' does, dammit."[23] Ruth agreed that "David is very strict with the gas and is very successful in holding me down."[24] By the time David shipped out to boot camp in 1945, she was driving alone, or so she told Bud, but she preferred to have Willie the cook drive her.[25] The truth is probably that Ruth just did not like to drive and eventually gave up trying.

Chapter 6

Tales of the stormy sea

After the shakedown cruise and a few days leave at home for Christmas, Bud was back with the *Bayfield* crew taking part in amphibious training exercises. Following repairs, *Bayfield* departed New York as part of a troop convoy bound for Scotland. At year's end, fewer than 800,000 American troops had been stationed in Great Britain. By the end of May 1944, there would be more than 1,500,000. Ruth, knowing Bud would land somewhere in the British Isles, sent him *The Adventures of Sherlock Holmes* and the names and addresses of people she thought he should visit. She could not have known how wildly unrealistic it was to think that Bud would get any time off. Once they arrived, the *Bayfield* crew was again busy with landing exercises, followed by a series of short underways to practice maneuvers and various tactical operations that would be used in the invasion of Normandy. A full scale rehearsal for Task Force U, under the command of Rear Admiral Don Pardee Moon, was planned for the end of April. The rehearsal, code-named Exercise Tiger, was meant to serve two primary purposes: one deceptive, the other to get the "green as grass" troops used to naval bombardment and live fire. As with most such exercises, events did not go according to plan.[1]

Tiger was to take place in Lyme Bay over three tides. Bud, who as far as is known never spoke about his Tiger experience, would have been among those assigned to land assault troops on the first tide on a shingle (rock) beach known as Slapton Sands.

> Martial "makeup" had already been applied to Slapton Sands so that conditions there resembled those on the Far Shore [Normandy]: two lines of concrete mine-encrusted tetrahedras had been laid with tide levels in mind, just as in France; steel piles had been driven into the seabed; barbed wire and minefields had been put down, and roads from the beach had been blocked. Americans pretending to be Germans would "defend" the beach against Americans pretending to invade it. Live ammunition would be used, the men firing over one another's heads. The invaders would bring interpreters, and "prisoners" would be "interrogated" for special planted, realistic "intelligence." There would even be simulated casualties, burials, and field cemeteries so that the medics and graves registration units could do their stuff. "Umpires" would report on the performances of the various units.[2]

> In the darkness just past four o'clock on the morning of April 27th, the first of Tiger's convoys, T-2A-1, dropped anchor in the designated Transport Area some thirteen miles off Slapton Sands. This was the initial beach-assault convoy, consisting of the four large attack transports, including the command ship, USS *Bayfield*, and a couple of LCH (landing craft equipped as amphibious headquarters), escorted by five O-class destroyers of the Royal Navy. The attack-transports were loaded with 4th Infantry, combat engineers, and other units equipped to crack open the "crust" of the beach defenses. An hour later, the thirty-man landing craft known as "surf boats" were lowered, ready for the troops to embark.[3]

Naval bombardment of Slapton Sands was set to start at 6:40 am, fifty minutes before H-Hour—the time set for assault troops to hit the beaches. However, *after* surf boats had loaded and set off for the beach, Rear Admiral Moon, for reasons not pertinent here, decided to delay the beach assault time (H-Hour) by one hour to 8:30 am. There is eye-witness and documentary evidence that troops going in on the first and second waves did not get word of the delay, and so were landed at the original time (Bud would have been in the 11th wave going in at the original time of 9 am), that there were casualties, and that the naval gunfire had to be suspended for the safety of the troops.[4] But, this friendly-fire incident pales almost to insignificance when compared with the massive loss of life that came on Tiger's third tide, when German swift boats torpedoed convoy T-4's tank landing craft, sinking two and damaging a third. *Bayfield* was not in that convoy, and Bud might or might not have known what happened to convoy T-4 that night, but, whatever he might have seen or heard, he would have been ordered to say nothing on pain of court martial. Hundreds more of Task Force U's soldiers and sailors died in Exercise Tiger than would die on D-Day. Bud cabled home on May 7. Ruth was relieved because she had "no mail all week." D-Day was less than a month away.

Two weeks after the invasion of Normandy, the family had had no word of Bud. Ruth focused her anxiety on his future education. "When things quiet down for L.C.V.P. [landing craft vehicle personnel] men be sure to ask about taking examinations for some of the specialized training", she wrote on June 22 while *Bayfield* was still off the coast of Normandy. "I don't believe you will want to be a farmer", she told him, responding to his having expressed that desire.

> To live on a farm is a very pleasant life. To make one's living on a farm, in this section at least, is not a very easy life. [Y]our uncle Gene [Smith] does not make his living on a farm. On the contrary, I think it is a rather expensive hobby of his—now your uncle Ted [Lucas] does make his living on a farm. But during the bad years he was about to lose it and if the brothers and sisters had not come to his rescue by assuming the debt—or at least each a share of the debt, he would have lost it—your father and I paid quite a bit, which we could ill afford into the place. I believe you had best have a profession and support for a country place.[5]

By "this section", Ruth most probably meant the Piedmont, which would include both Mecklenburg County (Deverill) and Surry County (Mount Airy), where Ruth's brother Gene had apple and peach orchards and worked as a banker. Montgomery County, Virginia, where the Lucases farmed, was in the mountains, on the other side of the fall line, its grassy hills best suited to dairy farming. Ford, the eldest of Davis Kawood's sons, had, like his brother Charles, studied medicine and become a doctor. The eldest daughter, Bess, married a salesman and moved to the other side of Roanoke, to Troutville, where she taught school. Rod, the youngest son, with financial assistance from Ruth and Charles (though Rod credited Ruth alone), graduated from Virginia Polytechnic Institute in 1926 with a degree in agriculture (dairy husbandry). Wanting to see something of the world, he went north and got a job in the Chicago stockyards. When he grew tired of that, he got a job at Southern Dairies in Washington D.C. He eventually landed in New York, where Charles found him. "A short stay and Charles sent me back to the farm to milk cows and plow corn."[6] Their father had died by that time, and the job of keeping the farm going in the midst of the worst depression anyone had ever seen fell to Charles's younger brother, Ted. These must have been "the bad years" Ruth referred to. The years were indeed bad, so bad that Rod had to leave the farm again to take public work. As he was, in his words, skilled in the use of the axe, pick, and shovel, he was made the labor manager at the former White Sulphur Springs resort, a short distance off the Christiansburg-Blacksburg road, which the authorities were converting to a "transient camp."

> I spent nearly three long years within its bounds. Many hundreds of transients, hobos and destitute men and older boys passed through its portals. At one time more than 380 persons were housed there. For many it was a short stop for clothes and food; for others it was a place of refuge; and for others it was a hide-out, as officers of the law seldom checked the rank and file...[7]

After the camp closed, Rod and others "picked fifty of our best transients and started working on a Work Projects Administration job on the Virginia Polytechnic Institute campus...the beginning of the stone buildings that now house the Agricultural

Figure 6.1: Ruth, Rod, Ted, Weasie, Davis Kawood

Engineering Department." Rod eventually went back to school, got a pharmacy degree, married a local girl named Wavie Harman, bought the old drugstore in town, and became the happy Montgomery County pharmacist, hayseed and historian he was always meant to be. That was around the time that the baby, Josephine, married a lawyer who took her to live in Delaware. Bud worked for Ted at least one summer, maybe more, returning often to visit, or at least as often as he could. Rod and Wavie had no children, but they had plenty of nieces and nephews and neighbors' children to keep them busy over the years. Before Rod died in 1982 of lymphoma at the age of 78, just a few weeks after Wavie, he set up a trust to provide those nieces and nephews and their offspring with tuition and education-related expenses for as long as the money held out. He never forgot the help he had been given.

The family would learn through a story reported from "aboard a Coast Guard-manned attack transport off France" in the *Charlotte News* that Bud had made it through the invasion without injury.

A week after he celebrated his nineteenth birthday, Lucas was piloting a landing boat in one of the waves which hit the French coast. Lucas' LCVP left this ship [*Bayfield*] well before H-Hour and went to a Navy transport where it loaded 25 or 30 soldiers and five bicycles. By the time his wave was going in, about an hour and a half after H-Hour, Nazi 88's [88 millimeter "anti-everything" guns known for accuracy, lethality and versatility] had the range and were dropping [34 lb] shells in the water among the incoming boats. Despite the shellfire, shallow water among old fishing stakes running out from the beach and a hard running current which threatened to broach [veer broadside] the boat, Lucas managed to beach his boat about 75 yards offshore from where the troops waded through waist deep water to shore, leaving behind them, because of the rough seas, dynamite charges they had carried. The Coast Guardsman's boat returned to this ship about noon of D-Day and began a round of duties as a dispatch boat, making trips to the beach to look for sinking LCVP's which had swamped or broached in the landings. Lucas, as other members of the boat crews from his ship, had little sleep in the first week of the invasion. His operations continued on D plus two [days], hours after the first raid by the Luftwaffe on the task force [U] during which a number of mines had been sowed in the anchorage area. On his trips to evacuate crews Lucas saw large geysers of sand and water caused by mines exploding.[8]

Another story about Bud, published in the *Charlotte Observer* in September, filled in some of the details: on the day of the invasion, a mine burst a barge in the anchorage area in two, trapping men in each end, "[a] storm was raging, the waters were rolling high" but "Lucas and his buddies" managed to pull 20 men out of the "churning waters."

> Every night the Germans came over in air raids, and the tracers sent up from his ship and other vessels made a weird background and the falling bombs and the rattle of antiaircraft fire, certainly destroyed any moments set aside for sleep.[9]

Bayfield remained in the anchorage area (about five miles off the coast) about three weeks, serving as a supply and hospital ship in addition to its flagship duties. Bud, according to the *Observer* report, was often "out with the smoke pot detail—a detail that circled ships and sent up misty or murky smoke", likely hexachlorethane based, intended to give the ships visual cover from aerial attack.

Bayfield returned to port on June 25. On July 5, she set sail for Italy by way of Algeria. Between July 31 and August 6, full-scale rehearsals were conducted off the beaches of Salerno in preparation for the invasion of southern France. On August 5, Rear Admiral Moon shot himself in the head on board the *Bayfield*, leaving behind a note and considerable speculation about causal factors that included Exercise Tiger. Rear Admiral Lyndon Spencer took over Moon's command.

The invasion of Provence began on August 15. Bud would have been among the LCVP crews putting 36th Infantry Division troops ashore east of Saint-Raphael. Hard fighting kept *Bayfield* in the area until September 10. Several days after leaving the Golfe de Fréjus, *Bayfield* joined a transatlantic convoy at Oran, embarked passengers at Bizerte, and set out for home, arriving safely in Norfolk on September 26. On September 28, Sm 1/C Chas. D. Lucas cabled his mother,

ARRIVE THURSDAY AT 130 PM 15 DAYS=BUD.

Sustained for nine months by letters from home, books, the nightly movies on board the ship and thoughts of country ham and cornbread ("Whenever I'm hungry I always seem to think of fried ham and corn pone"[10], and "I've often thought that if I ever have to die that it will be on a full stomach with the taste of hot, buttered corn bread still lingering"[11] and, often, "send cornbread"), Bud was more than ready to be back at Deverill farm.

While Bud had been on smoke pot detail, Martin and Susannah had been recovering from German measles, Ruth had been seeking permission from the War Priorities Board to build a four-room house on the knoll off the mill road, Mary Jo had been training to do canteen work at Morris Field, the county health officer, Dr. Hagaman, had been closing theaters, swimming pools, beaches and other gathering places to children 12 and under to prevent the spread of polio, and Camp Sutton had begun receiving Italian prisoners of war. "They are now termed co-belligerents", Ruth wrote Bud, "Heaven knows it is a problem, but I am opposed to any sob stuff about them, and it is beginning."[12]

While Bud had been rehearsing for the invasion of Provence, Ruth and the children had been visiting Aunt Irene at Myrtle Beach.

> The children are having a wonderful time. They went up to the swash last night + this morning + caught 15 crabs in all we had them for lunch today. They bath[e] morning + late afternoon and we have the usual struggle to prevent too bad sunburn.[13]

The "polio quarantine" was lifted while Bud was in transit. Summer over, David and the children were ready to get back to school. "We are all in harness again", Ruth wrote Bud, "and how I hate it!"[14]

Meanwhile, back in Europe, the British Second Army was liberating Brussels and the port of Antwerp. From the 12th Field Hospital in Cerfontaine, one Army Captain Maurice Rosenbaum took time to write to a sailor he hardly knew.

> Dear Buddy,
> Last June Mrs. Rosenbaum visited your Aunt Irene in Myrtle Beach—she sent me your address.
> I gathered from the letter your family is proud of your work in the war in the Navy + they feel you've grown into a fine man. I last saw you (I think) when you were about 12 years old + your Dad had gotten you your first rifle—I recall how proud he was of you + how he was helping you "grow-up".
> Of all the people I've lived + worked with, I know of only three I think of as "big men"—your Dad was one of that three. He was "big" because he understood human nature + knew how to do only "kindness" to others. He could see the good in people + knew how to overlook their faults

+ shortcomings; he did for others rather than ask others to do for him. He was "big" because he had a brilliant mind + used it to seek the truth in his chosen field of work.

If you are only one half the man your Dad was—then you're ok.—I hope as the years pass you'll take up where he left off—for he was, indeed, gifted + 'tis reasonable to assume you've inherited some of that mind that was his.

I've seen so much of death + destruction in England, in France, + in Belgium it has done me good to sit on my cot + write of your dad + recall the several months I knew him in 1937 + 1938—it makes me feel that some good in the world in spite of war etc.

The best of luck to you,
Maurice Rosenbaum[15]

Bud was home just long enough to sit for his portrait and be stuffed with cornbread and homemade butter. Francis Dayrell Kortheuer (1906-1995), an Episcopalian and former New Yorker, had moved to Charlotte along with his wife Katheryn in 1937 to paint portraits. He had painted Mary Jo, and would later paint David and Susannah. Ruth told Bud she thought "Mr. Kortheuer considers your portrait one of the very best things he has ever done and so do I."[16] To Ruth's delight, the portrait was on display in the drawing room during Christmas and dutifully admired by all visitors.

Knowing he would not be back for Christmas, Ruth and Mary Jo took the bus up to Norfolk to visit him. On November 7, *Bayfield* set out for Pearl Harbor via the Panama Canal. In December, just as *Bayfield* was beginning six weeks practicing amphibious landings in Maui, a riot erupted in Athens after Greek police, with British troops standing by, opened fire on a pro-leftist demonstration against the British-backed Premier Papandreou's demand to disarm in advance of the return of the Greek government (King George II) from exile. Twenty-eight civilians were killed and dozens injured. "By nightfall...British troops had declared martial law, imposed a curfew, disarmed 800 guerillas."[17] Ruth commented on the incident in a letter to Bud. "The British people, thank heaven, do not approve of their government's policy in Greece but, of course, neither do they [or] we like to see communism rise up to replace the government in every liberated country—certainly the British have chosen the worst possible means of combating it."[18] Bud saw things differently.

> Concerning the British foriegn [sic] policy in Greece—one can at least say it's forceful while the U.S. with the worlds greatest navy + best army is so damn timid in her diplomatic relations with Russia, South America, + every other little half pint country on the globe. Britan [sic] has shown us that she has the guts to use force when she thinks it necessary + she doesn't go around to see if Stalin will approve like we most likely would have. Won't we ever get over the fact that we are not the peace maker of all nations, that we can not do as Britan has done to Greece because of the "God can do no wrong" idea we have of ourselves.[19]

A few days later he wrote:

> [T]the British treatment of the Greek situation deserves our interst [sic] + concern + also our admiration. I have been trying to think of a principal [sic] that we are fighting for that would give a reason for the British polocy [sic]. The only one I can think of is "Make the world safe for Democracy" + the British are using the only effective method left to them. It is plain to me now that a form of government can survive only if it has sufficient armed power behind it. This means that we must have on hand + be willing to give up men + equiptment [sic] at any time. And if we have learned anything from experience the sooner the better or better "a stitch in time saves nine." I say, "Bully for the British + may our foreign policy some day be as forceful."[20]

Ruth remained unconvinced.

> ...I was greatly interested in your views on the British policy in Greece tho' not exactly in agreement. Certainly Mr. C[hurchill]. has won my sincere admiration for his honest + forthright action in going to Athens [on Christmas Day, in response to outrage over his "swindle democracy" remarks to the House of Commons[21]] + there bowing to the manifest will of resistance forces—certainly too his actions

at the first was as much motivated by a desire to reseat George (who is not a Greek) as king, as by a desire to fight communism. The result seemed to me to be a help to communistic forces rather than what we all desire—the displacement [here the letter paper switches from beige to blue] (I seem to have run out of paper) of such forces by a truly democratic form of government such as we enjoy. I started to put [G]reat Britain in—certainly England has a government more democratic than ours—but then there is India and other sections of the Empire.

>   It is all too much for me, I confess—I know that I have no right to express my opinions as freely as I do because it is mostly in criticism + I do not even guess at the solution. I am however much too interested to be silent—and I do try to be unprejudiced, except in the cause of justice and the liberty of each individual to win with his own mind + hands the best that he has it in him to acheive [sic]—

>   Try to write more often Buddy—when you miss a few days it is harder to pick up the thread—harder to write the next letter—of course I know there are times when you can't.[22]

Before receiving the above, Bud wrote to clarify his position further.

>   ...A few letters ago I expressed my views on the Greek incident + I think that I ought to make my views clearer because Mary Jo tells me that you disagree. First I don't think that we know the whole story. W.C. says that the E.L.A.S. inc. had for a long time planned to march into Athens and take over the goverment [sic] when they were liberated—wheather [sic] the majority of the Greeks favored the goverment that would be set up is another thing—that's the wrong way to set one up to begin with. But I'm not so interested in which side wins or not—it's this—The British have or at least one of them has (viz W.C.) definate [sic] ideas + objectives about what he is going to do. I don't think there are very many people who know what the very best thing to do would be, but they must have a plan + follow it with every thing they have got right or wrong.

>   What we, the people of the U.S. need, is a policy—a foreign policy that every one knows about + can fight +

> work for. F.D.R. has not shown us a copy of his famed Atlantic charter. W.C. stood up + stated his policy for Greece + he tried his darndest to stand by it—that [sic] what I ment [sic] when I said "bully for the British."...
> ...I'm glad you don't agree with me for one reason, because now we have something to argue about.[23]

Perhaps even more than country ham and cornbread, Bud missed lively conversations, "arguements", like the ones at home.

> I always like a good hot arguement [he told his mother] + there never seem [sic] to be enough here on board ship. I even have to force them sometimes by making questionable statements. They are usually pretty hard to defend but it's an arguement.[24]

In the Lucas household, "making questionable statements", or as some would say, being provocative, was just standard fare, like offering someone a chair or something to drink. It was a way of being hospitable, "entertaining" or a "good guest" to start a conversation about something you had read in the paper or in a book, or heard on the radio. This was how Lucases tried on new ideas, learned to persuade, identify fallacies, hone arguments. What Bud missed was just the sort of scene Hutch described in a letter: everyone save Bud in the library at Deverill, one evening after supper,

> [we] got into an argument on the subjects of India, the housing problem in Charlotte, the race question, industrialism, the British Empire, Greece, Turkey etc!!! I am sure that you can see David now! Honestly, he must even DREAM politics. It goes without saying that I got the worst of the argument since I am not an idealist in such matter but a pessimist. After David had gotten the best of us he went on up to bed in triumph. When I went up to bed around twelve o'clock I thought he was asleep so I cut the light on in the bathroom to undress by. Just as I was getting in bed he pops up and says, "Hutch, what do you think about compulsory military training after the war?"[25]

Bud hardly needed to remind his mother that December 25, 1944, "will be the first Christmas that I've been away" from home. "For my Christmas spirit I have to remember last Christmas + these are the things I remember best."

> Going out with the kids to pick out the tree + breathing the cold, stimulating air, I remembered how much better this was than just buying one. It was more our tree because we had choosen [sic] it from our own land, cut it down + dragged it home ourselves. We took pride in it. Decorating was fun; we all put on something + agreed on the final result.[26]

The tree was also "more our tree" because it was a naturally growing red cedar, rather than a commercial, cone-shaved balsam or blue spruce trucked in from Ashe County and sold at lots in town. While fresh, the tree's feathery foliage supported ornaments, but as the tree dried out, the limbs would gradually droop. By the fourth or fifth day of Christmas, one would start to hear the intermittent "tinkle...pow!" of colored glass falling through the tree and hitting the hardwood floor, a sad reminder that the holiday was nearly over, and soon it would be back to school.

The Navy wisely sent the off-duty sailors in Pearl Harbor camping for Christmas.

> Dear Mother, My Christmas on the camping trip was fine. I missed you all + home but I felt lucky to have had somthing extra that day. We had swimming in the surf, games, shows + movies + also an excellent xmas dinner. An exceptional attraction to that was shrimp cocktail. I had the most fun riding the surf. It would shoot you in very fast for about 30 ft then if you didn't jump up it would suck you right back in. One fellow rode in so fast that [he] couldn't avoid + hit a boy standing on the beach. He recovered but was more careful. The U.S.O. show was one that Mr. Clark [Rector of St. Peter's Episcopal Church in Charlotte] wouldn't approve of but I had nothing else to do + you just can't just sit solem [sic] faced when the others around you are so jolly. I thought how much the meaning of Christmas had changed in a little over 19 centuries. Any way, when

Figure 6.2: LCVP aka "Higgins Boat"

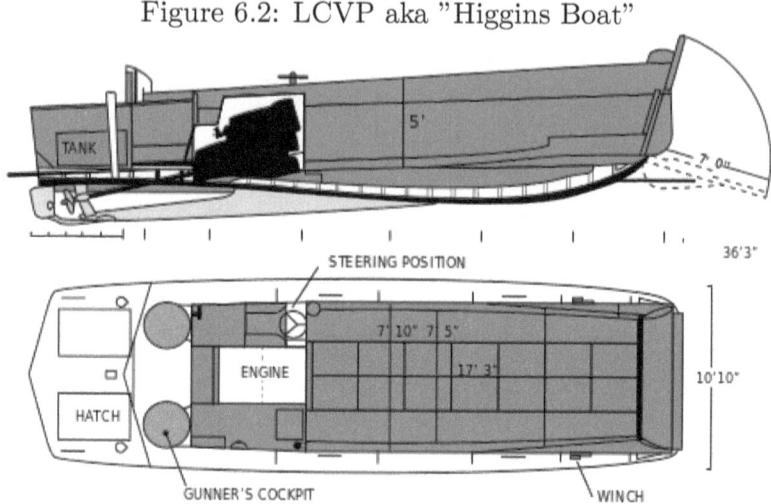

I got back, I let off my home sick steam by singing Grand Ol' Opera [sic] to the accomptiment [sic] of a guitar. I felt better afterwards even if I did act a little silly anyway the gang liked it. Love, Bud[27]

Running a surf boat (Fig. 6.2[28]) in the warmer waters of Hawaii was a break from the 50° seas around the British Isles. Bud described "how I'm occupying my time" in a letter to Hutch.

> ...I am one of four sailors on a barge, as you probably already know. The other three men are very likeable fellows and are just as salty as I think I am. And we are convinced of that more + more because of late we have had some fairly rough weather to prove our skill. It is dangerous when it's rough + we know it + enjoy it. The high waves make our boat roll + turn 'till anyone else might think that it would turn over. When we hit a wave head on with our flat ramp—smack!—we make a mighty splash then the wind whipps [sic] the water over us (+troops if any) in torrents. We love it + make the barge go faster so the splashes will be bigger. Once in a hurry I slipped roughly by a soldier sitting on the engine hatch. He was in the way so the rest of the crew bumped him around too. After a while I

saw his name on his field glass box with Lt. Col. before it. We had a good laugh later recalling that the motor mac [Motor Machinist's Mate or MOMM] had slipped + pushed his helmet over his face...[29]

Despite enjoying the boat division, Bud wanted more. At the end of November, he told his mother he had applied for admission to the Coast Guard Academy Preparatory School, a 3-month program designed to "prepare [enlisted] men for the competitive examinations held annually for entrance to the Coast Guard Academy" in Groton, Connecticut.[30]

> Where formally [sic] I had but one iron in the fire (radio tech) now I have two + that is the academy that you wanted me to look into some time ago. An announcement for the need has even reached the "B". I am doing all in my power to go. This ammounting [sic] to worrieing [sic] my division officer every day, asking him quesions [sic]. Today I told him that I didn't think they were doing much about it. He thought they were. The other boys that want it just want to go home. Of course that baits their hook for me too, but I plan to see it through.[31]

In December, the captain told Bud he'd been turned down because he lacked chemistry, but he could apply for the six-month program some time in the spring. Knowing he could not count on acceptance, or on being selected for the radio tech school, he talked the chief storekeeper into letting him strike (qualify on-the-job) for the SK rating, even though this would take him out of the boat division. He started New Years' Day 1945.

Chapter 7

We bawled church anthems in choro

Dear Mother,

I am now striking for store keeper. Today was my first day of it + I think I'm going to like it. As I told you Blackwood is in + has made 3rd class. I am starting out as "Jack of the dust" [i.e., in the storeroom] but it isn't so bad as it sounds, at least not yet. I have the keys to the can goods rooms + have to go down every time anyone wants any stores. You can leave off the Bt. 1 of my address because I am out of the boat division. Now it's S-1 Div. Most of the store keepers spend their time in the office + even at night to write letters etc. as I'm doing now. I'll have less time to read books + etc. now than I did have, but some how I think that maybe I'll like it better. Any way if I don't learn anything else I'll learn how to type. Today I learned what key I'm pressing without peeping.

My sack number was changed again for the 3rd time + believe it or knot [*sic*] for the 3rd time I got a top sack again. From now on I think that I'll be able to write more timely.

Love, Bud[1]

The change suited him, though it did require a period of adjustment.

My job is fairly routine now + I like it. I am able to keep

a little cleaner + I like the men that are over me because they give me credit for the little ability I do have + often for more than I've got for one of many reasons. My typing is progressing fine + in a few months I should be fairly average...[2]

...Well, today I have been cussed out left + right for not being generally "on the ball", but I'm learning. My General Quarters station is very much more important than it was; now my job is to take over anyone of the fire control circuits in case the man operating that circuit is sick or otherwise disable [sic]...[3]

The boats went over today + for the first time I was not in one. I felt like I was missing out on a lot of fun like target practice or a quick swim on the sly or maybe pulling some barge, broached, off the beach. Instead I had a 6 hour watch on the flying bridge but we did have some drills when a bunch of planes came over. My job here is to transmit orders (recieved [sic] verbatum [sic] from the fire controle [sic] officer) over my phones to a man who is on one of our guns.[4]

...As you see, I am fairly well satisfied with my new job (as well as I can hope to be). [Chet] Blackwood is in the office with me + also Wally, a very nice fellow. We've been on good terms every [sic] since I found out that he had read + liked [George] B[ernard]. Shaw's plays.[5]

The job did not, at least initially, allow Bud more time—or energy—for letters home. When they were not working or on watch, he and the other storekeeper gathered with others in the supply office to share food parcels from home and listen to records on a wind-up phonograph ("Now they are playing 'Come Out where ever You are' with the 'Voice' [Frank Sinatra] + worst of all they like it"). Though he seems to have enjoyed this opportunity to socialize, he confided to his mother,

> There is somthing that is annoying me; it's that I can't seem to consentrate [sic] on any one thing very hard or long. I have a lot of trouble memorizing poetry now + I can't do

anything with my calculus where I left off. It might carry over into my college work. I never was worth much in lib-arts to begin with, but that, I guess, was because I wasn't very interested. Interest has to take the place of intelligence with me. When I've got more energy—more soon. Love, Bud[6]

Bud was a conscientious correspondent who would try very hard to write about what he thought would interest his reader. He would sit with a blank paper for long stretches, just waiting for inspiration. He confessed to Ruth that, "Usually if I start to write somthing I get to thinking about it + if I do it seems awkward + unimportant. So in the end I just don't write anything."[7] This admitted self-censorship upset her almost as much as his poor spelling ("I want you to learn to spell now!"[8]). "Please don't stop to think + then decide the matter unimportant as you said in your last letter", she urged him. "Nothing I've written is important but it keeps you in touch with us at home and your ramblings etc. etc. will keep us in touch with you."[9] But Bud would remain self-critical.

> Did you know that very often the letters I send you I regret having done it because secondarly [sic] they are so short that I can see you saying that I might as well have made a V-mail out of that one + primarly [sic] they so often read like trite, sintamental [sic] trash; also as an additional thought my spelling is inexcuseable, but as to this resort to the idea that it is only a hipocrite [sic] who leads people to think that he realy [sic] can spell when after all without letting you know that he had to do it steals his knowledge from the dictionary—a slave to his pride?[10]

Ruth answered that his letters were "not trash + the spelling is not inexcusable—tho pretty bad and you needn't be so virtuous about deceiving people by looking up words in the dictionary."[11] About his difficulty concentrating, she offered reassurance, as she usually did. "Don't worry about losing your powers of concentration", she told him, "a little self discipline may be necessary now, when you are on your own + do not have any incentive or the pleasure of working with others on the same thing, but when you get in school you won't have any difficulty." By "school", Ruth meant any school, during or after the war.[12] It was a reminder. But Bud did not seem to mind it when he did not get into one of the Navy's vocational schools.

> ...I am very glad that I didn't get into radio + also quarter master. If I had, I would not be so well off + satisfied. The men that you work under + with make all the difference in the world. I am now more satisfied with my job than I have ever been since I've been in the C.G. + I want you to know this + not be worried.
>
> I think that you would maybe interested to know about some of my ship mates. I'll take them one at a time. "Del" is a very good friend of mine. He is about my size, black hair, but is older 20 or a little over + smokes a pipe. He is a pharmaisist's [sic] mate 1/C + is very intelligent. To be a doctor is ambitious + he was given a rate Ph 3/C when he joined because of his college training in that line. I have a lot of fun talking with him because (mainly I guess) we have common interest. He is the only one that I've been able to talk mathamatics [sic] to without seeming to be trying to "look too wise." I'm at a loss to talk about my favorite subjects because most think I'm trying to show how smart I am. So for me to find someone who at least partially understands me is wonderful—a discovery. To night I was able to discuss with him even tho' he has not too great an interest in math. [M]y pet problem of the bouncing ball that bounces forever ∞. Because each time it bounces it comes 1/4 the way up. The exact distance through which it travels can be found even tho it bounces forever. What a boon to my spirit that I was able to explain + he able to understand...[13]

At the end of January 1945, *Bayfield* departed Pearl Harbor for Saipan. David wrote Bud, thanking him for the air pistol Bud had sent him and Martin for Christmas ("very accurate up to about 20 feet and then mildly erratic up to 100 and from there on unpredictable"[14]), describing the construction of a lookout tower on the hill above the barn, and asking what Bud and his shipmates thought of the current U.S. political situation, which he described as a melding of Republicans and Democrats into "to Right and Left or Liberal and Conservatory or Reactionary + Communist etc." Claiming "You can classify any man except an 'American Firstes' or an 'Isolationist' some where on the swing of the pendulum", he illustrated his point with a diagram labeled "Pendulums of Government." In the diagram under "Right" he listed Churchill, Southern Democrats, Republicans, "Baily" (presumably U.S. Rep. Cleveland Bailey of West Virginia) and "Byrd" (presumably U.S. Sen. Harry F. Byrd. leader of Virginia's Democratic Party and the Senate's "conservative coalition"). Under "Left" he listed Northern Democrats, Labor, Russia, Communists, Nazis, former Vice-President Henry A. Wallace and President Roosevelt. He drew himself as being on the far right (right of "reactionary"), then Byrd, then their mother between reactionary and conservative (while noting that "Mother thinks" herself a Liberal). On the Left was Congress at "Liberal", then Roosevelt, then Labor, and at the farthest left he wrote "'Communist' (Wallace)."

David explained that "The Right" was upset because President Roosevelt had "fired" Commerce Secretary Jesse ("Jesus") Jones so he could give the job to Henry Wallace in return for his support during the 1944 election. As it had been in 1943, the concern was pro-labor Wallace having control of the assets of the Reconstruction Finance Corporation (RFC). "Write and tell me how you think and the men around you think", David instructed his brother, and "Remember this:"

Left ⟵⟶ Right
Less government ⟵⟶ More government
Less, change, More stabilization ⟵⟶ Changes—a New Deal Ira [sic]
You own the Government ⟵⟶ The Government Owns You
You keep what you make ⟵⟶ You divide what you make
Extreme right is called reactionary ⟵⟶ Extreme left is Communism and Nazisism [sic]

When you tell me their opinion's [sic] Classify them thusly: city or country, degrees of education, sections of country, Labor or professional. Don't talk about Dem. or Rep. any more their ideas have been thrown into a common pot and the Right and Left has [sic] eaten it up. Love, David[15]

We bawled church anthems in choro 57

Two weeks later, in a long letter he'd started in December but had not sent, Bud answered David's query about his shipmates' views, but did not offer his own.

> You want me to tell you some of the political opinions of the men here on ship + here they are in a nutshell—they know very little about the Wallace vs. Jones, they almost understand nothing about the peace plans of "the big three" [who were then meeting at Yalta]. They don't know because they don't care + are not interested They have some interest in the war—(how far we have advanced + where we will strike next) but not much more than that.[16]

The day Bud finished that letter to David, *Bayfield* was rehearsing off Tinian in preparation for the invasion of Iwo Jima. An Allied victory, never in any real doubt, was in sight, but, as everyone knew, much fighting and dying remained. As his mother and siblings were "all sitting in the library listening to the Symphony (Boston) reading—arguing, David drawing plans for a boat—Martin stringing homemade beads for his 'sweet-heart' Nancy Burton", *Bayfield* was embarking troops from the 4th Marine Division on the beach at Iwo Jima, following which she anchored off the invasion coast to serve for ten days as a hospital and prisoner-of-war ship. After nine days, casualties numbered around 7,000.[17] The photo of the flag-raising atop Mount Suribachi that won a Pulitzer and was later reproduced as a bronze statue was, of course, staged. A friend of Hutch's who served in the South Pacific during the war commented,

> The new bronze statue of 6 marines h[o]isting the flag at Surabachi [*sic*] is a testimonial to the power of advertising. It should have been a plaque reading "We the advertisers of the United States pay tribute to those who fought at Iwo." It is a fraud. 6 men, and one small flag pole. Advertising has dimmed the vision even of those heroes—though it can probably be safely said that those who <u>died</u> (distinguish <u>lived</u>) did not die for advertising.[18]

Exaggeration was often justified as "good for morale." The USMC was the first uniformed service (but by no means the last) to secure what would come to be known as a Public Relations Officer. It was during this war that, as never before, "Swarms of these, emanating from news ad agencies and newspaper and public-relations firms, attended the troops—in combat, not too closely—and provided for hometown consumption the necessary heroic-romantic narrative and imagery."[19] Bud was classic wartime PR material; good looking but not a movie star, cooperative but not seduced by attention, which, as Ruth's eldest son, he was used to receiving. When the *Charlotte News* published a close-up of him at his battle station in July 1945, his mother was naturally "thrilled", bought extra copies of the paper and wrote Bud for details. His answer: "The photographers [sic] mate did that to about every one on the ship. I am not exactly unique."[20]

At the first of March, with the RFC having been removed from the Commerce Department to keep it away from Wallace, the Senate confirmed Wallace as Commerce Secretary and *Bayfield* left Iwo for the Marianas. At Saipan, Bud made some big decisions which he shared with his mother in a letter dated March 10.

> I've just in these last few minutes decided how I now plan to spend the rest of my life. First I'm going to get real educated—physics, math, electronics, etc. then I'll take a stab at making a million or slightly under. If I see that I won't be sucessful [sic], I'll be a college professor, utilizing my education. If that doesn't work, I'll try to farm + live quietly not letting ambition mock my useless tail. And then if I'm not on the beam, I'll come live with you + eat ham + corn cakes + make bombs. Love, Bud [21]

It was a plan to which he would remain true, except for the bombmaking, which he eventually outgrew. When David learned of the plan, he foresaw problems.

> Dear Buddy, We'll have to work out an agreement, we both can't live with Maw, because after the other 3 have their education and after the government take all Maws money (no tax exemptions) some one will have to work. Maby [sic] we can take turns about? I have an idea—when we go out into the cold cruel world, let's don't look or get

a "secure" job, but let's get into all the "get rich quick" schemes in existants [sic], we might hit the jack-pot. Even if we didn't we would still have a lot of fun. After we graduate from college how about going "filibustering" and "Revoroosianing" en La America de Sur.[22]

On March 11, *Bayfield* and its cargo of 2d Marines began rehearsing for the invasion of Okinawa. On Easter morning, she "hove to off the southeastern coast of the Okinawa."

> As part of T[ask]G[roup] 51.2, the attack transport [*Bayfield*] and other units of Demonstration Group "Charlie" simulated a landing on the south coast to draw attention away from the actual landings at the Hagushi beaches. Although the ruse failed to fool Japanese, TG 51.2 received more enemy air attacks than did the real landings. *Hinsdale* (APA-120) and LST-884 were both severely damaged. The group repeated the operation the next day and, then, retired seaward to await orders. *Bayfield's* troops were not required at Okinawa; and, on 11 April, she got underway for Saipan, where they were disembarked on the 14th. She then remained at Saipan undergoing maintenance and repairs until 4 June.[23]

Ruth followed the news of the war closely and plotted Bud's supposed whereabouts on a (paper) National Geographic map. She surmised he was at Pearl Harbor for Christmas and "must have gone out" at the end of January "because we haven't heard for so long."[24] Guessing he might be in Guam or the Philippines, she implored him "Please don't get any of those tropical deseases [sic]—be very careful not to do any of the things you are warned against."[25] The day of the invasion of Iwo she wrote, "The news has just come that landings have been made at Corregidor and the Japs report at Iwogima (sp?) also—Of course I'm wondering if you are there. I suppose I'll keep that up from now on."[26] She did not hear from him until mid-March.

> Dearest Buddy, We were all so happy to have your two letters yesterday + one today—Of course we are all dying of curiosity as to your whereabouts. The Pacific is much too

> big and our bases are so scattered that we have only the imagination to tell us where you might be—That imagination, I assure you, has been having a field day these past three weeks.[27]

Toward the end of March, Ruth thought Bud might be in Saipan. It was not until March 20th that Bud was "alowed [sic] to say that I was at Iwo + to relate my personal expierences [sic], but that can wait. They are 'personal'. Love, Bud." His letter arrived home ten days later and Ruth was so excited that she forgot how to spell.

> Dearest Buddy, A letter from you this morning and we were so dissapointed [sic] that you didn't tell us about Iwo—tho' I'm sure that would be hard to do. Reports said Normandy was a picnic by comparison. You may know how releived [sic] I was to hear from you afterwards because I was certain from the timing that you were there. Now it is Okinawa and I suppose, as marines were landed, that you were there too—The reports, however, are that the landings were unapposed [sic], so I'm not so concerned over your safety this time.[28]

Bud chose not to write about his Okinawa experience, either; "Blackwood here just now read me a bulletin that allows me to say that I participated in the Okinawa invasion _____ It was o.k., they lived happily ever after + the next day it rained."[29]

President Roosevelt died suddenly on April 12, 1945. A few days later, David described the situation for his brother.

> Dear Buddy, The eulogies are over, and, to the great surprise of many people, the world still revolves about the sun, which is still burning brightly. Many have forgotten the good as well as the bad deeds, and all seem fairly content with President Truman. He may not be great, but also, he isn't a reformer who's going to set the world on fire. Two days after it happened, stocks and, in particular, the Utilities reached a 7 year peak. Varius [sic] trade reporters attribute this rise to the proballe [sic] overthrow of the "New Deal" and its Policies. I don't know anything about Truman. A lot has been said about him lately, but

We bawled church anthems in choro 61

you can not judge by these late-come essays. Everyone and everything slackened up on their critizism [*sic*] for a few (all except Pegler) day[s] and gave eulogies instead. Some were hipocritical [*sic*], other [*sic*] hysterical. Enough of this.[30]

David's use of "Enough of this" to terminate his argument suggests he had been reading Plato's *Socratic Dialogues*. Westbrook Pegler, whose syndicated column, "As Pegler Sees It", appeared in the *Charlotte Observer*, was a devoted critic of the Roosevelts and the New Deal. Perhaps it was the news of Roosevelt's death that inspired Bud to reread David's "Right vs. Left" letter, and comment on Roosevelt's proposal to institute a compulsory service requirement, which David had asked Hutch about the previous Christmas, and then written to Bud to oppose with his usual vehemence.

Brother, don't be for peacetime militery [*sic*] (compulsory) training for 18 year olds for these reasons. (if you want more argument on any, write and tell me) [in red pencil along the side of the page] I know what I'm talking about because of several long debates on the subject (I have read no material on the subject other than one statement by Mr. R.[)]...Think about this Question, Discuss it.

1. Mr. Roosevelt has not said that it would be military training. We would probably end up with a glorified CCC.

2. It would regimentate [*sic*] ideas with a low standard. government teachers, the common herd, false disciples.

3. Boy[s] would have the feeling that they were wasting their time. They would be right. There would be know [*sic*] war to stimulate them. There would be little room for advancement. You would be thrown in with the common herd.

4. It would disrupt. (self explanatory)

5. It would lower the ability of U.S. to defend herself. We have always been such great inventors because every man chose his own life and every one had a different and varied life. When you regimentate ideas and habit by force you destroy it.

[6.] What we need is a better government one that would have the courage to act when it saw what was coming. don't fool yourself, the higher up in our government

> knew what was comming [*sic*] long before it happen [*sic*]. If we would spend more time and money on our education and communications we would have a chance of avoiding war.
>
> [7.] You don't avoid war by preparing for it! do you think other nations will stand by and let us build up a trained army? boy, don't fool yourself![31]

The "one statement by Mr. R." that David had read was most likely the remarks Roosevelt made during an August 18, 1944 press conference, in which he introduced the idea of a selective service act. The idea eventually took shape as the May-Bailey bill for "limited national service", which the U.S. House of Representatives passed in January. The Senate, however, refused to go along.[32] Bud seems not to have known of the bill or its defeat when he wrote to David, arguing in favor of Roosevelt's compulsory service concept.

> ... [H]ere are my thoughts on the years [*sic*] compulsory military [*sic*] training for 18 year olds. I will only give my opinion on what the question itself as it is states—not as to what it will probably transform into. ([Y]ou mentioned glorified C.C.C., burden of low standard ideas, false disiplines [*sic*], etc.) Predominately [*sic*] against it are democratic principals [*sic*] + theorys [*sic*], but the ways + methods of making war have changed very much, things are different now—have to be dealt with differently, so it isn't a question of wheather [*sic*] it's against dem. principals + ideas but wheather we actually need it. I don't think that we need it drastically, but it would be a good thing. There are many things that 18 year olds don't + haven't learned from books + they will learn them fast + thoroughly in that 12 months. If the training resembles a C.C.C., burden of low standard + false disipline it will be just the thing. The cold cruel world has all these things + the quicker one learns about them the better off they are. To be able to live co-operatively with men wheather good or bad is a virtue.[33]

The importance of learning to live cooperatively was a refrain that Bud had heard at Webb School, and continued to play throughout his life. Even as he enjoyed a good argument and had difficulty "suffering fools", he valued getting along.

> So many people here around me are so fixed in their opinions that it is hard for me to find any pleasure talking to them. Of course you have to say something but this amounts to having said nothing at all. I think one of my best ways of judging how well I like to talk to a person even though he is not well informed on the subject discussed, is the degree of his willingness to change his mind or ideas without being ashamed of it. The person who will up hold his arguement through hell + high water is better than those who can't even do that, but mostly they are in about the same class—fools. Then there is the kind that will try to prove a point by giving abstract, boreing [sic] + sometimes irrevelant [sic] examples to prove his point. You probably come across such "personae" every day + you can to some extent avoid them; I can't. You could probably insult them + rid yourself of their company; but me—I've found it makes living much easier if you change your personality which includes your thoughts, mood + what you say (the language you use) to fit to generally be agreeable to the person you are speaking to. To walk with kings, nor lose the common touch.
>
> I have often regreted [sic] that I was not able to finish at Webb. I think that I missed a lot.[34]

Although the armed services had insisted (through the War Manpower Commission) that the May-Bailey bill was necessary to the war effort, most people felt its primary purpose was to blunt the effect of strikes (i.e., the power of the labor unions) that, along with manpower shortages, had sorely limited U.S. industrial productivity for the past three years. Its defeat was an undoubted victory for labor, whose struggles naturally interested the rank and file, including Bud and his shipmates. Labor, Bud told his mother, was "a big question + I am interested to know more about [it]. Mainly, I guess, because when ever you discuss labor you always have a lot of argument. And that's what I like."[35]

> ... [United Mine Workers' President] John L. Lewis is out of hybernation [sic] again. You've got to hand it to

him that he is very clever. He controls just about the most important industry + is able to, it seems, to fight the governent sucessfuly [sic]. Guys around me say to (in various expressions) eliminate Lewis + the problem is solved by that + the government taking over.

To mine coal with its dangers, hard work + etc. is not the most pleasant ocupation [sic]. Because of this some people seem to think that the miners deserve high wages to compensate for these hardships. They do, I think, but labor should (like tires, cars and other articles for sale) work on the principal [sic] of suppily [sic] + demand. Lewis is just trying to get a higher price for his article + is choosing a hell of a time for doing it. If he is charging too much for his article then somebody should say so + act accordingly. If he is charging a fair price then pay up + stop the mud slinging. The price of trucks, guns, tanks has gone up very much + the government is paying for them + the men who produce them are getting better wages + a coal miner too produces trucks just as much as the man who puts them together. To me it seems mearly [sic] a matter of math.

These darn tomatoes that we are loading now 'a days are packed in punk boxes that break open + scatter cans all over the store rooms. Then when I issue items they've got to be counted out one by one. Good boxes have a thin sheet of tar paper to keep water from weekening [sic] them. Maybe the coal tar shortage cause them to have to use punk boxes so that's my grudge against John L.[36]

Bud was a realist whose sympathies were usually with the underdog, even when the underdog was the enemy and "patriotic" expressions of racial hatred were sanctioned by military and civilian leadership. The Allies' Mariana Islands campaign had allowed them to construct air fields from which they launched "precision" bombing campaigns against Japan. When these were not particularly successful, the decision was made to try area firebombing (incendiaries). The first attack, considered successful, was on Tokyo and took place the night of March 9/10, followed within days and weeks by deadly attacks on Nagoya, Osaka and Kobe. It was in this context that Paul V. McNutt, the "platinum-haired War Manpower Commissioner, recommended 'extermination of the Japanese in toto'."[37] As reported in *Time*, "The onetime U.S. High Commissioner to the Philippines explained: 'I know the Japanese people'." When Bud read McNutt's recommendation in *Time*, he was offended. "What do you think of that?", he asked his mother. "Maybe he has some Indian blood in him + would enjoy a good old Indian massacre. I would like to know very much what you think about that." Ruth's answer was typically matter-of-fact.

> In your last letter you asked my opinion of McNutts proposal to exterminate the Japs—I'd did [sic] not know he had made such a proposal and of course cannot believe that we could deliberately set out to exterminate any people. Also I think Mr. McNutt must forget that there is an army of 5 or 6 million Japs untouched by battle. I wonder how many of our men he is willing to lose to acheive [sic] this extermination. If and when we have forced them to unconditional surrender I'll be satisfied.[38]

McNutt was not, as far as is known, an Episcopalian, if indeed he was any sort of a churchgoer. Unlike David, Bud did not need Ruth to remind him to go to church, because he was generally in the choir. But Bud's interest went beyond the enjoyment of music and group singing, though just what it was is hard to say.

> A protestant minister came over to give us services out on deck here. I had a short talk with him afterwards + he told me that he was from Charlotte, Michigan. I was almost sure that he was a Babist [sic] (from the ferver [sic] of his sermon) but he admitted [sic] being a Congregationalist or something like that. His sermon was good + a good change. He pointed out + discussed one of our everyday short comings (which is always a safe interest holder if done right). It was the vogue of having little or no interest of happenings before us but that we are always interested in what happened today or a few hours hence. We'll even rush for a paper a few hours early or the endless scuttlebutt we indure [sic] for just wanting to know what will happen. He did pretty good in the 10 minutes he used. Out here I think that I would like longer sermons, but they seem to want to get it over with as quick as possible. We seem to get an

> over dose of hyms [*sic*] + responsive readings. It is as if they were trying to make the service as painless to take as possible. Or maybe it's to do the job with the least amount of effort.[39]

On another occasion,

> We had church services on deck today + I went, but not without upholding the Lucas tradition of being a little late. The preacher was from another ship[.] the sermon was good, he did not bore us because he stuck to the subject. I've always thought it a good thing that preachers based their talks on a scripture because if they didn't they would wander all over the country. They do anyway but the scripture helps. To get back to the sermon. He rebuked us for having a religion of a six year old + justly so, but he offered no solution for the short commings [*sic*]. I wanted to go right up + ask him about it, but I could think of too many answers that he would give me, but if he comes here again I'll be sure + satisfy my curiocity [*sic*]. Always I'm more interested in the preacher than the moral of his sermon.[40]

"Being a little late" was indeed a Lucas tradition. For years, Susannah believed it was normal to process into the sanctuary behind the choir. Like the Roosevelts (also Episcopalians), the Lucases were not especially pious. The Smiths seem to have been Presbyterian, though Ruth's mother was a Quaker. The Lucases were vaguely Christian, except Charles was reportedly an atheist. Apparently, the Episcopal Church was a preference Ruth developed on her own. The children were all baptized after Charles's death in 1939, rather than as infants as is customary. Perhaps as a result of this late start, we see Ruth in the '40s putting rather more emphasis on attending services or Sunday school than she otherwise might have. At any rate, after 1939, the children were expected to go unless they were feeling unwell, but they did not invariably comply. Penitential seasons were observed as an example to the children.

> Tomorrow is Ash Wednesday [Ruth wrote to Bud]. I guess I'll give up my favorite beverage [bourbon]—The children

got inspired at Sunday school and Susannah is giving up funny papers—poor little thing! I'm afraid it will be a long six weeks. Martin hasn't decided on his form of self-denial yet except to say he was not going to give up "fat"! I gather he considers that is what he should give up.[41]

Public prayer outside of services was limited to grace before meals at Easter and Christmas, unless swearing is counted. Church polity was often a topic of discussion; scripture almost never. Asking for someone's prayers, offering to pray for someone and extemporaneous prayers were simply not on. Funerals were important but not obituaries. The dead were not referred to as having "passed" or embalmed, and resurrection was understood as a metaphor.

Their wartime experience apparently led Bud and his shipmates to conclude "the church" (presumably referring to the white Protestant denominations) should take an active role in shaping secular society. On the way to Iwo Jima, Bud wrote to Ruth about a conversation in the supply office.

> ...Religion was the topic. We agreed [sic] that the principals [sic] that Christ taught were not being taken as seriously as they should be + that the main reason for this was the church because that's its job + they are failing in it. Our thoughts, every day living + even our politics should be more strongly influenced by the church. These are not only my ideas, but most of us in here agreed. The ideas + principals should be taught more in colleges + the minister should not be afraid that he will not get next weeks pay cheque because he says what he should. To take care of this we thought that it would be a good idea if all ministers were payed [sic] by the government.
>
> Maybe our ideas weren't right, but I know there have got to be some changes made. You would be supprised [sic] at what little interest is taken in church here. They can't force a man to go to church but at least they can offer an insentive [sic].[42]

Ruth predictably disagreed.

> Dearest Bud,
>
> David, Susannah, Martin + I went to church this morning. Mr. Clark [rector of St. Peters] read the Bishop's letter and explained why we do not speak of "joining" the church as the sectarian denominations (Baptist, Methodist, Presbyterian etc.) do. It was in preparation for confirmation which comes the Sunday after Easter.
>
> I haven't answered your letter of Feb 15th your last for some time now. I haven't answered it, though I've written you many times since.
>
> It is a very difficult letter to answer—if I could talk to you, it would not be so difficult but I do not find it easy to express my thoughts + ideas on paper—However I will try to get a few of the latter across to you.
>
> First of all, of course you are right about the need to apply Christian principals [sic] to our every day and national life. Many people would agree with you, that the church has failed, but I cannot. I go each Sunday and hear these principals taught from the prayer book and then in the sermon shown in the application to our own private lives + our life as a nation in the community of nations. I am going to send you a copy of the bishop's letter as soon as I can get it. This letter will show you how the church stands on the matters which concern us all so deeply now. As I have always told you children, I go to church because I want to go and feel that it is a help to me to go—not because of duty or a feeling that I am virtuous because I go. Mr. Clark is not a great preacher, some times he is repetitious and somewhat tiresome, but always I can listen to what he says, and follow the ritual with respect and benefit because he is a real and true "follower" of Christ.
>
> He could be in no way different if his living came from the state. Quite the contrary he would lose his independence. History has proven what state control of church brings so I needn't go into that—Church is a habit — if you go regularly you enjoy it and miss it—regardless of the quality of spiritual "intertainment" [sic] offered. I have never been able to understand the viewpoint of those who go Sunday after Sunday expecting the same man who has been kept busy all week visiting the sick, burying the dead, greeting the newcomers etc. to preach a highly developed

> gripping and not too long sermon to the same audience. After all, he is only human!
>
> I think the bishop's letter when it comes will finish my answer for me. But always remember, the church is there—always open, always teaching—the lessons you learn depends on you.[43]

A couple of weeks after Ruth mailed that letter, she sent Bud a trifold pamphlet titled "The Episcopal Church" whose penultimate paragraph put the matter most plainly (though she did not call attention to this or any other part): "Those who most love the Episcopal Church and most deeply believe in it are the most conscious of their own shortcomings and their neglect of obligations." Or, as Bud once put it, "As always I wanted to go up + shake the preacher's hand + tell him what I thought of his sermon + as always I didn't."[44]

In April, Ruth sent Bud some photos taken by Cec and Skip Morris, frequent visitors who were both in the Army and stationed at Camp Gordon in Augusta, Georgia. Ruth did not own a camera, but even if she had, film and paper were in such short supply that few civilians had access during the war. For Bud, "It was wonderful to have the photos + It's hard for you to know how much they mean, I've never enjoyed any piece of paper so much." A few weeks later he wrote, "I just thought of the photographs you sent. I get so interested in them when I'm showing them to the fellows that I almost think I'm home."[45] From then on, Ruth made a point to collect photos for Bud and David.

The end of the war in Europe was very near. At the end of April, Ruth wrote Bud,

> Last night we had a false alarm to the effect that Germany had surrendered—I suppose it will come fairly soon however + then men and equipment will come to the Pacific in sufficient quantities to let us see the end of this war. Events are coming in so quickly that nothing seems surprising—Time has no meaning at all. Things that happened last week seem to live in the dim past.[46]

A couple of days later, the commander of the Army Air Base at Morris Field received orders to deactivate the Combat Crew

Training Station within 30 days. Everyone was moving to the Pacific theater, and with them would go Mary Jo's social life.

There were speeches but little fanfare when the Germans finally surrendered. Ruth wrote Bud, "I think everyone is more or less in a daze, as I am, and there has been almost no celebration. Of course everyone is thinking of Japan and feels that the war is only half over." Images of the liberated concentration camps began appearing in *Time* and *Life* magazines. Bud, along with much of the rest of the country, viewed them with disbelief. "The pictures + story of the German prison camp at Buchenwald is [*sic*] terrible. The photographs make it *almost realistic*." (Emphasis added.)[47]

While Bud and the rest of the *Bayfield* crew were enjoying a respite in the Marianas, with four-hour liberties ashore every four days along with the usual nightly movie, he had time to reflect.

> Dear Mother,
> The movie tonight was very unsatisfactory because just as things got so messed up that you couldn't possibly think of a way out, it started raining very hard + stopped the show. Now I'll never know how it ended.
> Circumstances have lately caused me to realize the prudence of being reserved. The trait that we usually ascribe to an Englishman + which is true as far as I have been able to find out from talking with a few. One of them as I passed close by his small mine-sweeper in a barge to hand him a message, hollered over and said "Are you happy in your work?" (This was at Normandy) I was so supprised that I said yes, without thinking, but later I did think about what he ment [*sic*] + I've never forgotten him.
> One day, a while back, I said a few words to a guy who was just ahead of me in the chow line. I hadn't seen him around so I thought he might be one of the group that had come aboard a few weeks ago. "A few words" is as far as I got, because from then on he was giving me his life story. He came up to the office with me + later left to return with an album of pictures. My insulting him just put wood on the fire so I left him with the first sucker who showed any interest.
> You can always be interested in some one about whom

you know very little. They are like that unfinished movie I saw tonight + seldom bore you.[48]

And before Okinawa,

> Sometimes I think that my Coast Guard years have not all together been wasted. I've learned to know people better. With one fellow I had been on board ship with for over a year I just got to know while standing a weeks watch with him...His pop died + he had to support his mother + the faimly [sic]. He had jobs that my foolish pride would have a hard time enduring but it has made him so that he can hold his own against the best.[49]

David had been planning since his 17th birthday the previous fall "to go in as soon as he graduates in June so he can get navy or C.G."[50] With graduation just a few days away, Mary Jo let Bud know that, after much consideration, David had finally decided on the Navy. Bud wrote to David to offer his thoughts on military service.[51]

> It's darn hard to believe you're going in. Among the things it gives you are mainly experience + experiences. The best way to get along is to be everyone's friend (but especially to your supers in rank) + always look out for number one. Mind you, I don't follow that proscription [sic]. It doesn't come natural to me as it does to some, but it pays good dividends in the long run.[52]

> The last time that I was home you said in these words that I hadn't changed abit [sic]. They made some sort of impression on me as you can see, because I have not forgotten them. Even now when I am almost 20 I feel myself that I have not changed. At one time I thought that I would be different when I attained that desicive [sic] age, but actually I feel like a kid + probably act like one. When I get home I'll want to do the same things I did when I left. I'll want to make bombs + build radios + do all the other same things...I'm pretty sure that you will have the same idea of the value of education + the desire to get ahead, that I do. The evolution of this idea is very transparant

> [*sic*]. You get so sick + tired of being a Seaman or even a petty officer + having people lord it over you. It's not that it necessarily should be different; it's just that it isn't. You know that you can't do anything about [it] while you are in but when you are out of it the laws of "getting ahead" are changed. Another thought—I have made the mistake, once or twice + even more, of showing that I thought myself superior in some way to someone. To think that you are superior to anyone, I have learned, is bad enough, but to show that you think it is social suicide besides a lot of other things. If I have to go through hell to get that out of my system, I think that it would be worth it.[53]

Bayfield's captain came down to inspect Bud's store rooms in May. Recalling Bud's interest in the six-month academy prep course, the captain let him know that the application forms had come in.

> Last night I looked them over in the ship's office [he wrote his mother]. I seem o.k. on every thing but my eyes. They require, with possible waiver, 20/20 all around. I have 20/20 + 20/25, I think. Also for my hight [*sic*] I should weigh 153; actually I'm 164 in dungrees [*sic*], but they said it's o.k. if the extra weight is bones + muscle + not fat. It's fat, but I might be able to convince them that it's muscle. I had forgotten about it almost 'till [*sic*] the captain called my attention on it. He seems more interested in the school than I am, but I would like to get in—not to be an old boy, 20 year man, etc. but to be with my first love, math, guns + radio.[54]

Picking up the letter after an interlude to watch the 1941 movie, *They Died With Their Boots On* (described by IMDb as "a highly fictionalized account of the life of George Armstrong Custer [played by Errol Flynn] from his arrival at West Point in 1857 to his death at the battle of the Little Big Horn in 1876"), he wrote his mother that he was "very impressed" by it.

> So much so that you can disregard [*sic*] my saying I was interested in radio, guns, etc. I changed my mind. I ask my self now + I am not. Even now when I am almost 20 I can

We bawled church anthems in choro 73

> make my mind up no better than a child can, but even at that I want no one to do it for me. These moods come + go often. Sometimes I feel as tho' everyone + myself are ruled by laws or principals [*sic*] or something so powerful that we can never free ourselves from them—I am an unfinished cog wheel whoes [*sic*] gears are slowly being ground into shape so that I will fit + turn as an infantessimal [*sic*] part of the universe.[55]

Navy Commander MacElvain, who had been sent to Charlotte in 1942 to run the shell plant and whose son Ford had gone to Webb School and was friends with Bud (the family were also Episcopalian) told Ruth he thought Bud could transfer to the Navy and get into the Naval Academy Preparatory School at Bainbridge, Maryland. Ruth passed the advice along to Bud, telling him "Mac" had said "be sure to inquire." Bud replied, "I will inquire into the Banbridge [*sic*] deal, but with not much gusto. When the war is over I want to be free."[56] A week later,

> It is 7:30 A.M. + the sun is just beginning to make things hot + stuffy. I am in a very bad mood because I missed breakfast waiting for the line to get short + it got to[o] short. It might be just as well because my physical for the academy prep school comes up this morning + I'm a little over weight. My chances of getting in are fair, I think, but I have no anxiety. I'll go if I can but I won't feel sad over not being allowed to give up seven years of my life to my country [*sic*]...[57]

Ruth did not understand that the prep course required applicants to commit to the four-year academy program (whether Navy or Coast Guard) *plus* several years of active-duty service as a commissioned officer thereafter, for a total commitment that was probably closer to ten years than to seven.

> I'm afraid a lot of people are much too optimistic about the time it will take to finish Japan [she wrote to Bud]. The casualties have just been announced from Okinawa. I'm hoping with all my heart that you will be accepted for the school... Please do go after the "Bainbridge deal"

> with "gusto" It will mean a lot to get your mind in "study practise" [sic] again for there has been quite a lapse... it will be a great help in getting in M.I.T. So put out your best effort.⁵⁸

While awaiting orders to report to boot camp, David was busying himself making post-war college plans. He ordered Bud to "Write for a Massachusetts Institute of Technology [catalog] Cambridge Mass—right away." As feared, Bud did not pass the physical exam (eyes). He was characteristically offhand in relating the news to his mother.

> Two of your letters came while I was swetting [sic] down in the "salt mines." In the first you were very exspectant [sic] of my going to the academy. Sorry to disappoint you. I'm glad to hear that I've got such a nice nest egg + thank you for the stock [probably a birthday gift]. Maybe I'll get educated some of these days. Then I'll set out to make a million. Being [promoted to] a S1/C gives me a lust for power. Love, Bud ⁵⁹

The birthday gift was most likely the shares of Coca-Cola Company stock that he later gave away. *Bayfield* left Saipan for the Solomons on June 4 "to load cargo and move it closer to the fighting."⁶⁰

> Tomorrow will sure be a hectic day; we'll be loading supplies again. We'll go ashore + I'll be in charge of a truck + a 6-man working party + they'll all complain about every case they pick up + make the same comments about storekeeper never doing any work. I can't help but make some enemys [sic]. I've often thanked my luky [sic] stars that [I'm] six feet tall. Mr. Barringer once told me that he had pulled off many a bluff by puffing out his chest + proved it when he took David [and] me to a wrestling match + made some men who were standing in the way move over. They threatened a little but they moved. I'm twenty; it seems such a short jump from the time I was 18. I dream of the time when I can come home + go to M.I.T. I want to work hard + become some one that you will be proud of. I feel that in a way the service is a part of my education + if it ends before I'm 21 I will be thankful for it. Love, Bud ⁶¹

Osmond Barringer, born in 1878, was the first Charlottean to own a car and build it an auto-centric garage. He was Charlotte's first car dealer – Chalmers, Stanleys, Buicks, Cadillacs, Packards, Oldsmobiles. Mr. Barringer and his wife Alice were frequent visitors at Deverill and enjoyed having the family, including Ailsie, Irene and Mary Denny, to homey suppers at Beechnut Farm. Like Bud and David, the Barringer boys served during the war (Army), though they were a good deal older. Before the war, Bud had sought "Mr. B's" advice on cars, e.g., whether his Model T could take a Model A engine, and considered him something of a mentor. They also shared an interest in dynamite.[62]

The day *Bayfield* set sail for the Solomons, David and 12 other boys (out of 40 or 47) passed the first set of exams to get into a Navy aviation program. David related to Bud,

> T]hey were hard both mentally and physicaly [sic] and nervously. They used the old elimination process right there on the spot. We took 5 tests and after each one they called us into a big room and read out the names of those who had passed.[63]

He thought he would not be chosen because of his eyes. (He was not chosen because the program closed.) He would "try for radar—eyes make no difference there, but the tests are hard and will be particuly [sic] so for me due to my lack of interest in radio and radar, what I really want is deisel [sic] school or to be a navigator."[64] (Bud had recently advised him "Don't mess with deisel [sic] school because you'll find yourself in a boat engine room sweating your life away."[65])

Primed perhaps by David's having labeled Henry Wallace a communist, Bud read with interest an article by Wallace in the May *Reader's Digest*, a subscription to which had been a Christmas gift from Martin and Susannah, a supplement to Ruth's gift of *Time* magazine (not up to her standards but "necessary during the war because you had so little time and w[ere] for the most part inaccessible [sic]"[66]). But, rather than writing about the article to David, Bud wrote to his mother.

I read Wallace's article + it seemed to me that his ideas were well explained + had plenty of good practical sense. It is not even a good arguement to hold it against him for being an "idealist" for Christ was one too. The thing to do is to think out his ideas by ourselves knowing as much about them as possible + then be for or against him. He is trying to appily [sic] the same kind of government "help" that worked such wonders with the farmers during the early part of F.D.R.'s administration to small buissnesses [sic]. There is alot of money tied up in banks that only gives interest to its owners. He wants to start this money circulating by govermentaly [sic] insureing [sic] it when it is reasonably lent to investments (such as a start for small buisnesses). The goverment will loose [sic] money but they will be many times repaid when the small buisness is a success + when the idle money is circulating. The success of small buisness means more responsability [sic] + more wealth for many people. He wants to subdue as much as possible monopolies to induce free compatition [sic] The main point is that he is not proposing goverment loans but is inducing civil loans. It is not difficult to see why the high + mighty capilatist [sic] is against him.

I am anxious to know if you are agin' him + if so, why?...

I have just read today's paper printed here on the ship. It says "President Truman asked Congress for a broad expansion of unemployment compensation financed with federal funds." Here we already have what we feared of Walace [sic]—unwise spending of goverment funds. It seems to me that the objection that he had to[o] much of [sic] financial power was used as a front to hide the real reason for unrest. The big capilatist feared government controle [sic] to allow small buisness to offer more compatition [sic].[67]

In answering, Ruth characteristically avoided arguing policy details and appealed to external authority, presuming, as many did, Wallace's guilt by association with "Communistic party" supporters.

I'm going to take a little time to answer you about Wallace. So much of what he says is alright—My beleif [sic], shared by a great many better informed and wiser people, is that, regardless of what he says, he leads inevitably to a communistic type of government. His attitude, plainly stated when his egibility [sic] for the R.F.C. lending powers was being questioned, was that only the pro German-facist type was opposing him. As a matter of fact, all those who had, up to the time of Hitler's attack on Russia, done all possible to prevent our helping England and other anti-Axis [powers], were his staunchest advocates. In my opinion the devil could probably write a very good sermon. I'll write you more—or better still, send you clippings from time to time. He will most surely be Mr. Truemans [sic] cheif [sic] opponent for the Democratic nomination three years from now—He will probably be supported by the Communistic party which is again out in the open—certainly by all these "fellow travelers" who label themselves in various ways, as well as by many good people who cannot beleive [sic] that these forces are moving in a direction which would be as abhorrent to them as to those whom they label "reactionary". I consider myself a liberal—Mr. Wallace would undoubtedly call me a "facist."[68]

Mr. Wallace, of course, would not have thought Ruth a facist, but there was some truth to David's estimation that she was perhaps more conservative than she liked to think of herself. It was Charles, according to Susannah, who got it from David, who was left-leaning, "radical" even; an ardent New Dealer who believed in things like desegregation and free medical care. Charles's politics had pulled Ruth left, and, with his death, she may have started drifting slowly back to the right, where she was more comfortable. It is fair to say she had contrarian or, depending on one's point of view, equalizing tendencies. Ruth read widely ("I don't think it is ever wise to read one paper or news sheet exclusively, especially such a one as *Time*"[69]) and enjoyed intelligent conversation, but she had stayed at college (Agnes Scott) only a few months and, like many women in those days, lacked a certain confidence in expressing her views. She preferred to try and work through persons of influence, who were usually men.

Maw is down stairs writing about inter-[racial] relations [David informed his brother in June]. She is planning (it's set right now) to have a research theme contest next year at Queens and Johnson C. Smith—the subject is "the housing problem in Charlotte." The "problem" is supposed to be deplorable. She is on the tail of Mr. Goddard [Dean at Queens College] at present. He made a speech somewhere and said that there had been enough discussion and that it was time now for some action. For the past three or four weeks Maw has been thinking up things for him to do, and she has some luluses. Mary Denny came down t[w]o weeks ago and you know what she thinks of him. Anyway Maw and her got to talking, Boy! I bet his ears burnt off.[70]

The discussion of Wallace's policies went no further, probably owing to *Bayfield's* busy schedule (Tulagi on June 12th, Espiritu Santo on the 17th, Tinian on July 9th, and back to Saipan where she took on passengers for delivery to Guam). Mid-July, *Bayfield* set sail for California. When Bud next wrote home it was from New Hebrides, and he had forgotten all about Henry A. Wallace.

> Dear Mother,
> Home, home, home is all that's on my mind now. Rumors are thick in that direction. They've already asked us what naval distric [sic] we want. I asked for Norfolk because it is the closest home. With 18 months of breath taking sea duty behind me (ha! ha!) I should be able to stay on land a while since they've passed a new order that you can't be shipped out again 'till everyone else in your distric has had their 18 mos.
> I don't feel so bad over having the SK3/c rate frozzen [sic] in my face but I hope to get to go to some school when I hit. Mr. Parker is the educational officer so I asked him about radio tech. school—no dice. Most of them are closing or closed soooo—I guess I'll always be a seaman + branded where'er I go, but my shining consolation is that what ever I am I'll get to see you now + then.
> Mr. Hunt, my new boss, is a pretty good chap...He got confidential + told me I was a good, clean-cut boy + also advised that I stop smoking (he doesn't smoke, drink, chew, etc.) + to add force to his arguement he said that his brother's friend—that's enough, you know the rest. He's a good egg + to hear the rest of the guys in the office talk—me too—you would think he was the only one with any morals.

We bawled church anthems in choro 79

> They've started talking about leave + shore duty now + I've got to get in it. Boy!—my moral [*sic*] is up. Love, Bud[71]

In fact, Bud did feel bad about his rate being frozen, as it meant all his work to qualify as a storekeeper might come to naught, including foregoing all the back pay he was owed. He was so annoyed that instead of getting off the ship with everyone else, he would opt to stay and wait out the freeze. But, at that moment, he, like the rest of the *Bayfield* crew, thought he was leaving the islands for good. He wrote his mother that,

> On liberty yesterday I decided that I had better get a memo [*sic*] of the island [Espiritu Santo] before I left so I bought some shells from the natives at inflation prices + made out of them + a pipe cleaner somthing that resembles a turtle. The reason I didn't bring a whole bunch of stuff back like some of the crew did is because I'm not to[o] interested in the place + I want to remember as little as possible of it + the rest of the places I've been.[72]

In thoughtful people, transitions lead to anticipation leads to introspection. Thinking perhaps of being home again, Bud found himself repenting of his shortcomings and neglect of obligation. He resolved (to his mother, at least) to clean up his act.

> I was glancing through a book on psycology [*sic*] + at the place I was reading it was mentioning some of the adult weaknesses left over from childhood. One of them was putting off things like not writing letters, etc. Another was lack of self controle [*sic*] like eating too much + smoking too much + another was just general disintegration of the mind + brain power which a typical result was not being able to read + enjoy anything but low brow reading. All three of these hit me square in the eye especially the examples. So now I've resolved to write letters when I think I should, don't eat so much, cut out smoking + stop reading funny paper books. You may not realize it but I'm in pretty bad shape.[73]

Around this time Wally, a fellow storekeeper and "ardent [*sic*] believer [*sic*] of Threau's [*sic*] ideas", said something else that hit

Bud "between the eyes." He said the crew "had gotten into the habit of being very vicious with our conversation."

> [R]ight away I realized that was just what I did to [fellow storekeeper Chet] Blackwood + others every day. It gets to be a habit. You don't come right out + say that he's a hypocrite, base, nitt witt; you just say it in so many words. I do it for somthing better to do (to make his character seem worse than yours).[74]

If indeed many years later Bud could still be vicious, it was not by habit. He was less successful giving up smoking ("It's just that everyone else smokes like a fiend + they are always offering them"[75]). But, he told his mother, he did cut down.

When *Bayfield* finally set sail for California, Bud was ready. After two months of pestering the ship's librarian for a book of plays someone had out, he found it on his desk in the supply office.

> The librarian probably had pity on me or else I was driving him nutz asking for it. It's eleven plays by Henrik Ibsen [introduction by H. L. Mencken]. When I found out that he was like Shaw, I realy [sic] wanted to sample them.[76]

He told the commissary officer (his boss), Mr. Hunt, that he would stay aboard the ship. "It's the only chance I have of getting the rate I've worked for 7 months for", he wrote his mother from Guam.[77] Two weeks later, *Bayfield* arrived in San Francisco and went into dry dock. On August 6, 1945, President Truman blew up the world's first atomic bomb over Hiroshima and David finally shipped out to boot camp at the U.S. Naval Training Center in Great Lakes. He was just one month shy of his 18th birthday. Bud arranged to fly home on leave, more than ready to resume his dabbling with dynamite.

> I had a swell time home [Bud reported to David when he was back aboard the *Bayfield*]. I blew out that little ventilater [sic] above the Oga when I shot off 4 sticks suspended by a string from a tree below the grage [sic]. I also planted 12 sticks in that first pile in front of the house.

> Quite effective. Also I put large rocks on a one stick charge. The fragments went about 400 ft. up . I had to go a little way out on the Lawyer's road to a powder house to get it + caps + fuse + the first thing I did with the caps when the man handed them to me was to knock them all over the car floor. Mother sat next to the case all the way back. She must love me very much, but when those 4 suspended went off she put her foot down and said no more. It shook the whole house.[78]

A diversion, if not a civilizing influence, was called for, and it came in the form of Dr. Hamilton Witherspoon McKay's 18 year-old daughter, Katherine Roddey Whitner McKay, a graduate of Chatham Hall and a freshman at Smith College who was taking flying lessons. How they met may be imagined. "My two dates with Katherine McKay were fun", he wrote to David, "I've written her. My first experiment with the art + even now I wish I hadn't mailed it."[79] Katherine wrote back immediately, perplexed as to why Bud had not included his address ("maybe I had had too many beers at the time"). He was right, she said, about her being a tomboy but wrong about himself. "It might be true that you have been in a social vacuum but you don't act it... The social life (club particularly) in Charlotte is mostly shallow + tiresome."[80] Bud and Katherine would correspond for about a year. Katherine would soon give up flying and eventually marry the youngest son of William Henry Belk, founder of Belk Brothers department store. Her brother Peter would marry David's wartime penpal Lillian Evans Lineberger of Belmont and Chatham Hall. Lillian's sister Harriette was at Chatham Hall with Susannah.

Mischief not out of his system when he returned to San Francisco, Bud spent the night in the brig after he was caught using forged identification ("I'd only had 4 beers + a shot of Shivelys when I was picked up").[81] The captain gave him and his ID-mutilating friend 60 hours extra duty ("Don't tell mom").[82] The personnel transfers on and off the *Bayfield* caused a certain amount of chaos and confusion as the crew prepared to get underway again at the end of August. Bud and Artie were the only storekeepers staying on. They agreed to switch jobs, Bud taking "commissary" (paperwork) and Art the canteen. Bud looked forward to not "slinging crates" all day. They and two others were the only ones left of the original crew, which left the ship's "chior" a "flop" except for Oswald who used to sing at St. Peter's and "wants it like I do, but the rest don't seem to want to make the required effort."[83]

Chapter 8

Rush to the fireside

The surrender of Japan had made sailors and marines serving in the Pacific eligible for demobilization (a massive reshuffling of personnel in the European theater having begun months earlier). The Advance Service Rating Score, aka the Points System, developed in 1944 to facilitate a "systematic and equitable transition" to a smaller, peacetime military, kept changing as the result of unrest on both the homefront and in the uniformed services.[1] Bud was disappointed to learn how few points he had.

> The new point system does not give any credit for sea duty or battle stars [Bud complained to his mother] but only for dependants [sic] + length of service + age. I have only 22 of the required 44. This is very discouraging but my hope is that they will change the point system as soon as they get rid of the old men.[2]

What Bud did not foresee was that the War Department's decision months earlier to halve conscription to 50,000 a year would mean a severe manpower shortage, such that staying with *Bayfield* even one more voyage would effectively make him indispensable.

> My main impression... [Bud ventured gently to explain to his mother, whom he suspected would be unhappy about his decision] is that they are doing everything to keep me. I'm the only man on the ship that knows right where all the dry stores are + to train somone [sic] to take my place

> would take a month or more. I realize myself that with my rate I'm better off here than any place I could hope for... Another slightly bright side is that every 4 months I'll get 3 points out here instead of 2 there, but it will be going down about 2 points a month soon, I think. But I don't care much either way; like last time things will be all planned out for us when we hit 'Frisco + they will be entirely different from what any of us expect. The complement of the ship will be greatly reduced + many will get off that actually don't have enough points to get out, [and] they will be shipped out again. But, what ever happens I will follow "Old Sawney [Webb']s" advice + "submit to the enevitable [sic] gracefully."[3]

As *Bayfield* got closer to Eniwetok, the heat and humidity below decks rose uncomfortably. "Even after you take a shower you feel just as messy as you did before."[4] Bud spent his free time arguing "about wheather [sic] an army can be made to function effeciently [sic] on a democratic system... It can be done + will be some day,"[5] playing chess with "the weather man + so the weather all over the Pacific is mine for the asking,"[6] and reading. He was particularly taken with a book that Hutch had recommended, called *Looking Backward*, which he had picked up in San Francisco. Its utopian ideals resonated on every level. He wrote to David, "I have been reading an excellent book."

> ...It was written by an Edward Bellamy back in 1875 + he fore tells of the modernistic social set up we'll have in 2000. It's a discription [sic], a very detialed [sic] + elaborate one of a Utopia that must have been very fantastic back in 1875 but is less so today. One of the more outstanding things it proposed is equality of material wealth for each individual.
>
> It is obvious even today that we are approaching this equality of material wealth. It is an arguable point so I will present mine. If you want to question the fairness of an equality of wealth here is an example. If two men are doing the very same job + yet one can produce twice what the other can, each doing his best, then if you consider fairly one should not be rebuked because, doing his best, he is not able to do more + the other complamented [sic] because he

is doing what is in him to do. Each, there fore, doing his best although not producing the same quantity should have the same reward for their labors.

Now you might say that there would be slackers because there would be no goal to work for. E. Bellamy over comes this by showing a system of rank not rewarded materialy [sic] but by the amount of athority [sic], responsibility + having more to decide for himself what he should do.

In his Utopia the people are educated 'till they are 21 + retire at 44. This is made possible because everyone does his share of work during his life's span. Everyone may choose his profession. + in case too many choose a particular profession, the working hours are made longer. A coal miner would have comparatively short hours with that of say a bank clerk. When you keep in mind that the book was written 70 years ago, you could almost think it impossible. The set up is so detailed + plausible [sic].

The man that takes a haughty or superior attitude or even thinks himself better than anyone else is a true fool. There are plenty of officers that come on this ship that think because they are better educated etc. that they have the right to be little Cesars [sic], but most of them ketch [sic] on quick (especially during invasions) that they are just human beings + equal in the hands of Providence [sic]. Amen.[7]

David's initial reaction has been lost or perhaps lies buried somewhere in family archives. However, this subsequent comment on Bud's letter gives the gist.

Brother—let me tell you something about socialism—About 20 years from now you are going to be very well off and way above average—and you are not going to want to give that mony [sic] and property up to a government to hand out. That socialistic state you talk about assumes (falsely) that everyone or most everyone will pull their fair share of the load—look at the stumble bums around you and think about having to share all your gains with them—When they spend all of their time playing cards, bulling and cussing and F.O.ing.[8]

When this advice failed to elicit a response, David observed, "You didn't say anything for or against socialism in your last letter", and asked, "does that mean you arn't [sic] one any longer and agree with me[?]"⁹ To which Bud replied,

> Yes, I am still a socialist but I don't want to set the world on fire. I use my socialistic ideas as a kind of guide in forming my ideas in approving or disapproving the changes that are coming about in our government + its policies. Take the fact that we have cieling [sic] prices on autos + minimum wages for workers to keep the rich from getting too rich + the poor from getting too poor. It is a step nearer the ultimate end, equality of material wealth. I had a long discussion with an Army captian [sic], a former lawyer, about socialism. I had a chanch [sic] to air my ideas + yet not be considered a rash adolecent [sic]. His aim in life was to make a pile of money by honest means if possible. From this it was easy to conclude that he'ed [sic] some hard knocks + I found out that he'ed had to work his way through college, waiting on tables etc. One can go through a lot of humility because of the lack of money—most think that they can shed this humility only by gaining wealth themselves + spend their lives to this end. Some few see no disgrace in being comparatively poor + have just as much fun out of life as anyone. The Barringers might fit into this last class to a greater or less degree. That is one reason I like + admire them so much.¹⁰

A 1968 article in the Charlotte Observer written after his death described Mr. Barringer as a pioneer and a dare-devil who was "born wealthy", but "managed to lose or give away most of his money", including land for a park and an elementary school.¹¹ Mr. Barringer's story is part of Charlotte's proud, and not so proud, history. The not so proud part has to do with his being the only child of the third marriage of the famed Brigadier General Rufus Clay Barringer, C.S.A., and his coming of age during the rise of so-called "fusion" politics in North Carolina, wherein the leaders of the People's Party joined with those of black and white Republicans to try and wrest control of the state from the white men of property who had, except for a brief period during the war, always governed—namely, the Democrats. For a time, the fusion strategy worked as intended. Following the election of 1894, "all statewide offices were in the hands of Republicans or Populists", including, most visibly, 1,000 black officials. The backlash against this "negro rule" (as the Democrats labeled it) was the statewide "White Supremacy Campaign" of 1898 (the year Ruth was born), followed in 1900 by a referendum on a state constitutional amendment effectively disenfranchising the lower classes who had dared to assert themselves.[12] Two days before the state was to vote on the amendment (it would pass with 58.6% of the vote), there was a rally in Charlotte, where it was "immediately obvious" that the citizens of Mecklenburg

> were standing Democrat by Democrat, white man and white man alike – committed by preponderant sentiment, to the passage of the constitutional amendment and the election of decent men to the State, legislative and county offices.[13]

At the head of the parade that followed the speeches was Charlotte's police chief Orr, Chief Marshall Heriot Clarkson – vestryman of St. Peter's Episcopal Church, Charlotte's city attorney and pro-tem mayor, and future state supreme court justice – and his assistant marshall, 22-year old Osmond Long Barringer. Following them was the Steele Creek Band and the carriages containing the speakers and their escorts, notable personages to a man.

Make of this episode what one will, it is related here not because it reveals anything unusual about the area's history or Mr. Barringer, during whose lifetime Charlotte became more segregated, not less.[14] Like Mr. Barringer, Bud spent most of his life in the company of whites who were cared for by blacks. Bud liked and admired Mr. Barringer for reasons other than his views on "race", if Bud even knew those views. Discussion of race, meaning race relations and the pursuit of racial equality, used to be taboo. Not, as today, out of shame, but long-standing custom born generations earlier of the need to preserve the institution of slavery.[15] Attitudes naturally shifted anyway. Bud, to the extent he was aware of the shifts, agreed with them. He was certainly not as concerned as Ford, his good friend from Webb School, who wrote to him regularly throughout the war about growing threats to white supremacy such as the elimination of the poll tax as a tool for disenfranchising the lower classes, blacks in particular (North Carolina eliminated it as a qualification for voting in 1919).

> What they don't seem to realize [Ford complained to Bud] is that if the negro is allowed the free vote, he will elect negro officials. I can't quite picture a negro mayor? Or even a negro sherif [sic]. These Dammyankees wouldn't like a negro mayor either, but they don't have the set up like some southern towns where the negro vote would be enough to swing an election. These yankees keep asking me if I think I am better than the negroes. I know darn well I am...[16]

Ford's conviction that he was "better than" was a reflection of his Alabama roots and parental attitudes—attitudes not shared by Bud's parents. Certainly, if Bud ever used racial epithets or negative racial stereotypes the way Ford sometimes did, there is no record of it. Most likely, Bud disagreed with Ford on the poll tax. One can imagine Bud responding to Ford's words in a number of different ways short of "a good, hot argument." One can also imagine him not responding.

Bud sent David (and Webb School) a copy of *Looking Backward*. Once David had read it, he wrote Bud an essay.

> Looking Backward
>
> Our 20th Century may ask "What induces a man to put forth his best endeavor, when, however much or little he accomplishes his income remains the same[?]" Dr. Leete answers that it is the same motive that promps [sic] a soldier on the field of battle—honor glory—esteem in the eyes of fellow men—Dr. Leete in his explanation says that human nature hasn't changed.
>
> In discussing advancement in industry—Dr. L explains how it is done by periodic competitive exams—the advantage of high grading being that the worker will be able to elect his type of work—
>
> Remembering human nature—while grading work of the type that can be tested only by doing (lath [sic] work,

machining—punch feeding etc.) it may be assumed by us—being imperfect humans—that much abuse will take place—brown noses and all—causing resentment. Remember—Dr. Leete holds forth honor and esteem as payment for endeavor. By substituting payment in esteem and honor for payment in money—a parallel to our present industrial system with its wage abuse may be drawn.

It may be unfair to draw back Dr. L's utopiaistic [sic] system of our own on only one of his many assumptions, but, considering their import, I think it not.

Dear Buddy—I haven't put much thought into this forthcoming statement as to its composition, but I have mulled over its contents many times—Man is basically an animal—as we think of a dog, or, horse—being bruetaly [sic] expressive—when a male animal wants a female animal, it goes and grabs one etc. We humans realizing that other humans are our most dangerous enemies, have, with our so called reasoning powers, come to realize that the only way to survive is to set up certain rules—our ethics, customs, manners—which make life easier.

Men—as is—would break these customs, ethics etc.—when he needed or desired—if he thought he could get away with it—Our policemen not only protect us from John Thiefs family but also Hieght [sic] Of Respectability's family. Social position and "what others might say" also act as policemen.

Our Dr. Leete neé Bellamy assums [sic] that 21st or 22nd or what have you—century man will either have lost his greed or be deprived of the way of making use of it. (greed) He assumes that man will have no jealosy [sic], no desire to make himself better than others at the expense of others.—Man is subject to greed, jealosy, hate, lust,—when he thinks he can get away with it in his own or other's eyes—conscience is an elastic constraint—a man with his reasoning powers, may twist it to encompass all passions. I think that "Looking Backwards" has served excellently to point out the falts [sic] of our own present system. His solution clash with our present human nature (By the by—in describing my human animal, I was using my self as the example—I believe it will hold true) Modification of his ideas—maby—Through the passing of time our minds might be made to mitigate passion and make this utopia of equalization possible.

> Of need—I must use History—Can you say that true civilization has advanced—are not people even more callous to suffering of others. Have they brought forth any better system for people to live together. [arrow pointing to previous sentence] (this is not a question) Life must always be a compromise between desire and restraint—We have advanced from the cave man, with no restraint. to the present, with a little. Do you think we can reach Bellamy world with its people of no desire. Buddy—I like my passion, I like to try to be better than the next man, to know more, to get more, to depend upon my own conscience for my restraint—Out of compassion for the under privilege [sic]—I want to help them, I don't want to lower myself to them.
>
> I have left the argument for competition, free enterprise, out of my argument, because its products have been of arguable value. In a 20th century materialistic sence [sic], they could be effectively used, but Bellamies [sic] thought and their modern counter part will be in contension [sic] through centuries.
>
> Bellamy if living, could point out things in my way of life to which I could only answer with a shrug, or "this is life" but with its admitted falts, it is more desirable. Maby "my way" could be coached by using the term liberty + freedom, not of want, not of food, not of shelter, not of the pleasure of security—these, Bellamy gives you, but—freedom of desire, that's what I want. It is a matter of degree of desire. The caveman had no restraint, we have a little, Bellamy is complete in restraint[.][17]

The essay-letter was the last from David before he was discharged. Bud replied to it promptly.

> I think that I have an arguement for Bellamy against your freedom of desire. It's hard to put it on paper but here goes. First Bellamy has already for the most part taken care of all material desires. After 2 or 3 generations under his system material desire will be wiped out. Why? Because it won't have any value of esteam [sic], honor matieral [sic] or anything. A boy or man who has been getting the best of food, clothes, education + etc. will look around for a guiding star somthing to hook his dreams onto. It is very plain that he

> will not want more food more clothing or more of anything material because no one admires that sort of thing. He will want to become the best in what he likes to do. God! it's plain to me as the nose on me face. Definately here would be freedom of material desire. An[d] as for the other desires there is where Bellemy [sic] so cleverly introduced the servival [sic] + reproduction of the fittest. You see, their [sic] will be no marriages because of "money" or material want of any kind. Instead they will be for "love" you can say which springs from <u>admiration</u> to a large extent. Marriages will be more successful then with the persons who are most admired by their fellow man. An[d] in this set up they are admired not by what they have but what they realy [sic] are.[18]

Bud did admit he "would not particularly [sic] like to live under such a system, because of its great personal sacrifice." Nor was he convinced such an arrangement could be made to work. ("I can see that the whole world would be much better off if we had it + it worked." and "It's just a matter of actually trying it out now to see if it will work.") Bud may have been a romantic (as most young men are), but his skepticism about the workability of "Bellamy world", not to mention his awareness that *he* would not care to live in it, make it hard to accuse him of idealism. Rather more consonant were *The Opinions of Oliver Allston*, a book by Van Wyck Brooks that Bud read shortly after finishing *Looking Backward.* As he confessed to his mother,

> When I am reading "The Opinions of Oliver Allston" by V.W. Brooks, I find that I almost never dispute what he says + when I put the book down + think that I must have agreed with everything he said I think that maybe I'm too easly [sic] influenced + have no mind of my own, but I have read somewhere that that is the characteristic of youth. We have not been obliged to form many definate opinions for our selves so we don't.[19]

In contrast to Bellamy's rejection of everything to do with the 19th century class system, Brooks's friend Oliver Allston had (like Ruth) "never lost his feeling for the Victorian age"[20], lamented that "Americans in general are no great shakes at conversation"[21], preferred the village to cities, and thought that "[o]ne cannot know what respect is unless one learns it in the country."[22] He was also a socialist who thought communism was not "in the American grain"[23], he considered it only natural for "younger thinking people" to feel sympathy with Soviet Russia.[24]

> We Americans are the most romantic of peoples. More than any other, we need heroes; and we cannot make heroes of people who only make money... Russia was the world's romance for fifteen years, because the search for social justice is the romance of our time.[25]

Mid-September, *Bayfield* embarked troops of the 81st Division in Leyte for transport to Aomori, Japan, which had been firebombed in July. The landing would be Bud's fifth (after Normandy, Provence, Iwo Jima, Okinawa) and last, but would "not be proceeded [*sic*] with the anxiety of danger that haunted the others."[26] Musing on the supply office typewriter, he wrote:

> For some reason I feel that I must jot down a few lines. We landed troops on the mainland of Japan, the Empire of the Rising Sun, today. Many boys like those around me and men like Cic [*sic*] or Don have died. They were just stepping stones to bring about what we are doing now... It now seems to me that at the time of Perl [*sic*] Harbor and the months that followed, we had very good reason to fear the Japs. This fear very easily [*sic*] turned into hate... Now that we have no more reason to fear them our hate for them seems a little emptyer [*sic*].[27]

"Cic" (Cec Morris) and Don (Don Dunne) were two of the "Syracuse boys" Bud got to know in 1942 when they came to Camp Sutton with the 801st Tank Destroyer Battalion. After the war, Cec and his wife Skip returned to Syracuse. Cec got into the insurance business but would drop dead (heart) in the summer of 1953. Don did not want to go back to Syracuse. His mother had died when he was two years old and he had been raised by nuns. He had a wife in Syracuse, but they were estranged. Ruth had made him feel welcome at Deverill; she was someone he could confide in—the mother he never had, he said. Over the course of the war he attached himself to the family through frequent visits, personal charm and steady correspondence, with the occasional parcel from overseas containing German army rifles, knives, etc. After the war, he and Bud and David would end up together at University of Virginia. To the grandchildren he was always Uncle Don.

After D-Day, when Don and Bette, his wife, seemed close to reconciling, Ruth invited Bette to visit Deverill, but Don was sent overseas before it could be arranged. To Don's distress, Bette stopped writing to him after about six months. In January of '45, a few weeks after the Battle of Ardennes, Don was thinking and writing to Ruth about what he would do after the war.

> [M]aybe I'll become a resident of the Queen City. Do you suppose they'll have me? You see Ruth—my life has been a lonely one—and I don't intend for it to be any more. Before the war I didn't know how to enjoy myself—didn't know or perhaps knew + didn't realize the happiness one can find in doing things for other people cultivating friends—real, close friends. Ones that you can talk to as I'm trying to talk to you now. People used to come to me with their troubles + I was a good listener—never had any advice to give in return—but would try to help by picking apart their troubles + looking for the cause of it—sometimes it worked—most always I never knew the results. What I'm driving at + I think you've seen it in me—tho they come to me—I never went to them. I'd close up like a clam when it came to talking about my own troubles—never felt that anyone cared. [N]ever trusted anyone—never shared any joys or sorrows and always wanted to. When Bette came along I thought she was the one who would share my life—but had I taken—no it was never given—had I seeked [sic] advice from a friend I doubt if we would ever have married—now too late. I know we'll never be happy together, for that feeling of trust so necessary just won't be there.[28]

Don was still with the 654th Tank Destroyer Battalion when he wrote Ruth from Merzig.

> There are still a lot of your letters that I haven't answered. In particular the one asking what I'm doing about Bette. Ruth I know you are right when you say I can't go thru life suffering the ill affects of a bad marriage. I know I'll never be happy, completely, unless some thing happens to change it. But believe me Ruth I have done all I can to change it. A divorce on my part is out of the question because the Catholic church will not permit it. It does sound a bit illogical and you are probably saying to yourself rite now "Balderdash" or whatever it is you say to yourself when something like this comes to your attention, but I mean it Ruth, I've done all I can to change the situation one way or the other. All I've got to do now, all I can do now is remember that I'm technically, legally, officially and what have you still married until or unless Bette dies in the meantime...That is the substance of my explanation. However I will not turn my back on advice that would possibly lead to a different solution.[29]

Ruth advised him to try for what is commonly called an annulment.

> I don't think I've ever made any reply to what you had to say in your letter of July 5 about your marriage—church, divorce, etc. To discuss these matters requires a great deal of courage (you may wish to substitute "effrontery" there) on my part, so I don't do it casually. I do not beleive [sic], however, that I have ever spoken to you of my profound respect for the attitude of the Roman church in the matter of divorce. I do not know if you are aware that the Anglican Catholic (Episcopal) is not so very different. No priest will marry a person divorced for any other reason except being the innocent party in a case of adultry [sic] That sentence seems incoherent but doubtless you understand what I am trying to say. But what I do want to say is this, I know a number of Catholics (Roman) who have gotten a special dispensation from the Pope I do know that the greatest persistence and effort was required and that it took time—but the point is—you will have to use this effort and persistence—it can be obtained—that I am certain of and have good advice to strengthen this faith. If there is a chaplain of any force whom you find sympathetic, go

to him with your story—And, above all, go and get things done while you can, with a clear conscience, as for annulment on principle and not because you are in love with, and want to marry some particular girl. And that, my dear, will be the first time you have a chance—I mean the falling in love. Now that's a lot of good advice—I hope you will take it because, for once, I'm sure it's good—and remember, I never advised this until last spring—Remember, I encouraged you in the hope that a reconciliation could be effected and that all would again be well. Now I'll say good night and write again tomorrow. I do not beleive [sic] you will be angry with me for speaking so plainly for you know I love you very much and want you to be happy. Ruth.[30]

Besides being generally good advice, the admonition to "get things done while you can", before falling in love was a gentle warning. In 1943, Don had raised the expectations of one Joy Fitzsimmons, a good friend of Mary Jo's, who knew Don was married but had (somehow) gotten the impression he was seeking a divorce. Feelings were hurt before she realized this was not the case. Although all was right in the end, Ruth knew the next time might be different. (Joy married a bomber pilot from Wyoming named Gordon Williams and the family adopted him, too,—"Joy and Gordon spent Sunday with us again. Joy says she can't get Gordon to go anywhere else, that he feels at home here!"[31])

In October, a typhoon blew *Bayfield* out to sea, following which she joined Operation Magic Carpet, ferrying demobbing troops home from, and occupying forces back to, the Pacific. David was home five-days on "boot-leave" during that time. When Mary Jo told him Bud was "very anxious to learn to fly with an airport and all above the house", he sent Bud his rendering of a "good layout for the 'port'"[32], and a few days later offered to "go partner with you for a medium plane when you learn to fly."[33] On the return voyage, Bud was "sacked up" for most of a week with a cold. He wrote his mother that he had "stopped smoking + resolved never to again", but his mood was "like the weather outside, dull skies, choppy seas + generally bleak."[34]

> How I yearn for someone that has an interest in the same things I have! I am almost amazed at the fact that no one in the whole ship's company is interested—well they aren't interested in anything enough to want to learn somthing about it. You would think that there would be many who would take advantage of the G.I. bill + go to school, but very few here want nothing [*sic*] but to go home + get a job. Most of them arn't sure exactly what job they want but they all want to make "darn good pay."
>
> I don't understand why most people are anxious to "get started" in a job after they get out of high school or even those that get out of 4 years of college.
>
> But, as for me—my ambition is to get an M.A. in M.E. for practical purposes. Then getting a Ph.D. (or at least makeing [*sic*] it my guiding star) in physics...
>
> You must think that all I think about is going to college + you're probably right. But here's one thing—I don't want to feel obliged to prepare for a "fixed" job in college + farm or maybe not do anything. In other words when I get "educated" there will be no strings attached...[35]

The next day was not much better.

> Tomorrow afternoon at the earliest we are due to arrive in San Francisco and for the first time I will not get to see you after a foreign expedation [*sic*]. Because of this, + my cold + the fact that the war is over + I can't get out I feel pretty low right now. So many fellows are getting off to be discharged + I too would be if I were married or had some dependents...
>
> After thinking over the cause of my sad state of mind again I am inclined to place some of the blame on the dizmal [*sic*] weather (although I've been out very little to observe it) + also the last book ("Dodsworth") that I read which was very sad. [Van Wyck Brooks had mentioned the novel in *The Opinions of Oliver Allston*.] I have resolved never to read anything by the author [Sinclair Lewis] again. There ought to be more books like "Huck Finn" around. There is too much of this cruel world stuff that Stinebeck [*sic*] thrives on.
>
> You can see from my other letters that I have given up telling you anything about the ship. That is because

> I have been on board two years and the very thought of anything on it brings painful memories + now every spare moment I have is devoted to reading, eating or shooting the bull... We have been at sea a full month stopping once only long enough to pull up next to a tanker + fuel. I have had no letters nor have been able to send any all during that time. I hope there is a good show on tonight—anything to relieve the monoteny [sic].[36]

And, Bud eventually came around to David's way of thinking about compulsory military training. When President Truman recommended to Congress a "universal military training" requirement (a draft)[37], he wrote David,

> I'm glad to hear you say that you are getting along o.k. in the Navy. As for me I'll never get along. If I ever have a son 18 years old + him have to get the military training that Trueman [sic] proposes, I'll give up my U.S. citizenship + I mean it. To my mind it's like giving your son to save your hide.[38]

Once in port, Bud had only ten days before *Bayfield* set sail for Jinsen, Korea. He used the time to telephone home and former shipmates, visit his godfather, John Rowold, in Los Angeles ("Be sure to write the Rowolds a note. It won't hurt you"[39]) and ride a roller coaster ("thought I would never live over the first hump – something had gone wrong and we had jumped the track. I could picture my mangled body among the wreckage. It will take days for me to get enough nerve to try it again.").[40] Ruth was distressed to learn that Bud was not able to get "off the ship" (shore duty) or even the 30-day leave he was due for serving in a war zone, but she remained hopeful he would get them "soon." As things turned out, however, she would not see him until *Bayfield* had made two trips to Korea and prepared to turn her command over to the Navy.

Meanwhile, labor strikes at home and abroad were delaying the return of troops from Europe, Don among them. Gradually, however, the demobbed troops were trickling in, restoring Mary Jo's social life.

> I really have been bad about writing [she confessed to Bud]—but ever since I got back from the beach + Mt. Airy the last of Sept. things have been buzzing. I'd no sooner hit town than I was up to my ears in weddings, luncheons, teas, shopping, sorority, bridge etc.—but best of all—the men are coming home—last Saturday 4 men called for dates—that hasn't happened since before Pearl Harbor. And this past week I spent with Fred Maness and his mother at their home in Lawndale—that's near Shelby... Lawndale was owned by Mrs. Schenck's 2nd husband [John F. Schenck (1865-1945)]—he died [last March]. It's nothing but a big cotton mill [Cleveland Mill & Power, built 1888] + the big house for the owner [Schenck's father, "Major" Henry F. Schenk, CSA]... It's practically the only non-union mill around—back during the trouble in 1936 [sic] Mr. Schenck made a speech to the workers about the dam [sic] yankee unions and ended with the Rebel yell—so the mill hands met the "flying squadrons" with guns + drove them away.
>
> Saw Dr. + Mrs. McKay [Katherine's parents] at the Club dance. They are nice people—They asked about you. That was the best dance in four years—down in the bar the whole room would rise with a yell to greet some returning hero—then you could hardly finish the welcome before some one else you hadn't seen for years would come in...[41]

Bud and Katherine McKay were "bouncing letters back + forth pretty good now", with hers (we have only hers) revealing little of note.[42] She signed letters "love, Kat" and called Bud, "m'love." Concerning a certain photo of her posing in front of her plane: "As cute as Susannah is, I'd like to murder her for sending you that hideous picture that was in the Observer." She told Bud she understood what he meant by "regretting the time you've spent in the Navy"[43] and not knowing "which me is doing the talking" ("What a marvelous way of expressing it"[44]), and "had to laugh" when he wrote that he was "practically converted to socialism" because she felt the same, having recently read Marx.[45]

"The trouble" Mrs. Schenck was telling Mary Jo about would have been the Uprising of 1934. The accepted view has long been that North Carolina thrives because it provides cheap labor in a business-friendly, union-free climate.[46] School children were taught its proud history, including Sir Walter Raleigh, the Battle of Kings Mountain, Andrew Jackson, the Civil War (lots of time on this), the Wright Brothers, Tobacco, and the Civil Rights Movement. They generally were not taught the lengths to which its mill owners went to *keep* labor cheap as well as segregated, and specifically not taught about North Carolina's role in the General Textile Strike of 1934, which had its roots in New Deal legislation and the terrible economic conditions the legislation was supposed to address.[47] At the time, Shelby was considered "the most thoroughly organized city in the piedmont,"[48] a hotbed of union organizing in North Carolina.[49] With 1,700 union members claimed in 1934, Shelby was "regarded as a focal center for the Carolina strike"[50], although strike headquarters were in Charlotte.[51] The first day of the strike, "not a wheel was turning [in Shelby] within a few minutes after the Monday morning whistles blew."[52] Once the Shelby mills were shut down [and this included Mr. Schenck's other mill, named for his first wife, Lily Moore] its "flying squadron [a motorcade of union picketers] dashed over the county... swooping down on Lawndale and Double Shoals several times [to call on workers in those mills to join them, and demand mill management shut down operations]... No violence was reported."[53] Cleveland Mill & Power in Lawndale stayed open until the fourth day of the strike.

> Shelby strikers' reply to news that President Roosevelt was to mediate the textile strike and that union leaders had called a halt to flying squadron activities was immediately to organize another cavalcade of 1,000 strikers and speed out of town... The strikers were in seven trucks and 70 automobiles... The squadron was poised this morning to swoop down upon the Cleveland Mill & Power company at Lawndale, six miles out of Shelby, where 500 textile workers have been employed unmolested during the strike. But an announcement was made at noon by mill executives that the mill would close temporarily at 2 o'clock. (September 5).[54]

The strike lasted about three weeks and ended in defeat for the union despite its closing 295 out of 521 mills in North Carolina.⁵⁵ At the time of the strike, Mrs. Schenck was still living in Richmond County (she and Mr. Schenck did not marry until 1941). Her story about her husband's armed mill hands cheerfully driving the "dam yankee unions" from Lawndale would be understood today, and at the time (although not in so many words), as a sort of metaphorical and ritualistic reaffirmation between "nice people" of white (a term that encompasses class and gender as well as race) supremacy as the prevailing institutional and social order. Earl Scruggs worked at the Lily Mill until 1945. Anyone from the area who did any sewing in the 50s and 60s probably remembers the Lily Mill label.

On the way to Korea, Bud read with interest *Clarence Darrow for the Defense*. ("I'm just past the part where he has formed a partnership with Edgar Lee Masters" whose wife was then a teacher at the Country Day School in Charlotte.)

> ...The more I read this book the more I'm inclined to try + see the strikers point of view. Every [sic] since I can remember hearing people around me talking of strikes I've gotten [sic] the impression that they were wrong, wrong under any circumstances. I don't know enough about labor—wheather they need unions in the South or not but I think that all workers whoes [sic] lively hood depends on skill work where they cannot go from one job to another because they are not as reaidly [sic] addaptable [sic] should be able to represent themselves forcefully.
>
> In this world of "might makes right" we get along sometimes only because someone is always submiting [sic] to be stepped on...⁵⁶

When he had finished the book, he wrote to David about it in detail.

> The book not only gives the events in his [Darrow's] life but gives a vivid picture of our social system from 1880 to not so far back. It makes you realize how marvously [sic] we have progressed toward making the U.S. more livible [sic] for the common laborer + for everyone. He was always for

the underdog defending rich + poor for the same reason. He fought the captalist [*sic*] by defending labor leaders. The captalist used every means possible to put down unions accusing union leaders of crimes + then doing their darndest to commit them + do away with the unions all to gather [*sic*]. He also exposed many terrible conditions + low pay that were imposed upon the workers. There were "black lists." There was a time when those who had joined a union had to meet in secret to keep from being put on the "black list." Pinkerton dective [*sic*] agents would filter in among the workers to find out who the union leaders were. The laborers often retaliated with violence because they were desparate [*sic*] but the union leaders knew that this turned the public against even tho they may have been justified in doing it or may not have even started. There were cases where Federal Troops were sent into a state violating states rights there. The troops hearded [*sic*] all union members into a pen for 6 mos. put the town + mining district under military rule + Tedy Roosvelt [*sic*] did nothing because the general in charge of the troops was one of his Rough rider buddies. He also exposed the conditions of the Penn. coal mines + defended the United Mine Workers Union in their blackest moment. You can see what a hard time they had organizing + getting where they are today. I hope you know that John L. Lewis is the head of them now...read the book; you'll find it in almost any book store...A funny thing happened to me after reading that book. The results of my feelings were somthing like loosing [*sic*] your best friend, first day at school + signing up for 20 years. It was the hang over after having read the book.[57]

David had just completed a three-week pre-radio course which he passed, but did not think he did well enough to make the cut for the primary school, which he told Bud he "didn't particularly care to go on through", a preference he had expressed previously.

> The work is simple and easy to understand, but the navy really means business and the speed of the course is astounding and the quantity of homework stupendous. We are schedual [*sic*] 11 hours a day—9 hr. of classes and 2 of study. Here is when and why I lost out—I was too slow in the simple algebra operations and since their [*sic*]

> was no time to study—my first grades were very low. This course has helped me very much and I've learned of my lacking—and their cure—namely—the wiping out of carelessness and developing of accuracy in mathematical operations—the cure has already been partially effected, but too late.[58]

In virtually all their correspondence during this time, the brothers discussed plans for college ("When we get out you will go to school for the love of property + I will go for the love of knowledge"[59]), focusing mainly on when they might start and the merits of M.I.T. versus Duke University's engineering programs. Somewhat in dismay, Bud informed David, "Did you know that you have to have two years of either German or French before you can get a B.S. degree? That is going to be a pain in the neck for me. I hate languages."[60]

The *Bayfield* commissary department moved up two decks. It was quieter, easier to read, but also easier to feel the ship's movement. One day out from Jinsen, Korea, Bud wrote Ruth this rather vivid description of being in rough seas.

> The water is very calm in contrast with the realy [sic] rough weather we had a few days ago. Then it was as rough as I've ever seen it. The flat bottom of the ship would hit with a jar that made the whole tub vibrate for minutes. If you stood at the bow, for one minute the ocean would come up at you + you'ed [sic] lost about 75 lbs of weight. Then you'ed shoot up + weigh 200 lbs. Then come down with a bang when the flat bottom hit + spray would shoot out each side + 40 mi wind would blow it over the super structure. It was fun for a while. At night in the sack I get [sic] a terrible feeling when we rolled that we were just going to roll right over.[61]

Ruth had reason to worry and no doubt did worry. Just a month earlier, the *Observer* had carried an AP story describing how two minesweepers were rolled and crushed in a typhoon off Okinawa, killing all but 6 of 33 of the crew of one vessel, and all but 1 of 23 of the other.[62] She kept her worry to herself. "I am very glad", she wrote to Bud, that David had made the cut for primary school after all, and had been sent to Gulfport, Mississippi.[63] Thanksgiving Day, Bud was in Jinsen on what he called a "sight seeing tour."

> ...I had two dollars worth of yen (15 yen to a dollar) but did not buy anything. I would like to have just given it to some of the wreaches [sic]. The town is filthy. The smell of garbage is all over the place. Rust + dirt are everywhere. The streets are cobble stone there are no sidewalks [sic]. The dirty wooden shops come to the streets edge. In the streets were carts puled [sic] by bulls, dirty, loud kids, women with dirty faced babies strapped to their backs, a little girl 5 or 6 carried a bab [sic], dirty faced sleeping with his mouth open looking as though he'ed [sic] been dropped on his face a few times. [O]ne of our fire raids would have left only the few cement or brick buildings standing. I never knew there was such porvety [sic] in the world. Only the younger generations have expressions of pleasantness on their faces. The kids in the streets are frisky but the middle aged or old for the most part seem sad. I know I would be too. the shop keepers do not seem to care wheather [sic] you buy their goods or not. I was glad to get back to the ship. I ate chow as soon as I came back + then threw half of it away. Reminds me of a story by Poe ["The Masque of Red Death"], I think, about a castle where outside people were dying of the black plague + inside the rich nobility were having luxeries [sic] of the best food + parties. [The host and all guests die in the end.]
>
> I am glad that I am an American, yes. but I would like to give up somthing to these people + help them in their persuit [sic] of happiness but that's impossible...[64]

Feeling generally powerless, frustrated, and self-critical, Bud wrote to his mother that he did not like his dependence on the ship's nightly movies and books "for pleasure. It seems a way of cheating yourself... I should actually be doing the things of my own imagination."[65] He was also disappointed in Mr. Hunt, who "seems to be stalling on my rate + I am going to speak to him tomorrow about it. Darn his hide. He burns me up. I'll see Thompson if he doesn't get it through in two days."[66] Evoking the "Rubáiyát" in a brief letter to David ("Dear Terd Face"), he wrote, "Korea is dirty, cold, The people are free and nothing more. The towns are flimsy and filthy + famished. Tomorrow I'm headed back sans mail, sans rate, sans stops."[67]

Bud finished *War and Peace* on the return voyage, and "wondered how she [Russia] became what she is now."[68] Americans today know that dropping the atomic bomb on Japan had had more to do with Russia than with Japan, who had sought terms prior to August 6, the day Hiroshima was incinerated. Once Japan was officially out of the way, the focus was all on Russia.

> Talking to these troops coming back on our ship [Bud wrote to his mother]. Their only concern is for themselves + maybe naturally so but they should at least know + have some opinions about the questions that are coming up every day. About Russia—they make a snap judgment + say—"well we'll be fighting her next"—or that we aught [sic] to put the pressure on + let her see our muscles. If our government waits for the public... for an opinion that will induce action they'll wait a long, long time. They act + the public will approve or disapprove but they aught to act soon + mold somthing like world cooperation to shape before the clay hardens.[69]

Bud phoned his mother as soon as *Bayfield* arrived in Seattle to let her know his rating—SK3/C—had come through.

> I won't be modest—It gives me a feeling of destinction [sic]. I'm not just a seaman that "go in + out of the hatches all the time." I bought a box of cigars, according to etiquit [sic], + upon offering them to my buddies informed them that I was a rated man.[70]

He tried to tell her he would not get leave and would probably have his "government job" for four more months "at the least." He told her he could not get off because the ship was "under manned + they can't get any ashore", but that he was "doing a lot of book work now + will know enough to take over in a month."[71] Ruth was worried he was not getting enough fresh food. It did not help matters that Bud had written saying he had hookworm (a parasite) when in fact he had ringworm (a fungus). She may have feared he was not asserting himself sufficiently, and needed encouragement.

> I want you to ask for and insist upon that thirty day leave. I know boys who have been in only a year who are out—discharged and back in school—of course the idea is that they have to take a chance on being drafted—but in my opinion it is a very remote one—now you are due a leave—take it !!!![72]

In a second letter written the same day, she is so frustrated she cannot stop thinking about it in between the usual bits of news from the homefront. She seems convinced Bud just is not trying.

> It was wonderful to talk to you again but I can't bear the thought that you won't get home. Please try to get a 30 day leave. ...There must be boys available. They have continued to enlist steadily and all the [military training] schools have been closed. They told David's class in pre radio that they were the last class and only 60% of them went on to primary. In addition a large number had resigned and taken sea or shore duty. I have heard that skippers are very reluctant to let satisfactory men go. So I presume you are very satisfactory. Ask for 30 day leave + agree to go back next trip. You can eat lots of greens and cornbread etc. and get in good shape...If you stayed until the B. sailed and worked—then should you leave it would just about work out 30 days—judging by the last...[After relating that Martin was due in a few days to have an operation to repair a hernia:] By the way it might be a great help to me if you could be home then...P.S. you can use Mr. [Martin] operation as a reason for 30 day leave + it is a reason. Don't let yourself be talked out of it!!![73]

Realizing her distress, Bud wrote to David, "Mother seems worried that I'm not getting off the ship but there is nothing I can do about it."[74] Ruth was not alone in her frustration. Families across the country were writing their representatives and generally complaining about their boys not coming home soon enough, and so were some of the boys.[75] Meanwhile, *Bayfield* moved up the coast to Everett, Washington. On a postcard to Ruth, Bud wrote "There is much more to the town than this but as far as I'm concerned the USO is the best place in it." On Christmas Eve, Bud went to Trinity Episcopial Church on the corner of 23rd and Hoyt and was invited to come back in the evening. "The minister [Mr. Jessett] was very nice + said he'd tell you I was there. 'Twas a beautiful church."[76]

Don was expected home from overseas the week before Christmas. The children heard Ruth and Mary Jo,

> talking about Don getting his marriage annulled and they immediately started maby he will marry you Mary Jo—oh I hope you do!! Etc—etc. Well, that wouldn't do—[Ruth explained later to Bud] so to stop them she [Mary Jo] told them a secret! [meaning a lie], that she was engaged to someone else. It worked like a charm + they feel very important.[77]

Afterward, nine year-old Martin was dying to tell Bud the "srekit", but restrained himself, writing only that "Marry Joe hase [has] a big srekit [secret] the only hint i can give you is that it happend [sic] to the Willemsis [Joy and Gordon] do not tell a sool [soul] ore i [sic] will get bold [bawled] out."[78] "I sent Martin's letter on through", Ruth told Bud, "I doubt if you can read much of it."[79]

Ruth made sure Bud heard regularly from Martin and Susannah, almost twelve that Christmas.

> Dear Buddy, [Susannah began], Some people from the Y.W.C.A. are out here to pick some greens (eating). I've a bad cold so I didn't go to school... Yor [sic] letter came too, along with a funny book, two papers, the New York Times, and a letter from Aunt Sarah, Mary Madison, and some railroad company. If Don says it's o.k. may I go hunting with you all? I've been practicing with the german [sic] rifles (unloaded of course). Won't you be discharged soon? Did you see any Geishi [sic] girls in Japan? The house is in an awful mess. Momma is Christmas house cleaning. I'm going to be in a play. I'm to be a cat called Cinders as usual. I'm always a cow or dog or cat or some animal... Martin and I went to see "Rapsody [sic] in Blue" while Mary Jo and Mamma shoped [sic]... Have you gotten your Christmas card yet. Write me soon Love Susannah P.S. My name in French is Suzanne L., S.L.[80]

Depending on one's point of view, Ruth supervised, or proofread, or edited the children's letter writing, e.g., over the word "(eating)" above, Ruth wrote, "Christmas!", the "!" signifying the affront she felt at the suggestion that guests of Deverill would be invited out to pick collards or mustard greens. Many delicate sensibilities of this sort seemed to lie just below the surface of Ruth's waking being. Her reprovals were usually sharp, or at least pointed ("P.S. It is DEVerill not Di !!!"[81]), with no explanation given; these were things she expected one to know. Whether or not one knew them did not matter. Aunt Sarah and Mary Madison were cousins, the daughters of Ruth's brother Matt. Sarah would later hang out with Bud, David and Don (especially Don) at the University of Virginia. If Don did not fall in love with her that winter of 1945-1946, he certainly became infatuated. Mary Madison, her husband Vance Cox, and their one year-old daughter were to move in with Aunt Irene, who did not particularly care for the arrangement, but "thinks it best", Mary Jo told Bud, "You know how Mary M. is rather domineering and you can't tell her anything."[82]

Between the transport worker strikes and his training schedule, David was not to make it home for Christmas. "Be sure to go to midnight service in an Episcopal church"[83], his mother told him. As a gift "from the family", David had sent Bud a Marlin lever action .22 rifle (delivered to Deverill)[84], and as much for being in the hospital as for Christmas, Bud had sent Martin a Japanese rifle, complete with bayonet, but no ammunition. The day of Martin's operation, it "snowed like everything"[85] in Charlotte, but Martin did not care. He had "about two dozen new comics", Ruth informed his brothers, "and won't talk to or notice anyone today, in consequence."[86]

That Christmas, everyone except Ruth and Susannah was sick, including Don, so the holiday was a quiet one ("the smallest in years"). It was just as well. After visiting his sisters in Syracuse and Maryland, Don had arrived in Charlotte with a camera that he had swapped for a German pistol, but no civilian clothes—his having been destroyed in a fire in his old boarding house. That winter, demand for consumer goods was at an all-time high, men's clothing in particular. The weather, too, was bad. "Christmas Eve", Ruth wrote Bud, "we started early to midnight service and couldn't get out of the drive way" (too icy). Christmas night, however, Ruth managed to get into town for a party at Paul and Mary Ann Sanger's, their first since Paul had left with the 38th Evacuation Hospital in 1942, and she was not about to miss it. The party lasted until four in the morning.[87] The following week, Sarah Smith came down from Mount Airy to visit. "Sarah is such a sweet girl and plays the piano beautifully. It is a pleasure to have her with us", Ruth told Bud.[88]

On *Bayfield's* second voyage to Korea (sans troops), Bud wrote about his latest literary undertaking, *The Theory of the Leisure Class* by Thorsein Veblen, published in 1899. Despite the "awkward number of 'high falutin' words" employed (said to be "a mixture of mechanic's terms, scientific latinity, slang and Roget's Thesaurus"[89]), Bud understood enough to be disturbed, perhaps as much as he had been by *Dodsworth*, the 1939 novel based on Veblen's theories.

> ...He uses the words "Conspicuous Consumption" which emply [sic] much to my mind. This foresaid trait is a predominate [sic] example of the idea that everything man does is done through a purely selfish motive.
> To explain; you give somthing to someone (This, you think can not be from a selfish motive) but it is. If you do not expect to get somthing back in return you get the satisfaction of thinking yourself a kind hearted, etc or if an expensive guift [sic], to let the sundried [sic] know you're B.T.O. [Better Than Others] etc. Maybe that's why it's better to give than to recieve [sic], it's more profitable if not materially then mentally [sic].
> ...The most disturbing thoughts I've ever had arose from the fact that my esteem, public + private, depended so largely on the degree of material wealth that I'm able to acquire. The evolution of this concept can be traced back to the first days of man himself + Veblen does it. So far he has offered no solution nor prediction; darn it. Bud[90]

Thanks in large part to Veblen, society today takes for granted the power of invidious distinction and the effect of performative

Figure 8.1: Bud's Dream House

wealth on social standing. But this way of looking at the world was new to Bud, who had been raised to believe that all persons are deserving of respect. This is not to suggest that Bud was or saw himself as anything other than a product of American culture. "What do you think of it!", Bud asked David in his next letter:

> This drawing by a future architect + friend is supposed to represent my "Dream House" at the present. The entrance at the right will have an iron grating with spikes at the bottom which will be lowered from the upper part of the entrance at will. This will be the entrance to a kind of cort yard [sic]. To the left are living quarters. The structure with the big glass window is my labratory [sic].[91]

In reply, David surmised Bud had been watching "'Frankenstine-Dracula' [sic] movies", wondered "where is an appropriate place for it?" and "where will the mulah [sic] come from." Still, David thought it would be "nice...in a goulish [sic] sort of way."[92]

Radio Tech school in Gulfport was in some ways not so different from David's days at Webb.

> Well, last night when I went back to my hut from the lounge where I was writing the first part of this letter—anyway,

> when I opened the door—a vision of gold braid, smoke and snafu caught me—the kerosine stove had blown up and had been put out with a fire foam extinguisher—3 officers were there and when I opened the door—they all turned to me as if they expected me to do or say say something so I said "whoosh" and they laughed ????? Boy! there is more chicken[shit] here now—the Commodore burnt the exc. and the exc. burnt Salt (our Lieut.—J. G.) and so he is burning us. Oh well, I'm not being worked too hard.[93]

Not long afterwards, David either quit, or was otherwise severed from, the school for reasons other than poor grades. A letter from Ruth hinting at the circumstances is all that is known.

> [Y]ou have plenty of time now. You must learn to control your facial expressions or it will cause trouble. I know just how you looked—remember I've used my hand on you in time past for just such a look!! I do hope you get an assignment to sea duty. You will learn more—be better off and happier.[94]

After three weeks at sea, *Bayfield* arrived in Jinsen and loaded troops before setting sail for San Francisco.

> With this extra weight we probably won't bounce around like we did comming [*sic*] over. No one got to go ashore this time + it's just as well. There are small pox in the town, some of our army has died from them already + some MP's have been knifed in the back + stoaned [*sic*]. The Sick bay gave us the pox vaxine [*sic*] day before yesterdy [*sic*]+ mine starting to iche [*sic*] now.[95]

Ruth continued to write to Bud even supposing "there is no use in me writing—you won't get any mail until you get back—but I'm afraid not to—you might get mail somewhere along the way"[96], and to David, reminding him to write. ("If nothing is wrong and you havn't [*sic*] any good reason for not writing, just consider all the things you know I'd say, said—in other words, consider yourself 'bawled' (sp?) 'out'!"[97]) She let both of them know Don had decided to study medicine at the University of Virginia if he could get in, and began nudging them toward Charlottesville. ("Would you like to go to the University of Virginia? It ranks with the best of the schools and is a wonderful country and climate."[98]) Don did manage to get into the premed program, but it was accelerated (two years instead of three), and he lacked the necessary grounding in mathematics. He eventually would have to switch to his first choice, languages.

On 8 February, Bud telephoned Ruth from San Francisco and gave her "the dope" on getting leave:

> Today I found the dope from Comdr. Hatch who got it strait [sic] from the Capt. The "B" will stay docked up 'till the 25th then move out into the bay + anchor 25th—1st of March then from the 1st to the 7th we'll go on a shake down cruise with the Navy relief crew + get off about the 8th of March. Then we'll get leave.[99]

Thirty more days was apparently too long for Ruth, who scolded him. "[Y]ou just haven't been persistent enough", she told him, though she eventually resigned herself. "If you get off at the end of the 30 days, I'll be partly reconciled."[100] Bud took in the Bay area sights, got lost coming back from "Okland", and found himself "saddened slightly to find out that even fewer people than I thought enjoyed poetry. Surely [no]one that truly enjoys poetry could fail to know some of the 'Rubaiyat'."[101]

> Comming [sic] back from 'Frisco on the "A" train an Ensign [crossed out] no he was a Lt. sat next to me + after the pleminaries [sic] I ask[ed] if he'd ever read the "Rubaiyat." He was looking so intently at the pocket edition I'd just bought. He hadn't tho' he had eaten at Omar Khayyam's in 'Frisco. I also asked the same thing of the O.D. [duty officer] as I came aboard ship a few minutes ago + he'd never herd [sic] of it.[102]

When not seeing the sights, Bud looked for, but was unable to find, ammunition for either the German or the Japanese rifle. He also had a comparatively long visit with Dickie Baxter who was waiting at Fort Ord to ship out to somewhere in the Pacific.

> I had liberty at one oclock so I finally contacted him by phone at Ft. Ord + he came to 'Frisco + we had a swell week end (got my liberty extended) It took him 4 hrs to get up here so meanwhile I got tickets to "The Two Mrs. Carrolls" with Elisabeth Bergner. It was very good. Today we went out to the Golden Gate park + went [horseback] riding then saw (in person) Spike Jones, the guy who playes [sic] with a wash board, horns etc. Stuff like the "Fu[h]rer's Face" is his stuff. All in all we realy [sic] had a time.[103]

With liberties so frequent, Bud was burning through his cash pretty quickly.

> When I think of the radio equiptment I could buy with the money I spend every liberty I get disguested [sic]. From now on I'm minimizing. They are making millions off the gobs [sailors] here in 'Frisco.[104]

He also got a taste of the labor unrest that he had been reading about for months.

> I had to get supplies from pier 56 'Frisco when we were doked [sic] over at Okaland [sic] a few days ago + here's the way my day went...I had to be over at P56 at 3 oclock PM with a landing barge so I start pestering the O.D. at about 1:oclock for a boat + crew to make the 45 minute trip over. Well, we start at 2, but due to the engine heating up a little it took an hour. That's fine. Well, I get to 56 + no supplies. They hadent [sic] been delivered so I wait 'till 5 Then finally a union truck driver whoes [sic] excuse was that his watch stopped drove up with my 800 gals of milk. Just as they got it out on the dock where a crain [sic] would lower it rite in my boat it's time to knock off + they do. I argued with them + even offered to pay them over time which they said that they don't work over time except when they get paid for it. The whole job would have taken less than 10 minutes with the crain but we had to load it by hand + that took 3/4 hour there. Well, we started back + right in the middle of the Frisco bay the engine konked out. In a little while we'ed [sic] hooked up to a tank lighter [flat-bottomed barge used to transfer goods and passengers to and from moored ships] that towed us to Treasure Is[land

Naval Station]. It was dark by then. I phoned the ship + waited another hour for a boat to come + towe [*sic*] us back to the "B". Then I had to go through the quarters getting a man here + there to form a working party—finally got the stuff in the reaffer [*sic*] boxes [reefer boxes are temperature-controlled shipping containers] took a shower + hit the sack at midnight.[105]

Figure 8.2: David and Bud

Chapter 9

Come you home a hero

On Valentine's Day 1946, the *New York Times* reported that the Army had lowered the physical standards for induction and "reached out for about 75,000 4Fs to make up the cumulative deficit in draft calls since V-J day", among them Hutch and Bud's cousin Gene, Jr. Hutch wrote to David that he hoped he would be sent to Germany, as "It would just be hell to have to stay in some place like Kansas", and chided him for not writing to his mother.

> Really you are just an old so and so. I spend all of my time taking your side with everybody who is mad at you for not writing. The only reason I do [is,] in a way[,] I am defending myself as I very seldom ever write. I know how it is. <u>However</u> you really should write every now and then and let us know that you are still among the living.[1]

Bud arrived home on leave on schedule, following *Bayfield's* transfer to Navy command, and, like Don, he was unable to find civilian clothes to replace those that, in his case, he had outgrown. The day before he left California, he had written to David that he had decided to "be a M.D. God knows why. Maybe I figure I'll never be worth a damn at anything else."[2] The decision was never very firm, but he repeated it about a week later in another letter to David.

> I'm home + have been working to get the shop set up in [the] smoke house. I've already spent about $10 for wiring for current from the pump room. It'll be a permanent job. (For 10 bucks it ought to be). Have already moved some equiptment up from the mill including the drill press. I've decided to go to U. of Va. may be a doc. but not positive.
>
> You [sic] probably get sea duty + even get in on the atomic bomb deal [testing]. The Bayfield is in on it but then it's on the West coast.
>
> I'm here in the library listening to the radio. Edward [parrot] is on the table next to the fire place + [S]pot is dreaming of rabits [sic] on the rug. Had a good time flying over. Got a ride out of 'Frisco in a DC3 owned by two x service Fliers as far as St' Louis. I got to sit in the co-pilots seat for a while.
>
> Been brushing up on my radio with that radio book of yours. Can't wait 'till Army surplus stuff get [sic] on the market but then we may have to hit R[ussia] first. [3]

Edward, a four-year old bird, green with yellow head and red-tipped wings, arrived at Deverill in the spring of 1945.[4] Ruth took him in as a favor when he was not getting on well with another parrot.[5] Edward, Ruth wrote Bud, loves to sing (no words) and being petted and talked to.[6] Mary Jo declared him to be "a thoroughly entertaining bird, but I know just what daddy meant when he used to accuse us kids of having faces dirty as the bottom of a bird cage!"[7]

> The parrot is very cute and furnishes a lot of amusement [Ruth reported]. He says "Hello Edward, hello!" "Hello, love!" "What?" and whistles and sings and laughs. Every time I call one of the children he answers and sometimes I'd like to wring his neck.[8]

Edward soon learned to wail, "Mama!" Ruth would let Edward out of his cage to stretch his wings on the screened-in back porch, and then be surprised when "the young devil" would refuse to return to confinement until enticed with his favorite snack of milky coffee and graham crackers.[9] Spot was a large fox terrier, a gift from "Mac" (the senior Dr. McLean), who thought Ruth needed a watchdog. Deverill had many dogs, including (during these years) Whisky, Flossie, Fitz and his mother 'Bama, short for Alabama, an Irish terrier whose master had left her with Ruth when he shipped to North Africa in 1943. Ruth also had a pony named Spot.

Bud flew to Norfolk to try to arrange a transfer from Alameda. Fortunately for Bud, Mr. Hunt, his former boss on the *Bayfield*, was the supply officer for the district and able to pull strings. Bud and Ruth's nephew Strother (Sarah's brother) got "the T" running, so all it needed was tires. When his leave was over, Bud drove with Strother and Sarah to Mount Airy before continuing on to Norfolk by bus. David was back at Naval Station Great Lakes, assigned to the mess hall, and Mary Jo was moving to an apartment in town with Julia Duff and a job at Belk Brothers selling ladies' dresses. "We all think it is the best thing for her to do since it is what she seems to want", Ruth wrote of the decision.[10] It was indeed what Mary Jo wanted. Except for Julia, most, if not all, her best girlfriends—Pat Stoyle, Joy Fitzsimmons, Nancy Wescott—had married, and she and Ruth were by this time "continually at odds."[11] In less than a year, Mary Jo would be married and starting a family of her own.

Hutch's father died (heart) shortly before he was to report. He went to his parents' home in Zebulon, Georgia to be with his mother. Ruth, looking forward to Bud's being discharged in May, focused on her spring cleaning, which she took very seriously. ("Do you want the pine room or the third floor?...I'm moving Martin or Susannah one [or the other,] and want to get them settled."[12]) Bud's time in Norfolk was the everlasting bore that he expected it would be, as he quickly tired of shore duty, frequent liberties, weekends off, and not having

> a darn thing to do. I just sit + sit—go out to get some fresh air then come back in + sit some more. Think I will come home next week end. I'll know I go nuts with boredom if I don't.[13]

The crowded buses between Norfolk and Charlotte landed Bud in the base hospital with mumps,—first one side, then the other. As he was recovering, he and Ruth corresponded about plans for "the 'T'" and school. Colleges were enrolling students in record numbers. Either because of his desire to "be an M.D.", or because of Don's being there already, a decision was made to attend the University of Virginia. Despite the previous discussions of M.I.T. vs. Duke, all Bud appears to have said to David about this decision was, "Do you want to go to U. of V. too?"[14] Bud was discharged on May 18, exactly three years after induction and a couple of weeks before he turned 21. David was sent to Camp Shoemaker, California and from there assigned to the U.S.S. *Pickaway*. He was to recall the experience many years later in an email to a friend of his daughter Jean who had asked him about it.

> Few events take place on a ship at sea. Three men serve one position on rotating watches. The sea is the sea, the watch duty is unvarying, the contact with other crew is very limited. A storm at sea is an event to remember, but is rarely encountered because ships get out of the way if possible. The event of the day is sacking out in your bunk. Entering and leaving port breaks the routine of watches. Loading ammunition can be fun!
>
> I can not remember having any particular feeling towards bombing of anything, nor did I observe any feelings by my shipmates. There was a feeling of relief at the ending of the war with Japan. We were so occupied in an unvarying routine that everything outside was remote. At our age, there was little abstract thought or thinking, much less feeling.
>
> While at sea, I stood watch as bow lookout. I was connected by voice powered phone to the bridge and reported any object in the way of the ship (logs, sea turtles, fishing boats, lights, mines...). While in a port, I loaded stores, chipped paint, cleaned the head... I was a seaman first class. My ship was the APA 222, Pickaway. I was at sea only about 4 months. It could have been 2 years as it felt. I recall no bullying or hazing. There was little time for socializing. There was much coming and going of men. There was little consciousness of age or culture or status. You could detect where someone was from. At the time I

was serving, the Navy had started to enlist deferred college students. They were identifiable.[15]

While David was at sea, Hutch in Army Diesel School somewhere, and Don in summer school at the University of Virginia trying not to "lose his head" over Sarah Smith, Bud was home enjoying himself and pursuing his pre-war interests. There is a photograph of him on Deverill's second floor balcony, probably taken by Don. He is lounging on the right arm of a bentwood loveseat, his right arm is bandaged above the elbow, his knees are bent and his bare feet are resting on a pillow propped against the loveseat's left arm. He is looking impassively at the camera, his left hand resting on the seat by his side, while his right hand rests on his knee, holding a cigarette. His entire chest is wrapped in gauze bandages. A burn of some sort? A bomb or chemistry experiment gone wrong, perhaps? The historical record is without clues.

In June, Ruth closed on the purchase of 90 acres on Deverill's northern boundary. She paid $42 per acre, using her share of the proceeds from the sale of the three "Hay Street" houses in Mount Airy, presumably rental, in her father's estate. She put the land in Bud's name. The year before, she had offered $40 an acre for the land between Deverill and McAlpine Creek, which David described to Bud as consisting of

> 19 acres of good meadow 15 of good field, (sheet washing in 3-4 acres however) and the remaining 15 acres in 5-6 year pines (7-8 acres) and World War I forest, mostly pines. The price of $65 per acre ["Old man Soule" was asking] is utterly ridiculous so I plan to offer $1800. I'm giving $40 an acre plus $200 thrown in for the terracing he has put in.[16]

Soule ended up selling the land to the Thompson Orphanage, instead. The 90 acres was an investment, certainly, but Ruth may also have had in mind Bud's stated desire to "be a farmer." It was to be the only acreage Bud would receive from her, apart from his one-fifth share of the portion that would be designated the homestead. He sometimes referred to his acreage as "the upper farm."[17]

The fact was, farming in Mecklenburg County was fast on the wane, with farms giving way to suburban development. The rate of this change post war had everything to do with something Bud had seen for himself while in the Pacific. As he had related to Ruth the previous year from Saipan,

> The truck that was hauling my supplies crossed a dirt road + about 1/2 mile up we could see that they [the Navy Construction Battalions or "Seabees"] were paveing [sic] it with asphault [sic]. When we crossed it again in about an hour they were getting closer + when we had to cross it again in 2 hours we had to turn around because they didn't want us driving across the asphault till it dried. That's speed. There are cases like that all around. One week I saw a bare space of ground + the next week there was a large warehouse there already full of supplies. The reason for this speed is due a lot to the men, but it's because they have modern equiptment + plenty of it to do the job.[18]

One of those Pacific Seabees was Bill Levitt, a man David Halberstam described as able to take on "on tasks that no one thought could be done and pulled them off."

> At night, Levitt sat around with other young men in the Seabees, all of whom had backgrounds in building and contracting, and they would brainstorm about their work—what they were doing that day, how to do it faster, and also what they would do after the war. The Navy, Bill Levitt said years later, provided him with a magnificent laboratory in which to experiment with low-cost mass housing and analyze it with his peers—a chance he might never have had in civilian life.[19]

It was Levitt, Halberstam observed,

> who first brought Ford's techniques of mass production to housing, up to then the most neglected of American industries... The typical prewar builder put up fewer than five houses a year... Levitt revolutionized the process of home building with remarkable planning and brilliant control procedures [that] made it possible to provide inexpensive, attractive single-unit housing for ordinary citizens, people

who had never thought of themselves as middle class before.[20]

Between the dearth of housing construction in the prewar years, and the boom in postwar demand, the U.S. in 1945 had a housing needs deficit in the neighborhood of five million units—units that, for the most part, would not be built in cities (row houses, apartments) but in auto-centric suburbs radiating away from their downtown business centers. Mecklenburgers with a family farm to sell or develop were positioned to make a small fortune by selling or developing the land for single-family housing, and many did. These were the years that Charlotte began its Atlanta-like sprawl toward previously undreamt of prosperity.

The Navy discharged David in August, a few days before his 19th birthday, and he and Bud soon joined Don at University of Virginia. They would at least initially be too busy with school to be writing their mother, so Ruth relied on Don for news.

> Bud and David are at work already [Don reported in October of '46] and seem very pleased with the room and meal arrangement... —Bud just got back a little while ago from choir practice + seemed to have enjoyed it so much he says he's going to continue. The choir he went to has a good reputation around here and there are a number of students in it. David was busy studying his Biology but the class text book wasn't sufficient so he got another from the library. I went to ask him some simple thing about the use of the slide rule + he wouldn't stop till he'd shown me all there was to it.[21]

A slide rule, it will be remembered, is a mechanical analog computer that was used for multiplication, division, exponents, roots, logarithms and trigonometry in the days before the electronic digital computer. Notably, if not amazingly, the Los Alamos research team of the Manhattan Project managed to complete their work using only slide rules. In 1946, any college-level math course required slide-rule skills.

> Bud + David both seem satisfied with their courses [Don reported to Ruth]—except that they're not in Engineering

school [here endeth any further reference to Bud's interest in becoming an M.D.]. I read Bud's first English theme last night and it wasn't too bad—no glaring mistakes—but when I tried to correct or rather point out what I thought was a bit of a weakness he put up such a loud argument I said no more. David saw my plight + said—you let him wait 'till [sic] he gets the paper back all covered with red pencil marks. It wasn't that bad tho. David is having a grand time delving into more Civil War history with books from the library. The only reason I can figure why he didn't get Math was the overcrowded conditions. When Bud + I got going on our Physics problems tho David is sure to enter in somewhere—especially when we get fooling around with the slide rule. When I went up to see them earlier this evening they were busy accepting rushing dates from the Fraternities. So far they've got dates with six of them. David is not as enthusiastic about them as Bud and Bud still wishes he had his T model up here—I can't begin to tell you the pleasure it is to have them up here. They've livened up the dining room and my whole life in particular. If we're not studying we're playing together or just talking—no idle moments with them around.[22]

I don't know what I'd do in physics if Bud wasn't here. He was writing his theme last nite on the Values of a College Education and it sounded pretty good—grammaticaly [sic] that is for his main thought was a slightly facetious idea on the "pecuniary motive." [ref. Thorstein Veblin's *Theory of the Leisure Class*.] Bud was trying to be funny about it [i.e. imitate Veblen's sardonic style] and David thought it was an excellent opinion. Both seem to have lost their original enthusiasm about fraternities because it takes up too much of their study time...[23]

Last nite Bud + I went to a lecture given by the Prof of Economics here on Socialism vs. Democracy. After it was over, Bud got into conversation with the Prof + on the way home made the surprising remark that there are so many interesting things besides mechanics in the world! If only Hutch could have heard him say that. And I don't think Hutch would, as an Anglophile, have liked some of the statements and view of the lecturer on Britain's present Gov't.[24]

Beside the choir and lectures, Bud was also participating to some degree in campus political activities; "Wallace Clubs" and the like. Henry Wallace, who would run against Truman in 1948 as Ruth predicted, had just resigned as Commerce Secretary, after going against the Truman administration in saying that the U.S. had no business in the political affairs of Eastern Europe, then under the control of Russia. Ruth sent Bud a clipping of an op-ed titled, "Mr. Wallace Takes His Stand." Echoing his 1944 comment about Churchill, Bud responded,

> I've only to say this—that at least he takes [underlined x4] a stand. God, I wish we'ed [sic] take some stand in the U.N. on the Palistin [sic] partition question. Or any question. We're not wining [sic] friends in Greece or China either. One is almost willing to become very disgusted when people like them, my roomate [sic], doesn't give a damn one way or the other about Greece, Russia, Wallace or anything, oh yes, I believe he did say that he was against Communism, but he doesn't know exactly why he is except for the fact that the Russians are Communist.[25]

In November, the *Charlotte Observer* announced Mary Jo's engagement to Wallace Duncan Gibbs, Jr., and their plan to marry at the end of the month. Parties ensued. The couple would, after an evening wedding at St. Peter's and reception at the Charlotte Country Club, honeymoon in Savannah and then move in with Wallace's widowed mother, Mildred. Don, who would have liked to be getting married, remained encumbered, and his girl friends, as he complained to Ruth, remained "unattainable." He had followed Ruth's advice of the previous autumn to "go and get things done while you can", but, as he informed her that fall,

> The news is sad concerning my annulment. The priest told me we haven't a leg to stand on + cited similar cases—in fact five of them—that had just come back from Rome refused. I still haven't given up hope but have started proceedings for legal separation which will put a big dent in my check book. When I told Bette the priest was going to drop the case she was ready to shoot me and got madder when I refused her request for a divorce.[26]

In reply Ruth apparently mentioned Cardinal Francis Spellman, appointed "Military Vicar" in 1939 to oversee the more than 3,000 military chaplains assigned to a war zone station, giving Don

> a sneaking suspicion that I'm going to write Cardinal Spellman (Vicar is right) and ask his help. Of course I'm not accepting as final the Monseigneur's decision. But his decision and reason for it will bear a lot of weight should the case ever be brought up again in Syr.[27]

As might be expected, Ruth kept up the pressure and Don resisted; he did not like thinking about his situation, much less writing about it.

> I've purposely sidetracked a question you asked me about my marital status in this and my previous letter simply because I just can't seem to write about it. There are so many ends and angles that need explanation for understanding I don't think I can do it right by writing so I'll wait 'till we get a few minutes together. OK?[28]

Don and the boys came home the following weekend. There was after all a wedding to prepare for and not much time in which to do it. Their wedding clothes and booze for the punch alone would, in addition to their studies, take them the better part of the month to secure. ("Bud mentioned something about a half case of rum and brandy a piece plus a half case of [S]outhern [C]omfort. Does this mean a collection of 36 bottles of each plus twelve of the last?"[29]) Finding time and space for a private conversation during this period would have been difficult. But, "The boys were wonderful at the wedding", Mary Jo wrote to Ruth from Savannah. "[D]idn't see David much but Bud really helped me through it all—hope he doesn't have bruises on his hand from my desparate [sic] grip."[30]

After the winter break, Don went to see a local priest named Blakely "about my difficulties":

> [H]e advised me against trying to see Cardinal Spellman right now and instead advised me to see a Prof in Georgetown—a prof. of Canon Law who knows all the ins and outs

> and has connections that would help to reopen the case. I wrote him last nite and asked to see him in Feb after exams. Then I got a letter from the Lawyer in Syr saying not to come to Syr until I hear from him. From the tone of his letter I smell a rat. He served the papers on Bette last Nov and still says the issue is in doubt... When I told Fr. Blakeley the story he felt sure the evidence I had would constitute an impediment that was why he suggested I see the Georgetown Prof. Something's got to work out!...[31]

Between these "difficulties" and his grades in organic chemistry and physics, Don was feeling pretty discouraged after February exams, and the fact that "Bud knows he's a genius"[32] could not have helped much. Don hitch-hiked to Washington, D.C. to see the law professor. His advice, if any, is not known. A year would pass before the subject again appeared in correspondence. In the interim, Don seems to have focused on his studies and otherwise enjoyed life as only a young man can, which would have both pleased, and worried, Ruth.

Bud spent much of his freshman year looking for tires and parts for "the T", and trying to keep it in working order.

> Bud finally got the generator fixed up here and we put it in yesterday [Don informed Ruth]... Bud really went to work once he got around to it + when he finished he was literally grease from head to foot.[33]

> We took it over to the gas station for oil yesterday + as we came back the motor conked out right at the corner. It's surprising how people come from nowhere cause in no time the streets were lined with spectators. It took us Bud I mean about five minute to get it going again with all the crowd giving us a rousing send off—Bud just came in quite dejected—he's not satisfied with the way its running + has decided (for now) to bring it back home + put another motor in it, then if he can still stand it he'll bring it back. He was really proud of his hand made gasket—and rightly so 'cause it works.[34]

Bud also had Aunt Irene's old Lincoln with him, but he decided to sell it when the insurance policy was about to expire. He thought it was worth about $300, but with Don's coaching, he got $375. As Don explained it to Ruth, Bud "feels inclined to mention a low price + work up—as tho he were doing the buying."[35] To replace the Lincoln, Irene let Bud have her Ford. "The little Ford drives very nicely," he told Ruth, "I didn't have a bit of trouble comming [sic] back up"[36] from Mt. Airy. A truck hit the Ford while Don was driving, not too seriously, but lawyers were involved and Don's ankle was sprained badly enough to put him on a crutch for about a month. Bud developed a strong attachment to "the little Ford."

Just how the three scholars were meeting expenses during this time is not entirely clear. The Servicemen's Readjustment Act of 1944 (G.I. Bill) paid tuition up to $500 and a stipend. All three had savings. Don and David found part-time construction work for what appears to have been a short while, and Ruth occasionally sent Bud and David checks. (At one point, the Veterans Administration cut off Bud's stipend when it was unable to locate him in the registrar's files and concluded he had left school.) The main drain on funds appears to have been the cars, which Ruth in the end probably paid for. This would explain why Bud told her, "I hope you won't be infureated [sic]", when he "looked into the prices of auto radios. There's the slikest [sic] little Philco 5 tube job for $45."[37] "The radio in the car may be good to keep Bud from some of his erratic driving", wrote Don diplomatically, "He has a tendency to slow down while fiddling with the dials + he sure likes to fiddle."[38] To Ruth and Don, the cars were transportation (the boys did sometimes take Amtrak's Southerner); to Bud and David, they were a hobby and a challenge. "I went riding in the Modle [sic] T out in the country today", David told his mother, "exciting isn't the word for it—its adventure. It just broke down once, and stalled once. A wire busted lose [sic]."[39]

Like Don, Bud and David were conscientious students, living off campus (dorms were reserved for in-staters), studying and eating together at Mrs. Hamilton's. "I'm still very happy about everything", David told his mother, "but, still realize how mighty lucky I am."[40] For recreation they went to movies (much enthusiasm over Olivier's *Henry V*), lectures, and away football games.

Most afternoons, when the weather was nice, they played basketball or tennis. In the winter, "With all the snow around none of us dare [sic] walk ahead of the other for fear of getting pummeled with snow balls."[41] "[T]he great snow fight Dave + I had against Bud + Dee [a classmate]" lasted an hour and a half, Don told Ruth. "My arm was sore for a week after."[42]

College women, always of interest to Don, did not interest Bud or David. Once, Sarah Smith lined up post-game dates for Bud and David, but Don "didn't mention [it] to them" ahead of time, "knowing their reluctance to meet 'such creatures'." He told Ruth he "figured if I told them they'd immediately say no."[43] Saturday afternoons, the three usually listened to the Metropolitan Opera, "each doing some kind of not too noisy study."[44] Bud and Don each joined the Book of the Month Club, and received as a "gift" a complete set of Shakespeare's works. Bud's reading habits began to pay dividends.

> Bud has been getting some real good marks on his English themes [Don reported to Ruth] and even the instructor's notes are pleasing. Every time Bud asks me how to spell a word I've taken to handing him a dictionary. Then he asks how to spell it so he can look it up.[45]

The instructor, Mr. Rushton, liked to read students' themes aloud each class, the worst and the best, as examples. Bud's themes were featured twice, once for the best, once for the worst. Bud told Ruth, "I knew (because I hadn't spent much time on it) that it was pretty bad, but I didn't know it was as bad as Rushton made it seem."[46]

As the academic year came to an end, Bud stopped smoking again and David brought up transferring to N.C. State "if possible because of numerous dissatisfactions here at U. Va."[47] Bud told his mother,

> As for David, I think that N.C. State would be much better suited to him and his interest. He, for one thing, is interested in agriculture and U. Va has no Agriculture school. As for me, my discontent is mainly with the instructors and also the petty discriminations they have here for out of

state students such as giving the State students preference in obtaining rooms in the "dorms." And we both recognize the advantage of being closer to home.[48]

Ruth was probably disappointed, as was Don, but Don could see the fit was not the best, and tried to help Ruth see it, too.

> I guess Bud told you about Mrs Hamilton telling us we would have to vacate if we came back to Virginia next year. [She said she'd promised the room to an "old lady", but Don doubted this was true.] ...You may be thinking that the boisterous activities of the three of us may be the reason actually—and I'm inclined to agree—but if that is so—if Mrs. Hamilton—or [her son] Adgate—thinks for one minute that I'd exclude Bud or David from the free use of this room they're both crazier than I've so far believed them to be. It's my personal opinion that Adgate is behind it all—mostly because we don't stop and gossip with him when he sticks his head in the door with a silly grin and a sillier remark expecting us to drop our studies and waste time with him... This seems to be a precipitating factor in Bud's decision to transfer to State next year. Neither he nor David can quite accustom themselves to the traditions of Virginia, feeling, like a good many of us, that stress outside of class room activities is placed too strongly on the wrong things, then they both feel that State has more to offer them in their particular wants and of course, this one I agree, it's nearer home... I'll sorely miss them if I come back alone but I think State has what they want and have tried to advise them on what to do about it...[49]

By the end of June, attention had turned to the peach harvest in Mt. Airy and getting more beds down to Irene's house at Myrtle Beach. The summer stood out for Don as the first time he had "really lived with you and the rest of the family." When it was over, Don was back in Virginia with a roommate who was "really quiet, so I have no one to argue with," and Bud and David were at Duke University.[50] At the close of the fall semester (his fourth in pre-med), Don switched his major to French. The correspondence thinned out after the transfer to Duke. Ruth's letters did not survive, and Bud and David were home frequently on weekends, obviating the need to keep in touch through letters. When Bud wrote, it was usually to ask his mother to send money or books or something he had left behind (most often his Parker pen, lab book, belt or shaving kit).

In February 1948, Al Hocker died unexpectedly at his home in New York. He had followed his usual routine of surgery in the morning, out-patient clinic in afternoon, theater with Margaret and friends.

> I was sorry to hear that Al Hocker died. I remember very little about him except that he was kind to me—gentle + soft spoken. I remember once that he bought me a modle [sic] aeroplane kit (the first I'd ever had) and when Pop saw what a mess I was making of trying to put it together, he just about built the thing himself while Al said that I could do it if I tried. He'd promised to buy me another if I put that one together.[51]

While at Duke, Bud continued to ask his mother for her views on politics, always hoping to find something they might argue about.

> How did you like the write up Howard Taft got in the new Life? Does it change your opinion of him any? I wish they could find someone like Wilkie again. And I'd like to know also if you favor H. Wallace's plan of allowing the U.N. to administer the Marshall Plan for European relief.[52]

Howard Taft of course died in 1930. Bud was thinking of his son, Robert Taft, aka "Mr. Republican", the senator from Ohio who was seeking the party's nomination for president. Felix Morley's glowing profile in the February 9 issue of *Life* was one of a series the magazine was publishing on each of the Republican candidates. Taft's being a conservative Republican aside (unlike Republicans today, not all were), Ruth would not have approved Taft's opposition to the New Deal and its programs, or his non-interventionist foreign policy stance. (Today, Taft would probably be considered a libertarian.) Wendell Wilkie, who died in 1944, was a Democrat who changed parties in 1939 to run against Roosevelt and beat Taft for the Republican nomination in 1940. The fact that Bud wished for someone like Wilkie suggests his politics were not as far left as some have assumed and one might think, given his apparent enthusiasm for (or at least interest in) "Bellamy-world", British "socialism" and Henry A. Wallace. At the end of December, Wallace had announced a seven-point "Wallace Plan" for European recovery (a counter to the Marshall Plan, which he initially had supported) that put plan administration in the hands of the fledgling United Nations. Wallace disagreed with the Truman Administration's increasingly tough stance toward Russia and apparently thought the U.N.'s approach would be more cooperative. Although Bud's experience at Webb and in the service had led him to value cooperation among individuals, he believed that "higher wages + better living conditions for labor, etc. would mean nothing if we lost the fight for national survival" and that "a foreign policy should be strong and if necessary backed by force, even the 'A' Bomb."[53] In asking Ruth whether she favored the Wallace Plan, he was (in effect) seeking her views on Stalin, Russia and the anticommunist ideology taking hold in much of the country at that time.

Though Bud subscribed to the *Wallace Weekly*, he was not a Wallace supporter (he voted for Dewey in 1948) or a communist sympathizer ("God forbid"), but, like Truman and Eisenhower, he thought "the best way to fight communism or anything else is to know all the 'angles' and thus be able to discuss + think clearly about them + draw a rational conclusion." He was so "erked [*sic*]" by the idea that "I can't be or have communistic ideas + express them publically [*sic*]" without being "blackballed" that he devised a scheme to print and distribute "incognito" "some very subversive posters", and "see what happens." If, as he expected, the posters were suppressed, "I intend to write a very fiery poster on freedom of speech."

> I very cautiously approached some possible collaborators but they all seemed to think that I would be edjected [*sic*] from this "Temple of learning?" So I broached the idea with my His. Prof. He thought it an excellent idea + gave a few helpful ideas of his own. Such as bringing in some vital issue (negros in our Univ.) along with communism. I hesitate mainly because I don't feel equal to the task. I

> would like someone to help me do the editing + planning. Henry hasn't spoken to me since I asked him. Phill agreed to (if Holly would give an o.k.) then backed out when he did. I even agreed to finance all opperations [sic], etc. (It wouldn't be much).[54]

As far as is known, the scheme to "toss a lighted bomb", as Bud put it, "into the midst" of Duke's "many dyed in the red conservatives" went no further. He hardly had the time, between his studies, his conventional extracurricular activities (including another fraternity rush season and his cousin Gene, Jr.'s wedding), and the drive between Raleigh and Charlotte (two and a half hours one-way without "misshap [sic]"[55]). He was still a fairly conscientious student, but not perhaps the best manager of his time. "There are so many things stacking up on me", he told his mother, "that I don't know where to begin. None of the work is difficult for me only long."[56]

> They are realy [sic] poring [sic] the work on now. I've so much to do that I feel lost + depressed all the time + this spring weather isn't helping matters any. Just when the weather gets nice two of my profs assign long research papers which require hours of work in the stuffy library. There's somthing meadevil [sic] about a college education.[57]

Another challenge was money management (the fact that he had started smoking again could not have helped).

> Dear Mother, your money came just in time. I didn't have a cent last nite before dinner. David came in my room and I asked him if he would lend me a dollar till tomorrow because I was reasonably sure that your letter [with a check] would come then. He absolutely refused, mentioning a debt of $11 that I owed him about a month back. Jimmy then offered to lend me the dollar—David seemed to have no objections to that even tho' he had some $20 in his own pockets at the time. I felt that somthing wasn't quite write [sic]. For me to have to borrow money from an acquatiance [sic] to eat when my brother stood by with $20. Well, I didn't borrow

> from anyone + consequently didn't eat anything last nite. Your letter came this morning, so I got breakfast + gave David 1/2 the check plus the $11 dollars. I figure that I'll need 10 or 15 more to feed me 'till my gov. check comes—I won't use that much now that I think again, maybe I can manage with what I have.[58]

Ruth had access to Bud's savings, and probably David's also, but the money she sent Bud and David for school was almost certainly from her bank account and not expected to be repaid. The arrangement was not reciprocal. Even when, by his own account, he owed her $457.50 for a new Ford he had just purchased, he instructed her to "send me the $20.00 you barred [sic] from me to get whisky and maybe send me a little extra."[59] Her financial support did have limits, but they were limits that Bud did not hesitate to press, as when he spent his allowance on a "slik [sic] little Philco" car radio and "wine, women + song" ("perfectly inexcusable I realize"). Toward the end of the year, Bud accepted an offer of membership from the Kappa Sigma (KΣ) fraternity ("I need $50 for inition [sic] fee. I think that dues are $3/mo."), and "the Frat" threw a big party. "David has agreed to come", Bud told Ruth, "He says he wants to find out what my brothers are like."[60] (The fraternity dues turned out to be $6 per month, which Bud paid for in kind by serving as the frat treasurer.)

When Bud returned to Duke in the fall, he had his '47 Ford Coach ("will you get me some insurance on the new car?") and his "nose fairly close to the grind stone."[61] He at least seemed to be aware he needed to manage his time better. ("I always start the year off with a bang then towards the end I grow faint of heart."[62])

> I am beginning to realize that I will have to do alot of my studying in the afternoons. If I manage one date a week, I'll be timing things close. I've stopped smoking, but I've taken up another habit almost as bad—drinking cokes (2 or 3 a day) because they are so accesable [sic]. They have despensing [sic] machines all over the place this year.[63]

He had developed more of an interest in the opposite sex, though he did not enjoy the traditional forms of mixing. "Maybe somthings wrong with me", he told Ruth, "but I don't seem to be able to have much fun at dances."[64]

> I introduced myself to a very charming girl in my accounting class whose pop works for J.A. Jones [Construction Company, one of the nation's largest] and who (she is) a math major—she is also taking physics and is on the business staff of the School paper. While walking from class with her a few days ago I mentioned that I'd finished my homework for that day in what I thought was the short time of an hour and a half. She said that it had taken her twenty minutes, but eased my deflated ego by saying that she'd had practice this summer while working in the Finance Dept. of R.J.Reynolds Tab. Co. When I first asked her for a date, she refused until she found out that we both knew somebody mutually, viz, Gene Jr.[65]

And he worried about his new car.

> I am, as yet, having no trouble with my new car. I am learning that along with the pride of ownership comes the worry of a new responsibility. For the first few days after the accrual, all my happy thoughts of a new car were marred by thoughts of wreckless [sic] drivers smashing, scraping the finders [sic], or somehow managing to distroy [sic] my car. Even when it rained, I thought of all the little rust spots that were getting started.[66]

Don's outlook improved considerably after changing majors; his grades improved, he had time for a part-time job and bought himself a car, and he spent the summer in Canada studying French. But, he and Bette were still married. In December 1948, following an interview with the Chancery Office in Syracuse, he was notified that his petition did not "possess the qualities necessary for acceptance for trial by the Diocesan Tribunal according to Canon Law."[67] Although he was able to recognize he was being discouraged from continuing his case, he just could not accept that this was because he had no case. He vowed to continue, and for all we know, Ruth may well have encouraged him to do so. But, within the year, he was also considering entering a religious order, as his sister had done. How seriously he thought about it is not known. One suspects it was not very seriously.

For whatever reason, Bud and David did not room together the first couple of years at Duke, which seems too bad, as Bud's roommates were not terribly studious. Ted Huggins, for instance,

> did not make his "C" average and therefore will not be able to transfer. I had told him that he wouldn't and have just collected $5 from him. I don't feel too bad about it either because he often played cards and played the radio while I was trying to study.[68]

In anticipation of a continuing problem, Bud asked Ruth to find a radio "that's around the house and not used",

> I would prefer to own the only one in this room because then I could say to my room mate "will you please cut off my radio?" and be much more likely to get it done than if I had to use your instead. Last year Ted played his constantly while I was trying to study. I can enjoy one, but only at certain times.[69]

Bud's fraternity elected him to represent it in the university Student Government Assembly (then divided into men's and women's assemblies), which in turn elected him to represent Duke in the North Carolina Student Government Assembly in Raleigh in May 1949.[70]

> ...The campus elections were over last week and our party won all of the positions in M[en's].S.G.A except vice pres. and there the runer [sic] up receives [sic] the office.
>
> Our man, George Skipworth, got axcepted [sic] for med school during the elections, I heard today, and is going to resign his office of pres. of M[en's].S.G.A This burns me up because so many of us expended much time and effort as well as our frat's. money to put him in office. I am esp. disgusted because I planed [sic] to be appointed by him to the Judicial Committee, which tries cases refered [sic] by the administration such as cheating, drunkedness [sic], etc. But now the vice pres. who doesn't particularly like me will hand out the jucy [sic] offices to men in his party...

> [At the N.C.S.G.A] I plan to present a bill... [that would allow the states] a way to take some of the coming Federal bureaucracy into our own hands and to administer our own affairs on a state wide basis and in such a way as to make things nearer to our own desires... I would want it so that, if possible, all Federal [medical] aid would be dolled [sic] out by a <u>Constitution</u> which the bill would set up...
>
> From what I have heard of the student Legislature last year,...the debates... were very hot and the Senate could not sit in the senate chamber because there were some negro student Reps.[71]

The North Carolina General Assembly had established the Student Legislature in 1937 to offer students at white North Carolina universities, colleges and community colleges practical experience in politics, the legislative process, and representation. As to the experience of representation, the practical reality sometimes was that the schools would invite any student who wished to attend to be in the "delegation." Delegations were to study current issues, write bills, and present resolutions for presentations at statewide meetings. Black colleges were not invited to participate until 1945 (for the 1946 session), upon the motion offered *sua sponte* by Ralph "Buddy" Glenn, one of 43 delegates from the University of North Carolina at Chapel Hill. Even though the motion passed 110 to 48 and would have carried by 19 votes even without the Carolina delegation, press reports insinuated or worse that "non-resident" students in the Carolina delegation, including one "on the GI bill", had "railroaded" the student legislature into making the invitation, thereby reprising the South's proud lament that hosts of foreign mercenaries were being hurled against her—again. The controversy was such that Carolina's President and Chancellor issued a joint statement, which disapproved a remark made in opposition to the motion to the effect that, if the motion passed, the General Assembly would cut appropriations to the university.[72] The Carolina delegation issued a lengthy statement on the poor press coverage, pointing out that among the "non-resident" students supporting the motion were delegates from South Carolina, Georgia and Virginia, "as well as from 'the North'."

> [Secretary of State] Mr. [Thad] Eure [who sought to make the student legislature retract the invitation] is quoted as asserting that a student not a resident of North Carolina, who was attending the university under the GI bill of rights, said "To hell with appropriations." The student [James Wallace] is a native of North Carolina now a resident of the eastern part of the state. He is not attending college under the GI bill, though if he were he would have had as much right as any other to speak his convictions.[73]

Twenty-seven delegates from five black colleges, five of whom were black, attended the 1946 session (the 10th). The 1947 session (the 11th) was canceled by the Student Legislative Council's executive committee due to low participation and an unspecified "racial question." The council rescinded its action ten days later, but Secretary Eure, who had immediately canceled its reservations for the use of the Capitol, refused to reinstate them, fearing that the student assembly was reorganizing primarily "to fan the flames on certain issues [i.e., 'the racial question']", with which he wanted nothing to do.[74] Thus, as noted in Bud's letter, the assembly convened its 11th session, but not in the Capitol. The next session (the 12th) (moved from the end of the first semester to the end of the second), was the one in which Bud participated.

> Since the dead line for getting in a Bill was May 9th, I had to draw one up in a hurry. And I am not too pleased with the result of my rush...In short it sets up a State Health Benefit Commission, which doles out state funds to the tune of $5 per day for hospital care and from $10 to $100 for major operations. My only "whereas" is "whereas it be the desire of the State of North Carolina to provide for its own citizens as much as possible without Federal aid and taxation." Which at least states my case.[75]

AP reported that the Assembly (which it termed a "make believe body") "passed a bill to eliminate segregation in graduate schools", but failed on public accommodations. A bill to require public school teachers to take "noncommunist oaths" also failed to pass.[76]

Dear Mother,

The experience I had in Religh [sic] was wonderful! I am already looking forward towards going again next year. One really needs two trials to get into the swing of things there. The main fault, I think, was that there were enough students there that did not respect proper procedure—some because they did not know it and some because they did and took advantage of the fact. None of us knew what bills were going to be presented by the different colleges—only our own. This is why I think our bills were not as polished as they could have been if we had know what they were before hand exactly. It is very difficult, under the pressure of debate, to amend a bill to suit your taste, and then be able to defend your amendment...

The Wake Forest boys put up a bill to require all Communists to sign affidavits (as if they really would); they spent 1/2 hour telling us how bad the Commies really were to get us to vote for the bill. They weren't very bright. I am enclosing most of the bills + wheather [sic] they passed etc. A copy and vote tally (by my motion) are to be sent to all the big shots in our state government.

The Duke delligation [sic] stayed in the Sir W. Religh Hotel + had a grand party 'till late in the nite. The girls from Duke were more interesting to me than the average because, I guess, they were interested in govt etc. which made them different...

The Carolina boys have this parlimentary [sic] procedure so much better the [sic] those of us from Duke. If possible I am going to try to get strict parlimentary [sic] procedure in the MSGA [h]ere next year with a parlimentarian [sic] handy at all meetings. I know more about it than anyone on MSGA, but compaired [sic] to the boys from Carolina that isn't much.

My bill was not on the agenda because of similar bills being already on I guess, I could have pressed its presentation but I didn't. Let me hear from you and send me clippings or anything about the Assembly in the papers.

Love, Bud[77]

Chapter 10

May I squire you round the meads

How exactly Bud spent the summer of 1949 is not known, but by the fall, he was referring to "Francis" Howerton as "his true love in Atlanta."

> Talked to Dean Cox... He said that I could not be absent from any classes but [i]f I wanted to go some where to come and talk to him. He doesn't want to tie me down so much as to keep me from just plain lazyness [*sic*] of over sleeping + carelessness. Wants to breed dependability. Told him about my true love in Atlanta, Francis [*sic*] said he might be persuaded to let me be absent some Sat. maybe.[1]

Frances's mother, Mildred Howerton, taught at the Country Day School while Susannah and Martin were there. Like Ruth, she was a widow, and they became friends. Bud is supposed to have met Frances through that connection, though just when is not known. Like Bud, Frances, was in her mid-teens when her father died, she had two younger brothers (no sisters), and was both smart and ambitious. She had dark hair and fair skin like the Smiths, and was something of a writer and musician. In the fall of 1949, Frances was starting her senior year at Agnes Scott College in Decatur, Georgia, Don was setting sail for Paris, where he would complete the requirements for a Master's in French from Middlebury College, and "the children" were off to boarding school—Susannah to Chatham Hall in Chatham, Virginia, and Martin to Webb School. A few weeks into the semester, Bud was announcing plans "to turn over a new leaf", having admitted to his mother he had not been "working too hard in studies."

> I am fighting mad at the way our Student Gov't meetings are carried out. Now there is little opportunity for a minority opinion. The meetings seem to have become gang meetings where the pres. is the leader of the gang. Had a Poli Science Quiz today—that's a very interesting course. One of the ques. was—did I favor gov't action to limit the Communist [sic] freedom of express. Naturally I'm not in favor of such.[2]

That Christmas, Dickie Baxter married Helen Wuliger Boyle of Charlotte at St. Martin's Episcopal Church. Bud was a groomsman, and Ruth "entertained at her home" the afternoon before the rehearsal.[3] The following spring, Bud was busy planning his own trip abroad – with Frances.

> I've heard from the A[merican] Y[outh] H[ostel] again. They want me to practice taking bicycle trips so that I'll be ready for the possible 30 mi. per day on the trip. They also make manditory [sic] the purchase of a bike here + not in Europe so that the group will not be delayed. Frances got the same info. too of course, and thought that maybe an unsponsored trip would be a little easier since there would be no forced rides etc. The only difference would be that the trip would be unsponsored and that there would be no groups. The same AYH facilities in every other respect would be available 'though. What do you think?—If I do plan to go on the spon' trip, I'd better get a good bike in a mo. or so and start practicing.[4]

> [And later:] I'm glad that you are going to wright [sic] Mace's [sic] about bikes—Frances just sent me a catalogue which had some good English modles [sic] in it for about 68$ [sic] from New York. Plans on this trip are jelling more and more...I wrote Frances & told her that the Russians would probably take Europe while we were over there & I may not be too wrong.[5]

What Ruth (or Mildred for that matter) would have thought about Bud and Frances biking around Europe unchaperoned may be imagined. No more about it was said. The *Observer* agreed to pay Frances for periodic reports on the trip. In June, Mildred and Frances, accompanied by fellow Charlottean Sarah Locke Blythe, drove to New York, stopping en route to attend the graduation of Frances's brother, Robert, from Andover Academy in Andover, Massachusetts. The now foursome continued on to New York and Montreal, where they met Bud. After touring Montreal, the group traveled north to Quebec City, where Bud and Frances boarded the R.M.S. *Samaria* bound for Britain.

> Dear Ruth [Mildred wrote in a postcard] We got Frances + Bud off yesterday. We had lunch with their group, then got them on the boat, then watched them sail at 8. It was most exciting. The weather is excellent so they should have a good trip over. They & we have had a grand time. I hope it continues as we go our separate paths. I'll call when I get home and give you details. M.H.[6]

During the ten-day voyage, 75,000 soldiers from the Soviet-backed Democratic People's Republic of Korea invaded the West-backed Democratic People's Republic of Korea, signaling to many the beginning of a communist campaign to take over the world. Washington issued pamphlets titled "What to Do in an Air Raid", and Charlotte organized "Civil Defense Meetings" (segregated, of course) where one could learn about "Bombs!, Blackouts! Air Raid Wardens! Fire Prevention and Protection! Emergency Medical Care!" Plans for the bike trip were not affected, however, and, as Mildred had predicted, *Samaria* was untroubled by inclement weather.

> ...The trip has been fun [Bud wrote from on board ship]—food, music & sun tanning. Everyone in my group seems very good. Shirly Anson (the Group leader) is pretty & nice to get along with. Frances & I have met alot of odd people & interesting ones too. An English Free-lance writer, a band leader two professors & of course lots of eager youths like ourselves. Fred, our waiter, furnishes us with

fresh milk, any no. of deserts & is very typically English & fun to be around.

The ship carries about 1400 with 500 crew. All the students (about 1200) arn't AYH (about 50%) but other organizations AY Abroad & Youth for Christ etc. F. & I are in the one % from the south.

Went to the English service Sunday. The Capt. read the service Except for the scripture; the Purser read that. F. & I thought it funny that he (the Purser) should be reading the bible on Sun. having the nite before called the dice in a horse-racing game of betting.

I find that the common Englishman thinks the service & the Church of Eng., as a whole, a farce & put little faith in it, or so I gather from the attendence [sic] & expressed opinions of the stewards & crew. I could see only 3 crew men there. I noticed also that a cynical smile appeared on the executive officers face when the Americans so loudly sang "Onward Christian Soldiers"...

P.S. I lift [sic] my sleeping bag in Sarah Lock's [sic] car. Please send it air mail I won't need it in England. Send it air mail to London, Gen. Del. EC 1—Don't delay. And wire me at nearest address on iteneary [sic] if you have done this. Bud[7]

Bud's sleeping bag was waiting for him in Mitcheldean in Gloucestershire, where he had had "a slight mishap along the road involving possible broken bones", requiring a train trip into Gloucester to get his shoulder x-rayed ("bone slightly chipped, arm in a sling for 10 days. Bike riding...not hampered."

I'm glad to hear about David's new investment the chain saw, [Bud informed his mother in a letter transcribed by Frances]. I hope there are a few trees left standing on the place when I get back and that he doesn't get killed in the process of making millions. Now that I'm thinking of home—I find that my hunger for corn bread has increased to the point where I would give almost a pound for just one pone here, good food is expensive and inexpensive food is not too substantial—mostly potatoes[.] Please, before I get to Paris, let me know where Don is + will be. Our stay for tonight is in Bath, which reminds me I've only had one genuine bath since I've been here but no one else has so things aren't too unequal. Frances, as you assured me, is able to take care of herself very well.[8]

Don, having completed his course of study in Paris, had left three days earlier for Spain.

> Colegio Mayor Generalissimo
> Franco Santiago de Compostela Spain
> July 11, 1950
>
> Dear Bud, Mama's letter telling me you were coming definitely to Europe finally caught up with me on my trip thru southern France before coming to Spain and I wanted this to be waiting for you to welcome you to Paris. I hope you had a good time in England. I'm sure you will in France. Are you alone, with a group or what? At any rate, if you need any help in getting to see the "classical" side of Paris (I don't mean Pigalle), I have a very close friend at the American House of the Cité Universitaire who will be more than willing to help. Besides I'd like you to meet her. Her name is Tina Romano—an Italian girl from Massachusetts. If you can find your way on the Metro or even on your bike to the Cité—the Cité is a group of buildings of all nations for students in the southern part of the city, don't confuse it with the Metro stop called simply "Cité" that is near Notre Dame—call Tina at the American House or leave a message for her. I'm sorry I can't be on hand to welcome you myself and show you how well I've learned the language + the city. I'm sure you'll recognize Tina—she's petite—5ft 1—not your type, I know—brown hair, brown eyes etc. cute is the word I guess. In fact I'm going to ask her to drop you a line at the same address giving you more details on how to get in touch with her. How long do you expect to be in Paris? I hope to get back myself on the 12th [of August] in time to finish my packing + catch the boat for home on the 16th. Please write me right away or tell Tina where you expect to be about that time and maybe we can get together for a nite of something.[9]

The letter never reached Bud. After visiting London ("So many people crowded into one place"), the bikers took the train as far as Slough, rode to Henley ("1/3 bicycles and 2/3 automobiles" on the road), and thence to Oxford.[10] Frances wrote her first report for the *Observer* from Rouen, where Bud discovered that "sidewalk wine drinking at about 10¢ per glass is the berries [a 1920s-era expression meaning highly enjoyable]." Bud and the other males of the group slept in a barn near Mont Saint-Michel ("I climbed a small stair case in one of the flying buttresses & finally got on top of the roof where I could see for 50 miles or more") and next day rode 30 miles to St. Malo. ("David will be interested to know that all scaffolding here is long pine poles & rope lashings."[11])

In Paris, shortly after the *Observer* published Frances's first report, Bud and Frances decided to ditch the group and get married. But for the legal hurdles, family might have learned about it only after the fact. As it was, they had just a few days' notice, enough only to send wishes of happiness, but not Ruth's ring, which she had promised to the first of her boys to marry. Ruth wrote to Don in Spain, hoping he would return to Paris in time for the wedding: "We are all very much excited of course—I think they were very smart and sensible and I don't think Frances's mother minds too much."[12] The wedding took place Saturday evening, August 5th, at the American Cathedral in Paris, the Reverend Mr. Dunbar officiating, the dean being on vacation.

The idea that this marriage was "arranged" by anyone other than Bud and Frances is as fanciful as the idea that Bud did not somehow believe in marriage. It is true, however, that he was something of a minimalist where romance was concerned. "I plan to put Frances to work at Duke", he informed Ruth the day after the wedding. "David", he said, "will have to find another room mate." The couple spent their "honeymoon" in a hotel "somewhere near Pigalle."

> Dear Mother, F. & I went to church this morning. The same church & same minister were there (which) married us at 6 Sat. afternoon. After 7 days of legal duping [gaming or conning], I was supprised to find that I felt better & even enjoyed the church sermony [*sic*]. The giving of the ring and Rev. Dunbar's words seemed simple + important.[13]

> Glad to know that Don plans to get here the 10th [Bud wrote his mother on Monday]. We planned to leave the 9th [for Geneva, Switzerland] but we will stay & see him... And do try to find us an apartment in Durham. F. & I figured that it would be cheaper to eat at the Univ cafeteria so a kitchen etc. will not be necessary. F. will probably be able to get a job at the Univ. so eating there will be convenit [sic]. Don't you think? If you can't get one—ok—but we'll be getting home late & time will be "dear", so try... Tell David to write[.] F. & I are still on good turms [sic] after 3 days.[14]
>
> We are always running into members of our group at the Amer Express & Post office. They were all very nice to us. Esp. Murry Barristine who acted as best man (at the church he was almost never was able to produce the ring—looking back it was funny, but very serious then) and inturpitor [sic] even though he has only 2 years of high school French. The mayor of the 17th District who conducted the civil sermony [sic] thought the whole thing very funny & it was esp. when I said "we" [oui] when F. should have...[15]

In the end, Don was not able to catch up to the newlyweds, who left August 10 for Geneva, Switzerland, the day the wedding was announced in the *Charlotte News*. After one day in Geneva, they set out by bike for Lausanne and got as far as Rolle, about 19 miles northeast of Geneva. From Rolle they took a 1913 sidewheeler riverboat across Lake Geneva to Lausanne, and from there a train to Venice. On August 16, Don set sail from Cherbourg on H.M.S. *Queen Elizabeth* bound for New York. By August 25, Bud and Frances were back in Paris shopping for "souvenirs" and looking forward to the return voyage. En route, the *Observer* published Frances's second and last article, "Local Bride Reports on European Tour."

Being an "unattached" reservist, Don expected to be called up as soon as he reported stateside; using Ruth as a sounding board, he debated volunteering, just to get it over with.

> From what little I know of the politics concerned, this [Korean conflict] looks like the beginning of what's been ex-

pected for the last few years. Then the doubt arises in my mind as to the advisability of getting a job. If it's going to be a long war it will surely include me sooner or later. Should I make it sooner or stick to the old Army maxim & never volunteer? The latter appeals to me when the thought of these past five years of scholastic preparation enters my mind and I've a feeling that if I once get back in again I'll not come out again—and that's not because I love Army life! I'd like to talk to you about this situation when I get home. From what I've read of the scholastic deferments I guess Bud + Dave won't be called for at least this year—I hope so anyway. Having finished with Middlebury I can no longer be classed a student—at my age still a student. In short I'd like to stay out of it as long as my conscience will allow me and I hope I'm right in thinking it will take the Army six months to catch up with me once I report in.[16]

The Army took less than 10 days to catch up with Captain Dunne, who was told he would be recalled for 21 months or as needed, with three weeks' notice to settle his affairs. He was in Saigon before Christmas. Before he left, though, he was able to secure a teaching position (French and Spanish) at West Point for 1952, but, as he predicted, he would have to extend his tour of duty by three years. The Syracuse matter continued to be a source of hope and frustration, which feelings had intensified since discovering "a wonderful companion" in Tina Romano. "I wish I could do something about it"[17], he had confided to Ruth from France. Now Bette, too, was wanting to remarry, and had even announced her engagement. "I went to see her" in September, Don told Ruth, "it turns out the boy is a Catholic and can't marry her until the church finishes our case", as if "finishing" somehow meant "grants the petition."[18] Don may have been in denial, but he was not optimistic. Even his representative in court sessions, one Father Murray, was giving him "but little hope." He just felt he had no other option. In March, Don was told that Syracuse had denied the petition. He could appeal to state court, but Rome had the final say. Tina wrote to Ruth with the news.

Le Chateau Middlebury College
Middlebury VT
April 30, 1951

Dear Mrs. Lucas...we had some very bad news from Syracuse. The whole affair is beyond our simple comprehension at this point, + I have asked Don's permission to go down to Syracuse myself to try to understand what has happened. The Tribunal voted in favor of Don's marriage (I hate to write that when it refers to Don + someone else) with Betty i.e. "that the allegations in your petition were not proved." This decision was reached on Feb. 27 + the letter informing Don of it was not written until March 19th. I received the news from him on April 5th, + it was a most unhappy day. The case will now be appealed to the N.Y. Court, + heaven only knows how long it will take them to decide anything. If they vote in our favor, then the final word rests in Rome. ...Since I heard the decision from Syracuse, I've been seriously looking for a job for next year. Up to that time my hopes had been high of actually joining Don [who would not return until December at the earliest.]...[19]

Don finally gave in. He and Tina married in December shortly after his return from Korea, in a civil ceremony in the living room of her parents home in Springfield, Massachusetts. By then Don was 34, Tina 25. In 1950, the median age of marriage for men was 22.8, for women 20.3. They wanted very badly to marry and start a family, and just could not wait any longer. So Don obtained a civil annulment pursuant to New York Domestic Relations Law § 140, most probably on grounds of fraud, specifically, that Bette had said she wanted children but in fact did not. It was a compromise; the Church did not specifically forbid civil annulment, and it would allow him to marry outside the Church. But, marrying outside the Church meant they would, for the rest of their lives, or until such time as the Church did relent (which it never did), be living in a state of mortal sin, without the comfort of the sacraments. It was either that or continue as friends. For Don, it probably was not much of a choice, and there is no evidence he ever sought Ruth's or anyone else's advice on the decision.

Just how the civil annulment came about is anything but clear. Records indicate that Don and Bette were married in the second half of 1940. Actions for civil annulments were subject to a six-year statute of limitations, meaning Don would have had to initiate a proceeding by the second half of 1946. That happens to be when he initiated an action for a legal separation (and when he told Bette he would not give her a divorce as divorce was expressly forbidden). Presumably, a claim for civil annulment could have been tacked on to the action for separation at a later date; however, no mention of it appears before October 1951, when Don wrote to Ruth saying, "there is a piece of paper that I'll need to furnish proof of my civil annulment from Betty. I haven't the slightest idea where it is."[20]

The compromise would be enduring and painful. Don's sister, Marion (the nun), would condemn the marriage, and the couple would carry the shame for the rest of their lives, simply because their perfectly legal marriage lacked Rome's literal blessing. This may somewhat account for their having persisted with appeals, even knowing it was all but pointless to do so.

> Just before the beginning of Lent [he wrote to Ruth] I received a nice long letter from Marion in which she told me of her conversation with a Priest and his shedding new light for her on our marriage. Not that she has given us her blessing but that she no longer condemns us and feels that what we have done is not so irrevocably wrong. For this I am quite happy for there are many things that bind Tina and I together not the least of which is a spiritual understanding that bring both of us closer to our Religion, thus closer to God, which after all is the aim of life. When I first told Marion of my marriage, she was heartbroken and so was I to see her take it the way she did. We are brother and sister again and I'm happy for that. The New York Court seems to have fallen into the same path as the Syracuse Court. Letters follow pleading letters with little or no information. It seems hopeless but I shall follow it thru to the best of my ability.[21]

In 1959, a priest would advise that their entering into an ersatz Josephite (chaste) marriage arrangement would permit them to receive the sacraments. By that time, they had had four children, and another was on the way. Still, for a while, they slept in twin beds. The arrangement lasted a few years (during which another child was born) before being abandoned permanently when the family moved to Bethesda, Maryland in the 1960s.

Once they were back in the states, Frances saw to it that Bud got his first set of eyeglasses ("he keeps commenting on how much easier it is to read"[22]) and the two settled into an apartment on Gloria Avenue in Durham. They apparently had no trouble adjusting to U.S. post war married life and Bud's senior year at Duke, and were soon expecting their first child in June. Bud would be 26 and Frances 23. Today, they probably would have waited a few years, but in 1950, no one was waiting. And anyway, barrier methods of birth control (condoms and diaphragms) were all that was available, and they were not particularly reliable. Having children was simply "expected", both in the predictive sense that children were a natural consequence of the marital relationship, and in the social sense that married couples were morally obligated to reproduce, which is not to suggest such things were ever discussed. The social expectation lingered many decades after the Pill, developed in the '50s, allowed couples (women) a choice in the matter.

From Paris, Bud had confided to Ruth that he was feeling

> very disgusted that David hasn't written. I want to know about the wood cutting job & how all the machinery is holding up—the truck, tractor, my car, the s. wagon etc. make him write![23]

For reasons known only to him, David had that summer become rather obsessed with his "wood cutting job" and was threatening to leave school with one semester to go. Ruth tried enlisting Mary Denny to persuade him to finish, but David was no more interested in her advice than he had been when she had tried to get him to meet with her "ex-pupil Chief Rhodes at the [Navy] Recruiting Office" in 1945.[24] David's dropping out was less of a decision than it was something resembling his abrupt departure from the Navy's radio school.

> I don't really think that he [David] was set on stopping when he discussed it with you [Bud wrote to his mother after a visit home], but he felt that he was force [sic] to take up a stand while argueing the issue & to be extream [sic] to get over his point. The more you disregarded his point the more extream he felt he had to become.[25]

For a few weeks Bud "tried to get him to study and get over the silly idea of not getting a degree", but David was not listening.[26] In January, David bought some land in Pollocksville ("no more than a cross road"[27] down in Jones County, near New Bern), moved the wood-cutting business there, and began leveling land on which to build a house. In April, the *Charlotte News* announced that he and Mary Lou Molloy of Charlotte, formerly of Baltimore, were engaged. Mary Lou was a graduate of Mount de Sales Academy in Catonsville, Maryland and Manhattanville College, New York. They had been introduced by one of Mary Lou's classmates, presumably some time after the Molloys moved to Charlotte in 1948.

> We behaved very correctly and traditionally for the times (which were also conservative) [as David would later describe the courtship]. We could talk. We were friends. We got engaged. I was still in school, so we corresponded.[28]

Bud and Frances visited David in Pollocksville, and Bud offered David some business advice "on the mechanical end."[29] "I'm almost as inthused [sic] as David about it", Bud told his mother, to her all but certain dismay.[30] When Frances let Ruth know Bud was planning to spend the summer (at least) working (and had bought a truck for use) in David's business, she voiced her concern.

> Dear Mother,
>
> Please don't worry about my being a financial burden on any body, you & David included. Of course I will not work with David if I cannot see my way clear to support my family. David knows this. I do not plan to invest any more money or effort in the pulpwood business if I can possibly

foresee that I will lose by doing so. I would be doing myself (& David too) harm if we both together could not make a go of things. I feel that I will have no trouble in getting a job later if I want it. In fact, I am seeing a Man in S.C. on May 7th about one which has to do with designing textile machinery. Actually Davids & my decision (as to wheather [sic] I'll be a help in the pulpwood business with him) will probably largly [sic] depend on wheather the cut-back is off by the time school ends or soon after. If it is not, I do not see how I will fit in or how David could have any need for me. I do not plan to do anything like this without plenty of thought & I want to discuss the pros. & cons with you when I get there... Right now I'm mad at David because he hasn't written me since I was down there week end before last & I have NO idea how my truck [GMC Army 6x6] is doing or anything else. And also I left my shaving kit down there which he hasn't sent yet.[31]

"The cut-back" refers, presumably, to demand for pulpwood. Whether demand remained low, or for some other reason, the matter for the most part ended there. David and Mary Lou were married May 5 in St. Patrick's Catholic Church, Monsignor John P. Manly officiating. Bud was best man. The couple moved to New Bern, where they lived for less than a year before David was back at Duke to finish his degree. In June, Bud received his B.S.M.E. from Duke, Frances gave birth to Eliza Catherine, and the family moved to Corcoran Drive in Clemson, South Carolina, where Bud had a position with the Deering Milliken Company that paid about $4,000 a year, or about $42,000 in 2021 dollars. Deering Milliken controlled a group of U.S. textile mills with research labs in Clemson and Connecticut. Each lab had a staff of about 40 mechanical and electrical engineers, chemists and physicists, "all applying their skills to textile problems."[32] Bud's work was primarily machine design and stress analysis. "My job seems to take up all my time", Bud complained to his mother. Still, the work was "even better than I thought it would be."

> [I]nstead of just spending my time on the drawing board, I'm drawing and seeing that the stuff I draw is made and installed. Of course I have to check every detail with Mr.

Klein but there I get my "learning." He is very good and has many inventions to his credit.[33]

Bud and Frances wrote to Ruth regularly that summer and fall (they had no telephone) about Bud's coworkers, the neighbors, the landlord, setting up house (painting, furniture, washing machine, etc.), Eliza's developmental milestones ("she will be an athlete if nothing else"), Bud's dentist and doctor visits ("sinus is bothering him + he won't eat eggs. Had two teeth filled + another appointment in Aug."[34]), and attempting to reinstate his veteran's life insurance benefit which he had allowed to lapse. "Thanks for taking care of it for me", he told his mother, "I should not have let it get over due—I remember Mr. Webb's speech on how bad it was to do such a thing."[35] In August there was a large party to celebrate Eliza's christening; compensation, perhaps, for wedding festivities forgone. Despite all these distractions, Bud was still wanting "to revolutionize the pulp wood business."[36] He wrote to his mother of his plans.

> I am working on a pulp wood loading & unloading devise [sic] which I call the "hydraulic hand." I plan to build it in the back yard & ship it to David when I get it built. I want to engineer somthing of my own & so this will be it.[37]

Hutch came down for the christening party and was a fairly regular visitor (he was still selling cotton and Clemson was in his territory). Their mutual friend Yerger Hunt Clifton also came for the party and stayed a few days. Clif, a year behind Bud at Duke, was a native of Jackson, Tennessee, and a graduate of Sewanee Military Academy, the erstwhile "Junior Department" of Hutch's *alma mater*. Nine months earlier, Clif had been in "very hot water with the board of directors and all the Deans."

> The humor magazine did a parody on the Duke family that was not nice but funny [Bud informed his mother shortly after publication]. Clif was not the editor but did all of the drawings & some writing. They may get kicked out of school. Pres. Edens went raving mad—said this had caused Duke to loose [sic] millions in grants. The top lawyers are

> working to see wheather [sic] the Univ. can be sued by Doris Duke. The cops have confiscated all issues they can find & stopping them in the mail. A few issues are still out & they are now collecter's [sic] items.³⁸

The subject of the January 1951 issue of *The Duke and Duchess* had been "the debauched, fictional 'Littleworth' family (a thinly veiled reference to the Dukes), and took the form of a scandal-filled series of genealogical vignettes accompanied by illustrations by staff artist Yerger H. Clifton '52."³⁹ Clif's drawing was of a "voluptuous naked woman, identified as Diane Littleworth."⁴⁰ It is not known whether it was Hutch or Bud who introduced Clif to the family, but like Hutch and Don, he had quickly become a fixture that could not be dislodged by minor scandal. Clif would eventually receive a doctorate from Trinity College, Dublin and take up the position of professor of English Literature at Rhodes College in Memphis.

Almost certainly Bud's boss Norman Cudworth Armitage, A.B., B.S., Ph. D. Columbia University, J.S.D. (patent law) New York University and an Episcopalian, also attended Eliza's party. He had joined Deering Milliken after the war (lieutenant, U.S.N.), and taken charge of the Research Trust (the section in which Bud worked), overseeing both scientific and legal aspects of its research projects in textile machinery and chemicals, new yarns (synthetic) and fabrics. He had started out in 1930 as an engineer for the Brooklyn Union Gas Company before switching to patent lawyering. Like Bud, Armitage had been athletic at school, and they both played on the company baseball team. His sport, though, was fencing. During his lifetime, he would win the national championship 13 times, make runner-up 9 times, and participate in every Olympic Games from 1928 through 1958. Frances, anxious that Bud should be successful in his job, was pleased when the Armitages invited them to dinner.⁴¹ She was perhaps less pleased to discover Dr. Armitage's socialistic attitudes.

> I also found out last night that Dr. Armitage is more or less the instigator of high rent around here. He could have had his house for $75 a month + he said he'd pay $120—that

$75 was too little—consequently all the other houses began to go up. + these houses out here in the beginning rented to the Research Trust for $24 a month for a six room house! Bud (did he tell you?) talked to Armitage about rent here + got the impression that Armitage thought $65 was fair enough for people in our status—in other words pay what you can afford to pay—I prefer the capitalistic system myself![42]

Figure 10.1: Bud, Frances, Pamela, Eliza

Chapter 11

My love is true and all for you

The U.S. was entering a decade of unprecedented technological change and economic growth fueled by Madison Avenue-driven consumerism. Bud and Frances would be largely shielded from its immediate effects by their income, their lack of a television, and the fact that they were living in a relatively rural area of the Jim Crow South. Bud, who had all his life been and felt financially and emotionally secure, adjusted readily enough to his new responsibilities as a husband and father, as did Frances to hers. It was understood without question that Bud would have the job and Frances would have charge of the house and children.

During the war, women had capably performed jobs previously held by males, but as soon as the war was over, the women quit or were fired because, it was felt, a man needed the job. The war simply had no effect on the belief of most Americans that married women should not take a job unless it was necessary to support the family. After her husband died, Ruth had not needed or wanted to go to work, but it was different for Mildred. Mildred may have wanted all along to go into teaching, even though she was married, but she needed to after her husband died. Fortunately for her, she had just finished getting her master's and so qualified for a better position than she would have otherwise. Mildred's experience doubtless informed Frances's thinking in ways few white, middle-class Americans seemed to understand or relate to in the post-war years. As David Halbersham observed in his book, *The Fifties*,

> In the postwar years the sheer affluence of the country meant that many families could now live a middle-class existence on only one income... The new culture of consumerism told women they should be homemakers and saw them merely as potential buyers for all the new washers and dryers, freezers, floor waxers, pressure cookers and blenders.
>
> There was in all this a retreat from the earlier part of the century. Now, there was little encouragement for women seeking professional careers, and in fact there was a good deal of a quite deliberate discouraging of it...
>
> The range of what women were allowed to do professionally in those days was limited, and even in those professions where they were welcome, they were put on a lower, slower track. Gender, not talent, was the most important qualification...
>
> Men were taken seriously. Women, by contrast, were doomed to serve as support troops...Only someone a bit off-center emotionally would stay the course. It was a vicious circle: because young women were well aware of this situation, there was little incentive to commit an entire life to fighting it and becoming what was then perceived as a hard and brittle career woman.[1]

Consumerism, the constant pressure to *spend* money on new things like vacuum cleaners, cars, vacations, etc., intensified the pressure many felt to *save* money, Frances among them. Bud tended to deal with these conflicting demands much as he had in college, by making lists and loose budgets, and then buying whatever it was *he* wanted to buy.

> Just to keep you up to date as to what my ambitions are [Bud wrote to his mother]. 1) get F's portrait painted by Mrs. Ferro (she does them for $150 which I don't think is bad) we plan to do this with the $140 some [*sic*] we'll get back from the Gov't. 2) a rad[i]o phono like David &

> Mary Lou's and with this a set of records & Book recommended by Tina's old Fr. teacher. (We planned to use the $140 for this alternatively though we really are trying to see our way to get both soon.) 3) A new 1951 English Ford (they are a little cheaper probably) and trade in my car so I can cut down on $25+ a month gas bill (nearer $30/mo) because they get 30-35 mi per gal. True, this car will probably keep me on the road 1/2 hr longer between here and Charlotte since they are not so speedy as my Ford but I'm growing more and more bothered by being in a speeding auto now'a'days. The AYH sent their forecast of trips today—we noted that the prices for trips were 10-20% cheaper than when we went. 10 weeks France & England (Normandy Wales) & Riviera $560 everything inc. I've got a great mind to try & talk Dr. Armitage into a 3 mos. leave. Wonder if I could. Frances would become her normal shape again with all the Bicycle riding & you could look after Eliza. We would want the Belg. Neth. Lux. Fr. tour though. 4 weeks & 4 weeks on our own as before except about $100 cheaper.[2]

The bike trip was, of course, a fantasy. They bought the English Ford *and* kept the old one, which did nothing to improve their financial situation. "You will never believe it," Bud remarked naively to his mother, "but it seems that about 1/3 of F. & my conversation consirns [sic] how to save money." Frances used her sewing machine to make things like curtains and dresses for herself and the girls. Bud made furniture.

> I've just finished a kitchen stool rather than buy one of some old pipe lying around [ ] I took it to the Lab shop and elec. welded it. That was my first elec. welding experience, really its fairly simple to do. Frances was in the shop watching (this was Sun afternoon) and left saying she had rather wait in the car for me than see me electrocuted.[3]

Frances and Bud shared a love of music. Besides the standard equipment of the 1950s—a turntable and mostly "barred" (often without asking) long-playing records—Frances played the flute and Bud the violin. Just when Bud learned to play the violin is a mystery. During the war, he had told Ruth that seeing *Phantom of the Opera* again had "inspired my resolution of long standing to learn to play the violin." He told her that he wanted to take lessons at Davidson and "see how I make out", but as he played by ear, he was probably self-taught.[4] He and Frances formed a trio with Bud's coworker Dick Van Fossen who had been at Duke with Bud. They met Thursday evenings to play hymns mainly, for want of sheet music. Occasionally, they were joined by other Clemson area musicians. Dick was to Frances "a true friend" who would sit with Eliza so she and Bud could go to the movies. Dick also sang with Bud in the Holy Trinity Episcopal Church choir in Clemson, where they were cast as (singing) magi for the Feast of Lights.

Bud and Frances enjoyed conversation and had, during these years, a relatively active social life. They encouraged Hutch to stay with them when he was in Clemson, they would visit Ruth and Mildred in Charlotte, and almost every week there was a bridge or dinner party, in addition to concerts and lectures at the college. By November, David and Mary Lou were expecting. Frances and Eliza rode down to New Bern with Irene for a visit ("quite peaceful after riding with Bud"[5]). Reporting afterwards, Frances told Ruth, "I hope he [David] + the mules have settled things", adding diplomatically, "He's certainly had his share of hard luck." His luck evidently did not improve, as he sold Bud's truck in February saying he needed the money.

In February, the *Saturday Evening Post* began publishing Whittaker Chambers's book, *Witness*, as a serial under the title, "I Was the Witness", recounting his experience as a member of the communist underground in the 1930s, and his case against the highly respected Alger Hiss, whom he had accused of being a fellow traveler before the House Un-American Activities Committee. At the time, public sentiment favored Hiss over Chambers, but not Bud. Bud read the first installment and informed his mother he had found it "interesting."

> F[rances] & so many people I've mentioned this to are too ready to condemn all of the man's ideas because they condemn the man. Too bad—not many people think much for themselves, nor do they need to in this age.[6]

My love is true and all for you 157

Ruth visited Bud and Frances in March, as usual bearing gifts of food and household necessities. Clif followed shortly thereafter.

> We gave him quite a work out [Frances wrote to Ruth]—we biked about 6 miles, looked over Pendleton's Church [St. Paul's Episcopal Church of Pendlton, South Carolina, established 1819]. They [Bud and Clif] attended Sunday.[7]
>
> [Bud wrote later to say] I am sure Clif gave you all the details of his & my going to the Episcopal Church at Pendleten [sic]. The organ was given by Mrs. John C. Calhoon [sic] and I suspect the organest [sic] came with it. On the wall facing the congregation are 4 Huge tablets with the creed, commandments, etc writen [sic] on them in gilded letters. The minister (a Mr. Cole) is about my age. I am playing with the idea of forming a chior over there (they have one—10 year old girl). Nealy Hicks says she will play the organ and Joe Young said he'll sing bass. I need only a soprano & an alto.[8]

Bud remained surprisingly sentimental about his 1947 Ford, and tried to persuade Ruth to buy it using his best "sharp sales man" pitch.

> My Little English Ford is still in Greenville awaiting a part from Charleston to make it work like it should. I really hate to see my old Ford go and would keep it if I had one good argument against all of Frances's not to. Why don't you get it. While Clif was down I listened to the Sta. Wag.'s engine [Ruth's car] and heard an ominous knocking and saw a rotton [sic] place starting at a bolt on the left side—It will be more trouble than it's worth in another year and you may have to get a re-built engine for it in one or two years. My car will give good service for 4 more years at least. It does not need any oil in between the $2000 [sic] mile change and is in very good shape otherwise. They are selling for about $875 in Greenville. Of course I would have difficulty in selling her at that price but $775 (I feel like a sharp sales man, uncomfortably so) should be what I could get. And even with that money on my loan it will take me 12 more months to pay off the debt on the little Ford. So I feel that it would be a good idea if you would sell the Sta

> Wagon (for $500 if it's still possible and not to the Ford Dealers but to maybe Skidmore since he gives best prices, I think). Then buying my car wouldn't be such a shock to your finances. If you think all this descussion [*sic*] has possibilities, Frances & I will drive both cars up a Friday, leave my car and see what the Sta. Wag will bring Sat. (That is if the little Ford ever gets fixed). You could pay me the balance any time you can.[9]

After Mr. Andersen at the Veterans Administration in Philadelphia denied Bud's appeal of the decision not to reinstate his veteran's life insurance benefit (despite Ruth's having paid what was owed), Bud wrote to South Carolina's 3rd District Representative, William Jennings Bryan Dorn, a freshman Democrat who would one day chair the House Veterans' Affairs Committee. Dorn persuaded Mr. Andersen to reconsider. Bud later reported to Ruth that he had

> won my insurance case and can now re-new my policy by filling out a form, having a med. exam, and paying back premiums ($47.50). Mr. Hicks [Bud's lawyer] was very helpful and wrote long letters to all S.C. Congressmen in [*sic*] my behalf. And didn't charge me a thing. What should I do here?[10]

There can be little doubt that, whatever else Ruth might have advised him to do, she would have told him to write thank-you notes—those simple exercises in perfunctory charm for which Bud lacked any aptitude. He never outgrew his aversion to this "most unappealing task" and was, weeks after winning his case, still procrastinating.

Bud and Frances were dutiful parents who, like most of their contemporaries, knew nothing of Piaget, Kohlberg, Erikson, Maslow or Spock, but did the best they could based on their own experience and advice from grandparents. Like all parents, they sometimes worried about not doing enough.

> Liza [Bud wrote to his mother] is real cute now she can walk and bite (with her 4 teeth) and play by her self for hours. It's disturbing how little I get to see her during the

working day. 10 min in the morning, 35 min at noon 70 min at evening & that's it. I'm almost tempted to get a job teaching here except my salary would be at best $3000 per year instead of $4000. Then I'd have plenty of leasure [sic] time plus 3 mos vacation.[11]

By August, Bud and Frances were again expecting. Pamela Howerton was born the following spring. By 1953, Bud was becoming restless working for Dr. Armitage.

I've had an opportunity to do some reading [he wrote his mother], being away from work like this [at home nursing a cold]—all sorts of stuff—among them E. L. Masters' "Spoon River Anthology." He makes one think about what one should try to aim for or do during life. Anyway, even before I read him I'd decided that I want to try my hand at building airplanes—In fact, I'd already written a letter to Cesna [sic] Aircraft Co. but Frances hasn't typed it yet. They make small private planes so that I'll likely have an opportunity to work on the whole plane rather than part of it as would happen on the larger ones. Maybe I'll be able to get home more often by flying home if I do get in the airplane racket.[12]

Ruth by this time had seven grandchildren, all girls. Don and Tina one, Mary Jo and Wallace three, Bud and Frances two, David and Mary Lou one. Ruth was said to have favored boys, but perhaps no more than society in general. David used to joke that she believed in primogeniture,

the tradition that the eldest son inherited all of the land and responsibility for all of his siblings. By this same tradition, the second son, me, was supposed to serve in the army or navy. Likewise, the third son was destined for the clergy. You would have to know my younger brother, Martin, to get the import of this.[13]

David also liked to say that Ruth had done "all things in her power to keep [Bud] out of the service", but had no problem letting him join when he was only 17. He of course knew that, given the fact of the draft, there was nothing his mother could have done to prevent Bud going in, and that the circumstances were very different when she consented to his joining in 1945. The truth was that David had been Ruth's baby boy for almost seven years. It was only natural for him to resent being supplanted, but he never quite got over it. After Duke gave him his B.S.C.E., he moved the family to Keokuk, Iowa for work and Susannah, who was majoring in French at Bryn Mawr, set sail for Paris to spend her junior year abroad. Martin was presumably in high school somewhere, not applying himself.

In April 1954, Bud and Frances bought a house and the family moved to Towson, Maryland, just outside Baltimore. He was still in the textile machinery business, but he was making more money (about $5,500).

> The job? well sometimes I think that I just wasn't born to "work" [Bud wrote to his mother]. The hours are good—I eat lunch here (Frances fixes it) and leave at 4:30 with Sat & Sun off. Right now I'm mad because the Co. opens all mail and very often I don't get literature & catalogs addressed to me in care of the company. Just being reminded of it now makes me mad all over again...Took Liza to the Episcopal church here in Towson—very crowded—sat in balcony and F. gave me a sucker to give Liza when she began to get restless. [S]he did in the middle of the Sermon & so did I—he kept making statements then saying "that's religion!", so we left. I do like the churches down town—"old" St. Pauls reminds me of St. Peters in Charlotte.[14]

After a couple weeks, his enthusiasm had not improved. "Becoming adjusted to a new job, I find, is not easy", he wrote to his mother. He was only 28, his work bored him, and he was beginning to drift ("I often wonder if I'll ever find my niche in life"). Aptitude tests offered but small insight.

> I have a spread of abilities which keeps me in the upper 15% of the masses in every thing except clerical work and that in the upper 20%. My ability to learn and verbal (understanding words & speaking) were in the upper 10%. They said that I should make a better writer than an engineer a better teacher (verbal) than accountant. The interest tests

> were not so convincing to me—they just said that I tended toward outdoor—music— artistic—soc. service work instead of clerical—computative—mechanical stuff. But that <u>is</u> my work <u>now</u> anyway and that may change. Whereas my <u>abilities</u> won't—or at least not so fast.[15]

He would remain with the company for slightly less than a year. David, whose interest in civil engineering dated to high school if not earlier, was the first of the brothers to "find himself" career-wise. The move to Keokuk had been good for him.

> Glad to hear David is doing so well with his new job [Bud told his mother]. By "doing well" I mean <u>liking what he's doing</u> which is what one's aim should be. And thinking of that—maybe Martin will like shrimping—think I would too.[16]

It is doubtful that Bud truly believed Martin would like shrimping, as shrimping was hard physical work, and Martin had always avoided strenuous exercise of any kind. Bud on the other hand liked to work with his hands, and did not mind hard work, but probably not full-time and year-round. He liked engineering, he just disliked working for someone else (as do most Lucases), or merely for money which, like Thoreau, Bud considered true idleness or worse.

> A manufacturer of certain textile machines (speaking of my present profession) seems interested in obtaining my professional services so we are to meet at his plant in Philadelphia the 29th [of June]. Everything will be, for my part, on an honorable basis. I will keep my job here in any event for a while because I like it fairly well & because I've gone into partnership with an engineer friend, Frank Holford, and I want to see our development thru to the finish. We are making Pawleys Island like hammocks by a labor saving process (patentable we think). We plan to sell them mail order if possible. I've already made one test modle [*sic*] which is pretty good but could be better.[17]

The house in Towson was, by all accounts, "much nicer than the one in Clemson"[18], and Frances, Bud told his mother, was soon "swimming" in the suburban milieu.[19] Among the new neighbors was the psychiatrist treating H.L. Mencken, who had covered the Scopes Monkey Trial for the *Baltimore Sun*. "Tell Hutch", Frances instructed Ruth, "that his [Mencken's] hope of ever being normal is nil + he's not very entertaining any more."[20] Towson winters were cold. Frances soon had Bud and the girls ice-skating with her in the local parks. Bud and Frances became interested in the *Great Books of the Western World* program, founded in 1952 by Mortimer Adler and Robert Hutchins of the University of Chicago, who thought good things could result from the shared reading and discussion of significant works of Western literature. Bud felt inspired to form his own, racially diverse discussion group, the first ever in Baltimore.[21]

> As you probably know [Bud wrote to his mother], I've been taking a Great Books leader ship [*sic*] course at the Pratt Library here and hope to get a mixed group starting Sept. Everyone says the negros [*sic*] need educating but few do anything about it. I'll be helping myself too—learning myself and seeing how I would like teaching as a profession.[22]

Visitors to the house in Towson included Clif, Susannah, the Molloys (Mary Lou's parents), Frances's brother Robert and his girlfriend Ann, and Dick Van Fossen, who occasionally took the train up from Clemson weekends to visit. (Frances thought Ann was too good for Robert, and was quite pleased when he lost her to Dick.)

> He [Dick Van Fossen] and I went to St. Michel's [*sic*] and All Angles [*sic*] [Bud wrote to his mother]. The Chior & Dr Finn were excellent. What an excellent man! Most preachers are passively inclined towards the affairs of the world right around them. They are for being good but not so much for <u>acting</u> and <u>doing</u> good too. He accented the fact that the church was not an end in itself but a means for each to "build his house upon a rock." The "house" he said did not refer to the church but to the non-distructable [*sic*] part of men.[23]

Martin also came to visit and was persuaded to stay, probably at Ruth's urging. At 19, he had still not graduated high school and had no discernible ambitions. Ruth hoped Bud and Frances might succeed where she had failed.

> I'm not at all sure he finds our rule any less confining than that of Charlotte [Frances confided in a letter to Ruth]. His job has possibilities. It is in a branch (2 miles from us) of a down town dept. Store which hasn't opened yet. It is primarily physical labor—carrying stuf here + there, handing out instructions to various dept. heads + the like + if he proves himself they will keep him permanently when store opens. Hours are now 7:30-4:30 6 days a week, I think. The 2nd semester of night school opens in a week or so + he is currently investigating it. We tried to send him off to Young People's group tonight but then Molloys showed up. We left him to babysit one night + he had to change Pamela's diapers which amused us greatly. Liza pesters him constantly + he already misses use of car. He is paying us $15 a week room + board which he thinks is too much.[24]

Martin may have benefited under the new arrangement, but it did not change his trajectory. Like Bud, he was just biding his time until something more appealing opened up.

> Dear Ruth, I know you are probably even more worried about Martin after talking to Bud the other night [Frances wrote in February]. His cold is better + he has moved back up to the attic to sleep. Liza seemed to disturb him before up there but maybe it will be better. He was home from work yesterday nursing his cold but went back today. The assistant minister at Towson Trinity who leads the young people's group came to call in Martin's behalf this morning. I think his name is Noble—a West Virginian in his late 20ties. I would guess. I tried to give him a picture of the situation and he took your address with the intention of writing you. We are still trying to persuade him to get started on his high school—just to keep him occupied if for no other reason. It is too late for him to get into Towson High now or really any place and with his record (as it is slowly being revealed to me) I don't know where he'll get in. He is going to Gt. Books with Bud + reading the stuff. Both have been busy with the hi-fi set. The young people's group will be some help. He keeps talking about going off

> to the beach as soon as summer comes so I don't know. I feel that if we send him out completely on his own or back to you that he will go off on some wider tangent + find more trouble to get into. With no car he seems relatively tied down here + less apt to meet up with objectionable friends. He can walk to bus line + go any where + Bud has offered him use of the bike... Well, hope Martin can get back to some sort of normal status in the near future.[25]

By the end of March, Bud had started yet another new job, but was feeling generally "up in the air about jobs", as he had been "for some time."[26] Martin was probably feeling the same, though he did not have a family to support. Frances wrote to Ruth that Bud was "contemplating going... to N.C. State for a Masters in the fall", and that Martin "spends all his time reading Spillane + Van Wyck Mason, it seems, despite our influence." Van Wyck Mason was a veteran of the Great War who wrote historical novels about the American Revolution and Civil War, among other things. Frank Morrison (Mickey) Spillane, was a veteran of World War II who wrote comic books and crime noir novels. His most famous character was detective Mike Hammer. Hammer initially targeted gangsters, but as the country fell under the spell of McCarthyism, Hammer started going after communists.[27] Both authors benefited from the 1950s paperback revolution, which allowed many more people to buy instead of borrow. Not that Martin necessarily felt the need to choose. He used to brag that if he happened to come upon a library book he wanted to own, he would simply keep the book, tell the library he had lost it, and pay the nominal fine. He did not say how often he did this.

> You were so right when you commented that you never knew what was going to happen next in Towson, [Frances wrote to Ruth]. Martin came by Monday to pick up clothes. Gay as a lark. Mr. Benson had given him a raise + title of night watchman so he is sleeping (I think) at the store. [He had rented a room.] Mr. B. had taken him out to dinner Sunday + home for supper. We offered him a free meal in return for baby sitting one night. He refused saying he could get a free meal any time... Mr. Benson seems to have more or less taken him under his wing for the time being.[28]

My love is true and all for you 165

After two months in the new job, Bud quit and went to work for Mr. Benson. He and Martin then commuted together, 45 minutes one-way. Frances told Ruth that Bud was "relatively happy" with the work, "says he likes it better than any he's ever had before", but still planned to go back to school in the fall.[29] He wanted to

> see how I like teaching. I have not made any final decisions as to exactly how I'll do this but I have written for Graduate School Catalogs of N.C. State & Chapel Hill (Duke does not give Master's Degrees in Engineering). The State Catalog arrived a few weeks ago and it seems that I'll have no difficulty getting in grad. school & that it will take a school year before the Degree & I can start teaching. If, as may happen, I do not relish teaching so much as I now believe that I will, the higher degree will stand me in good stead when I seek a more digestable [sic] type of job than I am now able to find My immediate aim will be to get as high a paying job as I can find now—sell the house before the Fall term—move (F. wants to live in Charlotte so I can study and things will be cheaper). My salary when I first start teaching will be around $3500 or about $2000 less than I'm making now. But I will probably be able to get a summer job to raise the total to $4700 so I won't be too much worse off and I will be a lot happier, I believe. Martin seems to be fairly happy. He is having to work long hours and as a result is both making some money & keeping out of trouble. Seeing that he was determined to buy a car, I helped him to get as good a buy for the money as possible—now "repairing" it keeps him more than occupied. I got him covered with my insurance agent but it is only temparoy [sic] while they investigate him.[30]

Now four, Eliza began accompanying her father to Sunday services.

> Liza + Bud have finally started attending Church of Nativity regularly—4 Sundays now. Liza loves the Sunday School—tells everybody she goes to school + much to Bud's disgust prefers "Jesus Loves Me" to Beethoven.[31]

For her part, Ruth was planning another wedding. "Send us details about Suzannah's plans!", Frances enthused. "Mother said she was having 40 attendants." Ruth and the groom-elect, Harry Morris Clabaugh "Jim" Hewson, Jr., of Charlotte, planned to attend commencement at Bryn Mawr.

> You and Jim could make it here your first night [Frances suggested]. We have beds enough and then leave early in morning for Bryn Mawr...I think Bud wants to go along. Then you all could stop by on the way back. I'll put you + Suzannah in the beds in the attic with Liza + Jim in the basement by himself.[32]

The wedding took place August 20, at St. Peter's, the Rev. Mssrs. Grey Temple and Brian Griswold officiating. The noon wedding was an hour late starting because someone forgot to pick someone up, and by the time Bud gave away the bride, the atmosphere in the full, unairconditioned sanctuary was sweltering. The attendants numbered only 21, including Mary Jo as matron of honor, David, Martin, Wallace and Hutch as ushers and the oldest four nieces as flower girls. Martin was said to have embarrassed the family by losing his virginity with one of the bridesmaids following the reception in the Terrace Room of the Hotel Barringer.

Like the Lucases, the Hewsons had moved to Charlotte in 1934, but when and how they met is not entirely clear. Hutch is the prime suspect, as he and Jim were at the University of the South together, and the Hewsons and Sullivans both attended St. Martin's. After the war, Jim had gone to Harvard law school on the G.I. Bill, following which he clerked for John C. Parker, Chief Judge of the 4th Circuit Court of Appeals in Richmond, Virginia, before opening a practice in Charlotte in the fall of 1951. It was around that time that Don began mentioning "Jim" in his letters to Ruth. As Mary Jo was by that time long married and gone, and Susannah still at Chatham Hall, the initial draw appears to have been purely social. Sunday afternoons in the library, sherry and politics, argumentation, maybe some supper. When, like Don, Jim was called to serve in the Korean War, he and Ruth corresponded. The flavor of the friendship can be tasted in the one letter between them known to have survived. Note: the "vatican appointment" Ruth refers to in the letter was probably Truman's nomination of General Mark C. Clark (an Episcopalian) to be ambassador to the State of Vatican city, made in October 1950. Vehemently opposed by "Protestant church circles" on the grounds that appointing an ambassador to the Vatican violated the principle of separation of church and state, and by Senator Tom Connally (D-Tex.), chairman of the Senate Foreign Relations Committee on the grounds that Clark had been somewhat careless with the lives of Texas National Guardsmen under his command in Europe, Clark had withdrawn his name from consideration in January.[33]

>Dear Jim [Ruth wrote in March 1952, when he was serving in the Mediterranean], I must begin with an apology but I will make it brief—to wit, an abject apology for each day, including Sundays, that I have failed to write since your most delightful and unexpected letter came.
>
>I am, of course, much too far behind to ever hope to catch you up with my affairs—as usual, they have been of little interest to anyone except myself and so can be passed over with a simple requiem. Susannah's, I've no doubt you have at first hand and probably with elaborate detail. Martin has managed to extricate himself from Latin by the simple expedient of flunking out of the course. Bud, Frances and Eliza are thriving. David and Mary Lou have a small female named Katharine Ann and Mary Jo and Wallace are expecting a son, or should I say, SON [but were blessed with a daughter instead].
>
>Mr. [C. Alfred] Cole's departure [from St. Martin's to become Rector of St. John's Episcopal Church in Charleston, West Virginia] is a matter of sorrow to all [Mr. Cole was a graduate of Duke and the University of the South]. A beautiful friendship, I feel sure, has been nipped in the bud. I offered him any books of mine he cared to have and he very modestly chose only the best. I miss him very much.
>
>Your mother reports you to be "running around" over Italy looking for cheeses. Are you sure she read your atrocious writing correctly—or did you type?
>
>Your comments re the Vatican appointment should be treated with silent disdain. However, I must confess to

amazement that one of your intelligence should have fallen into this snare and delusion which seems to have infected our state department. That is, a belief in the preternatural wisdom and power of the Roman curia. [Anatole] Von Hugel [(1854-1929), founder of St. Edmund's College, Cambridge] says "all the world knows how apparently incapable of dying is the Roman Curia's thirst for the old temporal power and its hunger for external, political recognition and influence amongst the governments of the world." You will I'm sure, admit his right to speak with authority of the R.C.

I've a wonderful new book—or books—two vol. Davison's Poetical Rhapsody [English Poetry 1500-1700, pub. 1814-1817]—ed. by A. H. Bullars. Do you know it? His father was Sec. of State to Elizabeth and the poems are otherwise unpublished [ ] works of his contempor[ar]ies and of his own. Donne. Raleigh. Sydney, Spencer, Campion, so far—there are others. I think Susannah will like it.

Hutch is out of town for a couple of days. He apparently expects daily to receive an answer to the letter he wrote you. Amazing. He was in Georgia several weeks ago on family business and went up to see Abbo [Abbott Cotton Martin (1899-1974), Professor of English at Sewanee, considered an authority on Wordsworth] over the week-end. Poor Abbo had no coal and no fire and Hutch nearly froze to death. Clara, I think it was, gave Hutch a bag of coal for the fireplace Sat night. Can't you picture them, hovering over it and clutching their drinks in shivering hands as they disposed of John—you, et al!

This grows lengthy I miss you a very great deal and will doubtless continue to do so until you get back, in spite of the fact that I've forgotten what you look like—are you short and rather stout—a little squint-eyed — with ears akimbo—do write and tell me—I've no picture of you, you know! Love, Ruth

Pretending to "forget what you look like" was Ruth's way of letting you know she was due a visit. Jim was of course not short and rather stout, but a not bad-looking beanpole. The year he married Susannah, 1955, was also the year that the case challenging whites-only restrictive covenants on one of Charlotte's public golf courses was decided. The case had made its way through the courts in the wake of the U.S. Supreme Court's 1954 decision in *Brown v. the Board of Education of Topeka, Kansas* which declared that separate schools were "inherently unequal" and must desegregate with "all deliberate speed."[34] Mr. Barringer, who had donated the land to the City, infamously chose to defend the covenants' enforceability. He won all the way up to the Supreme Court of North Carolina, which had to rule in his favor because it knew "of no law that prohibits a white man" from conveying land "upon the limitation that it shall not be used by members of any race except his own..."[35] The U.S. Supreme Court predictably denied review, having decided many years earlier that the 14th Amendment applies only to state action, and there was no state action in the Charlotte case, since the covenants provided that title reverted upon use of the property by non-whites, just the way title to land passes to heirs upon the death of the owner—no further action needed by the state or anybody else. Following this, Charlotte did what it should have done to begin with: bought out Barringer's interest (i.e., the reverter clause) and desegregated the golf course. Charlotte, a town with no integrated hotels, restaurants, restrooms, churches, hospitals, cemeteries or theaters, a town which had for decades loved and lauded and accepted substantial gifts from Mr. Barringer, without reference to his white-supremacist views, would eventually do other things she should have done to begin with, but only when pressured to do so.

The Engineering Department at North Carolina State accepted Bud into its graduate program, and he and Frances and the girls moved to Raleigh the winter/spring of 1956. "Bud seems to be getting along fine at State", Frances wrote Ruth in March. "So far, good grades + adequate ones on his graduate record exam. He had his pneumatic loom project approved—for research + thesis which pleased him greatly."[36] That summer, Uncle Ted's heart condition, which had slowed him down considerably the past several years, took a turn for the worse. The stress of not being able to work as hard as he felt was needed, of watching the farm fall into neglect, had been more than his heart could bear. He died the following February, just as Bud was inquiring about teaching positions. Bud wrote to Aunt Weasie and asked his mother if she would like for him to take her to visit the family, "Tho I will probably have to go to classes, etc. and interview for my teaching job."[37]

Clemson Agricultural College (today, Clemson University) began as an all white, male, military school. When Bud applied to teach in the Engineering Department, Clemson was admitting white women, but was still segregated. Clemson would stay segregated until 1963, the year that future Charlotte mayor Harvey Gantt was admitted. Clemson offered Bud a position teaching engineering mechanics starting fall semester 1957, and Bud moved the family to Pendleton, South Carolina, just as the Little Rock, Arkansas, School Board and the local chapter of the National Association for the Advancement of Colored People began to implement, over Governor Faubus's dead body, their plan to integrate a single white high school with nine students. Charlotte City Schools were also being integrated, but on a much smaller scale. (Charlotte had not bothered to develop a plan to integrate, there being "no real [insurmountable] pressure from the community and the prevailing [white] attitude [being] just to 'wait and see'."[38])

The national press gave Little Rock far more attention than it gave Charlotte. North Carolina Governor Hodges, whom the world would later shame into granting clemency to two Monroe boys, 7 and 9 years old, who had been sent to reform school for having allowed an 8 year old white girl to kiss one of them on the cheek, did not need to call out the national guard to let 15 year-old Dorothy Counts, one of 4 Black students to enter Charlotte's white schools that year, know that she was not welcome at Harry Harding High School.[39] Hundreds of Charlotteans, mostly students and their parents, took care of that.[40]

Like the years in Raleigh, the years in Pendleton were busy and fairly happy. Bud and Frances continued to visit friends and family and attend concerts and political gatherings. Except for two miscarriages and colds (someone almost always had one), everyone stayed basically healthy. "There's really no news here, no sickness, sadness or anything", Bud wrote his mother in June, "Except that I am sad about the bomb testing" (presumably a reference to Russia's refusal to agree with the U.S. and Britain to suspend nuclear weapons testing).[41] Earlier that year, Bud had been sad about the appointment of R. C. "Moon Pie" Edwards, the college's first director of development, to the post of president.

> All the faculty here are distressed at Edwards being made pres. of Clemson. All the deans tell the faculty they are distressed too, but announce to the newspapers just the opposite. Everyone feels helpless... Everyone agrees that the football team will be bigger and better in the comming [sic] years... Even the newspapers seem cool towards Mr. Edwards. An editorial in the Anderson paper said they thought the Trustees had made a bad choice. Maybe he will be the Achilles' Heel of the Trustees, who are for the most part very uneducated businessmen. The two most vocal are Brown & Cooper...[42]

The loquaciousness of board president Robert Muldrow Cooper (1887-1966) and board member Edgar A. Brown (1868-1972) may be put down to their having been in the state legislature. The concern with Edwards, who had come to the college in 1956 after a successful career in the textile industry, appears to have been his lack of academic credentials, made more worrisome by his visible enthusiasm for the football team, which some considered undignified. There was also his position on desegregation (Gantt applied in 1959 and had to petition the courts to require the college to desegregate). In August 1959, N.C. State awarded Bud his M.S.M.E. In 1961, the Department reportedly decided not to renew his contract after he questioned its refusal to give an interview to a qualified black candidate. "Bud could not keep his mouth shut", Eliza was to recall her mother saying of this, and other, incidents. Possibly, Bud planned to leave anyway, to pursue his Ph.D under the sponsorship of Ed Byars (1925-2020, B.S.M.E, M.S.M.E., Clemson; Ph.D. Engineering Mechanics, University of Illinois) a colleague who had managed somehow to spend the war at Clemson and had left the previous year for West Virginia University to chair the Department of Engineering Mechanics.[43]

One Saturday night in the fall of the year Bud moved to Pendleton, Martin was on a date with 19 year-old Lillian Eleanor

Morris when he spun out his car on Old Sardis Road and was thrown into the street. Lillian broke her leg. The following August, Martin and Lillian were married in the Matthews Methodist Church, the Rev. Mr. Paxton T. Dixon officiating. There was no reception. According to the *Observer* announcement, Martin was then a graduate of East Mecklenburg High School and a U.S. Army reservist who had spent six months at Fort Chaffee, Arkansas. He and Lillian were working in retail, she at Ivey's, he in auto parts. Lillian's people were from Union County. The talk in the family was that they were "mill people", even though her father was a carpenter and his father had been a cabinet maker. Mill workers and their families lived in mill towns, built along the rivers. The river fed power to the mill and the town fed it labor and that was all it did. The whole family worked, with no time or perceived need for school. Being a mill worker or from a mill town meant a person was barely respectable, uneducated, uncultured, used to living hand to mouth, and bad with money. Anybody was better than a mill worker—even Martin. Facts did not matter—what mattered was that Martin was the way he was, and now there was someone to blame, namely Lillian. The couple began their married life like most Charlotte newlyweds in those years, living in the apartments at Selwyn Village. The following year they had a child, a girl, giving Ruth an even dozen granddaughters in addition to five grandsons, four courtesy David and Mary Lou, the fifth and latest from Don and Tina.

From Pendleton, Bud moved the family to Hamden, Connecticut, where he was to attend Yale University until he could get into West Virginia University. Eliza was to recall clarinet lessons and singing in the children's choir at St. Thomas's New Haven ("reminds Bud of St. Peter's"[44] Frances told Ruth).

> Dear Mother, We are finally pretty well settled [Bud wrote from Hamden], all the rugs, furniture, etc. in place. And even the curtains hung. I even have the comfort of my hammock in the basement where I will study. The desk you gave (?) us is very nice & handy, with all its pigeon holes. The children went to school for the whole day ('till about 3PM), came home for lunch, and seem to like their

> teacher... I wrote a company near Boston Mass. about my invention [possibly a spring of some sort]. It will be exciting if they become interested and offer a chance to make some money from the patent... I am really hopeing [*sic*] that the Barry Corp. people will take this patent stuff off my mind to a large extent.[45]

Ruth, being the youngest of five, had, over the years, accumulated many household furnishings, which she stored in the barn and the mill and doled out as, one by one, the children married and set up their own households. Bud's reference to "The desk you gave (?) us" was a tacit acknowledgement that the desk was on loan, as were all such "gifts" from Ruth, to be retained as long as one wished or until such time as Ruth found a more suitable place for it, in which case she would recall the item and offer a replacement. Sofas were especially susceptible to involuntary exchanges of this sort.

The move to Hamden put Bud and Frances closer to Don and Tina. Don, by then a Lieutenant Colonel, was teaching at West Point, and Tina was teaching at Ladycliff in nearby Highland Falls.

> Much has been going on [Frances wrote to Ruth shortly after settling in Hamden]. Bud has registered & met several profs whom he liked a great deal. Currently he is peddling his patent. To Boston yesterday, to N.J. tomorrow. It's nice to be so close to all these places. We drove to West Point Sat. + visited with Don + Tina + introduced them to friends of ours from Clemson (he) who is teaching in English Dept. They seem well situated, nice house. West Point is very beautiful. Shame it's a military school. Don is having physical therapy for an hour a day. The doctor at West Point conflicts with Dr. at Walter Reed + Don is struggling along. I know it must worry them a good deal. He did not have the second operation. It's only 80 miles from here so we may go up again.[46]

Don's years in the tanks of the anti-tank battalion had taken their toll on his cervical spine, but he had not begun to feel it until years later. His first operation in June 1959 had not done the job, and it would take another six months for the doctor at Walter Reed to persuade the West Point doctor to try something different. Don would have to be in a cast followed by a brace for months after the surgery, but, as he would tell Ruth, "the pain that was constant the last two years disappeared with the operation."[47]

> The children + Bud are studying hard [Frances wrote to Ruth in October]. Bud doesn't like it here, primarily because it's not home + it's thickly populated but he is enjoying his courses in vibrations. He's also waiting tensely for a reply both from N[ational] S[cience] F[oundation] scholarship (won't hear until Dec.) and from company interested in his patent. He likes his patent lawyer here. Won't Wallace be surprised if Bud does "sell" it?[48]

Being married to Wallace, a man of medium build and swarthy hue with pronounced ears who always gave you a big toothy smile when he was sneering at you, had hardened Mary Jo's conservative/capitalistic views. Wallace's father, a dentist, had died in 1943, and Wallace, the eldest of three sons had gone into the real estate business just as land prices were rising in response to the post war housing crisis. Wallace did not think much of the Lucas boys and is credited with saying that while most parents want their children to be smart, the Smiths (meaning Ruth) sent their children to "stupid school." Bud got along with Wallace for Mary Jo's sake.

Bud did not enjoy Yale. "I am disappointed not starting work at W. Va. this spring term", he wrote to his mother in January 1962, "but the difficulties are plain and no doubt out weigh such a move now."[49]

> There have been about a 2 out of 3 ratio of graduate doctoral candidates to fail their preliminaries this semester [he wrote in mid-February]. One student took his own life, but I don't know whether he was a graduate student or not. I haven't reached that point yet but sometimes I do feel down in the dumps. It seems that I am already behind on my work. They really pile it on at times. The only bright side at the moment, is that I ought to be well prepared

for W. Virginia Univ... "Mrs." sent clippings about the Charleston Episcopalians. It has been in the N.Y. Times.[50]

"Mrs." was Frances's great aunt, Olive Lubbock. Mildred, Frances's mother, had gone to live with Olive and her husband Frank around the age of six. "Mr." and "Mrs." Lubbock to all intents and purposes became Mildred's parents. The clippings "about the Charleston Episcopalians" concerned the decision of Clemson College president Dr. R. C. Edwards to withdraw his invitation to the Rev. Dr. Albert T. Mollegen, a member of the faculty at Virginia Theological Seminary, to speak during Clemson's Religious Emphasis Week. Stories like this used to fuel hours upon hours of analysis and spirited dissection on Sunday afternoons in the library, especially if Hutch or Clif was visiting. Dr. Mollegen, it seems, had run afoul of the House Un-American Activities Committee. Matters had come to a head after four members of St. Phillips Church, Charleston, heard that Dr. Mollegen was going around lecturing on "Christianity and Communism", and they leaned on the college's trustees.[51] A follow-up letter to the editor of the Charleston *News & Courier* observed that "Episcopalians Country wide seem to be taking the lead...against the infiltration of the pulpits" by communist sympathizers.[52] The *Courier* also reported claims by an Army Air Forces major that government records showed theological seminaries, church-supported universities and church publishing houses had been infiltrated by subversives, a majority of which were Methodist, with Episcopalians second. (The debate in the library would have been, "Why only second?") Bud's time at Yale was short.

> How time flies! Here it is the end of the semester and my last class is tomorrow. Everything as usual has piled up and exams are all next week, but it will be a relief to finish—and then not a relief to start German. Frances & I plan to go to Morgantown [West Virginia] after the children get out of school and look for a house—we will have four days then German starts. Not much time for vacations. I am really looking forward to a much less frustrating situation. I don't think the children will have quite as good schooling as here, but Eliza may do better with less pressure.[53]

David and Mary Lou by this time had moved back to Charlotte, and David was working for the City. In June, Martin and Lillian produced a baby boy, Ruth's seventh and last grandson after the SON finally born unto Mary Jo and Wallace the previous July. The child was given his paternal grandfather's name, and Bud was asked to be his godfather. Writing to Ruth around this time, Bud, remarked,

> Looking over your last letter—I can't imagine you and daddy not being mature when I was born, but of course you would remember better than me. Aunt Irene said that Martin was going into some sort of business—I shutter! [sic][54]

Bud was not the only one to "shutter" at the thought of Martin in business for himself. Nor would it be the last business Martin would start. In between these entrepreneurial failures, Martin continued to work in retail. At one point he tried selling real estate, but that did not work out either.

Ruth offered to keep Eliza and Pamela that summer as she often did, but their parents had enrolled them "in the music school here [Eliza clarinet, Pamela recorder] and arithmetic for Eliza. Also swimming lessons", Bud said. At the end of June, he and Frances drove to Morgantown as planned to look for a house to rent.

> We found a 3 BR house within walking distance of the children's school, town, and old college campus. It's fairly big & old but has a new gas furnace all for $110/mo. Ed [Byars] persuaded me to teach a class a day for $300 per month plus tuition, & nice office and other benifits [sic] so you will need to send me only about $150 per mo. after September. ...Tomorrow the German classes start. I picked up the text books for the course today. They look pretty stiff but everything will depend on the teacher. Classes are from 8 to 10 AM every week day. We took the children by to see the house just before we left Morgantown and they liked it. Pamela did not like having the smallest bed room again and cried some but it is larger than the largest bed room in the apartment here.[55]

My love is true and all for you 177

In her letter to Ruth, Eliza was brief and to the point. "We got a house with no yard in West Virginia."[56]

Figure 11.1: Pamela and Eliza, Morgantown

Chapter 12

Why must true lovers sigh?

Two portentous events occurred during the summer of 1962, the first being Bud's realization that German was going to be a problem after all.

> Dear Mother, I've been putting off writing you for some weeks it seems because I have been having such a hectic and discouraging time with the German. I had such high hopes of [f]inishing off the requirement here and not having to bother with it at W. Virginia, but the pace here was too fast for me. I cannot memorize 500 words per week although I am getting so I can memorize about a hundred or so. I hope that one or two semesters of German at W. Va. will do the trick.[1]

The second was Frances's decision to pursue a graduate degree in psychology at West Virginia University. "I think she might as well do it since the main cost will be the effort she must expend and not finances so much", Bud told his mother.[2] Neither he nor Frances imagined how difficult it would prove for both parents to be in graduate school at the same time. There was one last trip to West Point before leaving Hamden.

> We visited Don and Tina this weekend (spent the night Saturday) and found him with the cast off, only a simple

> brace to hold his head in an erect position, and in very
> good spirits. He thinks the operation was a real success
> because he was relieved of pain when he woke up after the
> operation. They went in from the front of his neck this
> time which was not a new approach but new, Don says, for
> the army. All in all things seemed alot better than the last
> time we were there. We saw the Smiths there at West Point
> too, they came by Don's, we knew them in Clemson he is
> teaching English. Oh yes, and Tina will be teaching part
> time at a Catholic girls school in town, 5 contract hrs. per
> week, French, she seems to be looking forward to the job.
> How she finds time even now for all that mob [referring to
> the six children] is beyond me. They will move into a 7 Bd
> Rm house soon though, which will help.[3]

After a week of waiting for the moving van (there being little such traffic from Hamden to West Virginia), Bud rented a U-Haul, and the family caravaned to Morgantown, "Pamela assisting and Frances and Eliza in the car also loaded since we almost did not have enough space in the truck."[4]

> I had a difficult time finding anyone to help me unload the
> truck. It was Saturday, but I finally asked the Sheriff (sp?)
> since I found a parking space near the jail back of the court
> house and he was in. He ask [sic] around the court house
> square but no one he asked (they were obviously men who
> had been in his jail a few times) wanted to work. Finally
> one of them said he knew of someone who had a faimly
> [sic] and wanted to work within a few block [sic] walk and
> he'd go and get him. The man he got turned out to be
> a good worker but mentally off and unable to keep a job.
> Eliza and Pamela got an excellent example of how not to
> eat lunch. He burped, chewed with mouth open, etc. but
> he was friendly and liked Thomas [the family cat].[5]

Ruth continued to send a monthly check, occasionally more for specific expenses such as summer school, occasionally dresses and sweaters for the girls, sometimes a robe or trousers for Frances and Bud. She might have chosen to give larger sums less often, but the checks and gifts were a way to keep in touch. Regular contact was what mattered.

> I am glad that Ed pressed me to teach part time [Bud wrote to his mother a couple of weeks after arriving]. I signed up for four courses, a full load this time, but I may have to drop one since these and my teaching load (2 classes) may be too much for me. The courses here are more what I want and there is a much greater variety to choose from (about 3 times). The head of the Psychology Dept. and also Frances' advisor, Prof. Courtis [*sic*] [Dr. Quin Fisher Curtis, Department Chair 1941-1968] I found out tonight sings in the chior here and will sit right next to me next Sunday when we start up again after being recessed all summer. I believe that there are more midwesterners here than southerners among the faculty, also some Easterners. Frances and I had to stand in a recieving [*sic*] line at the Engineering College Reception last evening for me to make this estimate, but midwesterners have a reserved friendlyness [*sic*] that I like. Lillian phoned this afternoon (Friday) and invited me to the christening but was not surprised that I could not come. We had a very pleasant conversation and discussed Martin's loosing [*sic*] his business partner and on the lookout for another etc. too bad or so it seems, but of course I don't know any details. I did agree to be a God father and to approve David's standing in for me on the occasion. Should I send some present or something? Maybe I should wait till it (little Charles) can read and send him the new Revised Translation [Revised Standard Version of the Bible, published September 30, 1952]? Or better, become very rich as all excellent godfathers should become—or better—<u>be</u> rich allready [*sic*]? Or how about a nice silver porringer? Does he have one? Let me know any ideas you have.[6]

Ruth sent Martin and Lillian a silver baby cup on Bud's behalf, which Bud approved after the fact, thereby reaching the summit of his Methodist godfathering experience. In fairness, Martin and Lillian were not exactly churchgoers and may not have noticed. Frances and the girls were, by Bud's report, happy and getting settled in Morgantown, and Bud as usual made time for choir, despite his heavy load.

> Frances seems to be having an enjoyable time going back to school and meeting all sorts of people [Bud wrote to his

mother in October]. And Eliza and Pamela have already more than enough playmates to keep them busy. They haven't centeralized [sic] the schools here so much yet and many of their school mates are also neighbors too. My studies seem to be going along fine except that I am probably taking too many hours and the work seems to pile up too fast. I'll probably drop one of the <u>fun</u> courses so that I can reduce the tension. The [Trinity Episcopal Church] chior here is fun for me—We sing fairly simple pieces that sound good (which means they were written by Bach, Purcell, Handel, etc) There are around 30 members of it and the director is on the music faculty, a serious midwesterner who does a good job or at least the best job he can with what fate has given him.[7]

The studies are really becomming [sic] difficult now and sometimes I think that maybe I'm not up to it. The math is difficult in the extreme and takes very long hours of study to learn. Ed has said that he is glad he got his degree before all this math became required.[8]

The children are getting along fine in school, music lessons, and art lessons. And Frances worries some over her studies and tests but seems to enjoy most of it. As for me, I have to take too many courses that are required and for which I have no interest in because they are the vogue. I expected some of this but I am somewhat dissappointed [sic] at the amount... The Episcopal Minister, Father Chapman, had Frances and me out to dinner last night along with two other couples. I like him and would have liked to have heard him discuss his profession or books he had read, but no we discussed dogs all evening or at least his guest did. And it was impossible to get the subject changed.[9]

Father Chapman, Bud would later report, was "just a very ordinary, everyday sort of person", the sort of person who, sadly, showed he lacked the aesthetic sensibilities most Episcopalians take for granted, by failing, for instance, to dim the sanctuary during the celebration of the Feast of Lights.

Morgantown winters were colder than in Towson, which made for good ice-skating. The family visited in Charlotte over the holidays, as they did most years. Late one January afternoon, after the family had returned to Morgantown, Ruth slipped on wet leaves while walking up the trail from the creek and broke an ankle. Fortunately, there was a worker on the grounds who (eventually) heard her cries for help and came to her rescue, or she might have frozen to death alone in the woods. Inquiring after her health, Bud told his mother he hoped "you are not imobilized [sic] very long because the rest of you may go to seed and a 'nice' doctor may keep you inactive longer than otherwise." Ruth used her weeks-long convalescence to read books about the United States War of Independence (1775-1883).

> Frances...is really worried about her stistics [sic] course [Bud confided to his mother just after they had finished their first-semester exams]. The math was hard for her. She probably should have taken college algebra again beforehand. I hope that your ankle is mending fast and giving no pain. You could be getting in some good reading. Have you read "Lord of the Flies" by Golden? It's pretty gripping but there are probably many other recent books that are more enjoyable. It's a good yarn tho. Thanks for the clipping about Clemson. I've been keeping up with things there fairly well, but we don't take a paper regularly, however. I buy one once in a while. I find that I'm less interested in such now. Don't know whether it's my studies, being in a less controversial area, or what.[10]

There being no political news he wanted to discuss (1963 was the year that Congress debated the deteriorating situation in Vietnam and passed the Equal Pay and Clean Air Acts, that civil rights protests across the country were erupting in violence and that President Kennedy was assassinated), Bud returned to the topic of Father Chapman.

> There were only a few people at church this morning, a combination of snow and the Univ. being out. Father Chapman asked everyone to come forward and then delivered his sermon from their rear. Afterward, I heard that one olster [sic] at least was ruffled. But I would prefer some really thoughtful and well thought out sermons dealing with things and

> people as they really are in relation to what Christ really said. However, I might as well hope for a mericle [sic]. Let me know all the details of your "well getting." Love, Bud[11]

Influenza hit Morgantown mid-February. Mid-March, Pamela "was the first to go to a doctor this winter."[12] "We use the student health doctors here, the last of whom is a fellow Episcopalian."[13] After flu, the girls went through mumps, followed by measles, but being considered old enough to stay home by themselves, only they, not their parents, had to miss school.

> Frances is having a few quizes [sic] these days and worries some but less than she did at midterm [Bud told his mother in April]. My courses are going more smoothly this semester, probably because I can see more usefullness [sic] in them than the 1st semester ones. I will probably want to take a language this summer, but I could study on my own and really do better than a rigid course approach.[14]

In May, Bud's Uncle Ford died at his home in Blacksburg, age 68. Like his younger brother Ted, he had been diagnosed as having a heart condition several years before. The family spent a couple of weeks vacationing at Irene's beach house in June, following which Eliza and Pamela spent the summer with Ruth, and Bud took another stab at German.

> I hope you and the children are enjoying these plesant [sic] Summer days [Bud wrote in late July]...My German is comming [sic] along, but it is not easy for me. However I believe it is possible for me to do it and get finished at least by next Jan. Don't let the children exhaust you. They like to read books and such. I expect them to have grown almost beyond recognition when I see them again.[15]

In the fall, Frances took a teaching position to cover the cost of help with cooking and cleaning; tasks for which she felt personally and solely responsible. Her sense of duty was not unusual. As David Halberstam has pointed out, Betty Friedan (1921-2006)(author of *The Feminine Mystique*), believed "[i]t was her job as a writer to make more money than she and Carl [her husband] spent on a maid— otherwise her writing would be considered counterproductive and would be viewed as subtracting from rather than adding to the greater good of the family."[16]

> Frances' job is pulling in about $750 for the 9 mos. after various deductions. If I get a 3% return on investing the new school money [Bud had just sold 15 acres of the "the upper farm" (the 90 acres his mother had bought for him during the war) to the school board], then both of these will bring in about $100 per month over what was comming [*sic*] in before along with your $200 per month. So I can likely get along now on $100 from you per month as well as last year. I am very grateful for your help but if you find a more worthy "bottomless pit" just let me know, because I can very well dip into my own money. I started this letter Sunday and here it is Wednesday! We really do get in more or less of a rut during the week—everyone off to school in the morning—study at night—a dash of play after school in the afternoon.[17]

For the avoidance of doubt, Bud also felt Frances was personally and solely responsible for housekeeping, complaining to Ruth the following year that "Frances is spending too much time on studies so that the house goes to pieces so that I have to raise hell every now and then."[18] The focus on work and school took precedence over almost all other activities. The girls had no idea President Kennedy had been shot (on a Friday, about 1:30 p.m. Eastern Standard Time) until they arrived at school Monday morning and found it closed, Eliza was to recall. Nor could they find time for the usual holiday visit to Charlotte, though they blamed it on weather-related hazardous driving conditions. At Bud's suggestion, Ruth gave Eliza and Pamela a piano for Christmas. Bud had thought he might give his mother a reel-to-reel tape player/recorder so they could talk to each other, but she could not bear the thought of having her voice recorded, so he gave her a book instead.

> I had really planned to give you one of those tape recorders for Christmas and sent the book as an after thought [Bud wrote just after New Year's Day]. I sent Aunt Irene a tape

letter with singing... If she seems to like it I may yet send you one. I agree that our accent sounds pretty low class but it is just a matter of overcoming a little pride. It is a more basic way to communicate as well as being much cheaper than the telephone. 10¢ to send a 1/2 hour reel by mail.[19]

Morgantown winters were the children's primary source of recreation during the school year, and skating gave the parents a much-needed break from their graduate school grindstone.

After church and noon dinner we went skateing [sic] and toboganing [sic] with the Mosses and Curtises and what fun it was. It has turned some warmer the ice seemed unsafe except way up on a mountain pond in the Cooper's Rock park near here. We used their ski run for the tobogan [sic] run. The four children are getting quite good on their skates, especially Eliza. But they enjoyed the tobogan most. They would come down very fast and often spill over or end up sliding backwards. Exams are comming [sic] up in about two weeks for me and Frances. I'll be glad when they are over so we both can relax somewhat mentally.[20]

The children are learning pretty fast to play the piano [he wrote to his mother in February] and they seem to enjoy it as well! The terrible tension of Frances' takeing [sic] those comprehensive exams is over and we are just getting back to some sort of equilibrium.[21]

[In March, he wrote:] It is Saturday night and everyone is reading. Pamela has a cold which I believe I've caught. Frances is studying as usual. She is determined to finish her thesis this semester. I hope she can but it will be hard. My course work will be all finished this semester. I plan to get the German off by the end of the summer. Then study for and take the preliminary exams in the fall. These will be the most difficult hurdle. You are right about our "falling off" on letter writing especially me. The days are too much alike and even the weeks seem to rush by. I used to plan on being able to catch up studies on the week end but it is easier to do somthing with the children (ice scate [sic], walk, etc.) than to have them and me mope around the house.[22]

Father Chapman's ordinariness eventually wore down everyone's enthusiasm for the Episcopal service.

> I am so sorry about the rest of the family. They have stopped going as of Easter. But I really can not blame them much. There is little in morning prayer or sermon that has meaning to the girls or to Frances or to me for that matter. But I keep going I guess, because I love to sing. The girls tried Sunday School, but they did not want to continue.[23]

> [Later in the year, after the family began attending the Unitarian Universalist Church (which Veblen considered an improvement over the other Protestant denominations because it rejected the Trinity and was thus less anthropomorphic), Bud would write:] At church today we had an interesting talk on the influence of the ideas of biological and historical evaluation on literature in the 19th centry [*sic*]. For a change—the children enjoy Sunday school and actually for the first time <u>want</u> to go.[24]

Bud and Eliza continued with the Holy Trinity choir, but avoided services led by Father Chapman. "I can withstand Father Chapman only once in a while," he explained to his mother.[25] In March, they "finally did break down and buy a car, a red Volkswagen, which Frances mostly drives." The old car (presumably the 1951 English Ford) was "on its last leg", but Bud hoped it would last until the end of the semester.[26]

> Our plans for the summer are slowly beginning to shape up. [The girls had already said they wanted to spend the summer with their grandmothers in Charlotte.] We will probably stay here until the first part of July because Frances wants to finish her Master's work and I want to get started strongly on my German. And we probably won't go down to the beach 'till August.[27]

That summer, Congress passed the Civil Rights Act and a joint resolution authorizing President Johnson to do whatever necessary, including the use of conventional military force, to defend any country in southeast Asia (i.e., South Vietnam) against communist aggression, not that Bud or Frances noticed, so absorbed they were in their studies. Frances finished her thesis, and although Bud had not completed his course in German, he told his mother things were "going smoothly." He gave her this accounting of how he planned to spend a typical week over the coming year. Teaching: 6 hours, attending: 18 hours, auditing: 4 hours, choir: 4 hours, studying: 10+ hours. Minimum total hours: 41. He told his mother, "If I am not finished by the end of this year I am leaving anyway", adding:

> I have also obligated myself to organize a children's chior in a poor town near here, but I hope that it won't take much time once I get it going.[28]

A third portentous event occurred in October of 1964. Members of an Anabaptist Christian movement with a community in Farmdale, Pennsylvania spoke at a Unitarian meeting that the family happened to attend. Afterward, Bud, Frances and Eliza made the hour-long drive north to Farmdale to visit this "place of brothers" (*bruderhof* in German). The three of them were, Bud told his mother, "impressed."

> Briefly, everyone owns all property in common as did the very early Christians; they eat and work together, but the family group is maintained. The children are educated in the community thru the 7th grade and then sent to the public schools. Some are helped to go to college. They make educational toys and play ground type things out of maple. All big decisions are made by "life" members by unanimous consent. There are no rules. They also publish books on a small scale now but since their founder was a publisher they plan to expand more in this direction again (they were greatly restricted in this during WWII). They have picked up all sorts of people in their moves. From Germany, they were forced out by the Nazis in the early 30's and went to England, then to Paraguay in the early 40's , and here in the early 50's, collecting people on the way. The first community here is still in Rifton, N.Y. and this one we were told was the third, started three years ago. I really didn't intend to say so much about them, but they did and do seem

out of place and thus interesting. Someone at the Unitarian meeting asked Mr. Hind (from the Society of Brothers) if he had read Walden II. He had some 10 years ago and thought the accent and dependence on science would prove unworkable. I think he used two words "too cold." Eliza asked the young girl whom he had brought along if the children in the community got spankings. "Sometimes", was the answer. I'll stop with the comment that I am supprised that they are able to survive.[29]

Frances had given Bud a copy of B.F. Skinner's *Walden Two*, published in 1948, as a joke because he was, in Eliza's words, "always talking about utopian goals." The book would, according to historian Timothy Miller, have "a greater impact on 1960s-era communalism than any other." Miller said the book followed "a classic formula for literary utopias:"

> [A] visitor happens into an ideal intentional community and describes what he sees in glowing terms—in this case a community that uses the relatively new social science of behaviorism to provide its members, living in near-paradise, with lives of agreeable work, abundant leisure, and intellectual stimulation. Members build their own low-cost, efficient buildings; they can choose which jobs to perform, with compensation in work-credits reflecting the desirability of the work; planners and managers steer the community's life and work for the benefit of all.[30]

But for the excesses of the 1950s, the consumerism, the paranoia over communism, and the fear engendered by the Cold War, the *Walden Two* vision might not have been nearly so attractive as it was in the 1960s. Just how personally attractive Bud found it is hard to say, but he was definitely intrigued, and he was still writing about the Farmdale visit a couple of weeks later.

> I think that if you would come up and visit this "Society of Brothers" with us [he told his mother] you would not say (as you do in your letter) that the group is practical. I have been reading a book about their history and basic approach and it seems that they are the ultimate in impractically [*sic*]. For example, they will accept into their

community any and all who profess to be seeking a Christian life. Whereas Walden II seems to be "practical" in that nothing is accepted unless it can be justified as putting forward the aims of the community, and everything is rejected if it can be proved (scientifically) not to forward the aims. At anyrate [sic] the "Bruderhof" commitment is practical to the extent of using the most modern methods to manufacture the toys they sell. And they do seem to work and hold together—although the book telling of their history tells of factierial [sic] disputes which almost doomed the community in the '20's... I'll send you this book about the Bruderhof when I finish if you are interested.[31]

The 1964 presidential election perked up Bud's interest in politics somewhat, enough to predict Goldwater would receive no more than 40% of the popular vote (he got 38.9% nationally, and 48% in Mecklenburg County). "And when you consider," he wrote to Ruth after the results were in, "the 20% or so who vote Republican no matter what, that leaves only about 18% of the 70 million voters who really thought Goldwater had something better."

> Here in W. Va.[his letter continued] the two party system exists [as it did not in the Democrat-controlled South] and as a result there seems to be a realistic opportunity for one's vote to have some effect. At any rate there is alot more interest in local and state candidates. Almost everyone votes a split ticket. I voted for the Republican candidates for governor [desegregationist Cecil H. Underwood, lost to Democrat Hulett C. Smith by ten points] and sheriff. A two party system of some sort in the southern states might be a very good thing there. Of course I would like to see a strong democratic-socialist party or at least one that is more "people" concerned instead of property, national security, etc. diverted... I hope that you are not too dissappointed [sic] in the election. Regardless of what sort of man Goldwater is or the sort of pres. he would have made, I cannot agree with most of the sort of people who gave him support [most notably, Ronald Reagan and Ayn Rand].[32]

If, as it appears from Bud's comment, Ruth voted for the Republican, it very probably was because of the "sort of man

Goldwater" was (his mother was a devout Episcopalian), which is to say the sort of man Ruth thought he was, based on her limited information. She would not have voted for Johnson merely because he was a Southern Democrat (she insisted "Texas is not the South.") Nor would L.B.J.'s infamous television commercials have influenced her, as she did not own a television set. She may have viewed Goldwater as a man of principle; many did. She might have distrusted L.B.J. as too "pragmatic." Truman never trusted him, either. She may have remembered the cloud of Box 13 over his election to the Senate, or his maiden "We of the South" speech. Or maybe she remembered what he had done to the courageous, consumer-oriented chair of the Federal Power Commission, Leland Olds. She had a long memory, and any number of reasons to vote against a man known to all as the consummate politician, in other words, decidedly not "a man of principle."[33]

There can be little doubt that Bud was as close as he was ever going to get to a party that was "more 'people' concerned." The Democrats under L.B.J. were serious about civil rights and poverty. There was reason for hope. The arc of the moral universe seemed to be bending.

Frances's brother Robert, a graduate student in electrical engineering, was to visit that Thanksgiving, and Bud hoped to interest him in one of the early online dating services.

> It will be nice to see him again [Bud wrote to Ruth]. I think he plans to start back to school the spring semester at Ga. Tech. or N.C. State one. I am going to try to get him interested in a person-to-person contacting service which uses a computer. A sociology professor at UCLA ran one for 6 years and wrote a book about it—very interesting, actually using computers to help individuals instead of faceless masses.[34]

Robert was not interested, however. A few years later, Bud would make the same suggestion to the newly-formed Twin Oaks community, but they "didn't think much of the idea", either.³⁵

Around the time of the election, Frances had been very near completing all the requirements for her master's. Bud and the girls, according to Bud, were looking forward to the pressure letting up.

> My studies are going fairly well [Bud wrote to his mother], but I do have a load enough so that I always seem to be behind in everything. Frances is to take her oral exam Nov. 13 if all goes as planned. And shortly after that we can all relax, I guess. Anyway the children and myself will be thankful.³⁶

But the pressure did not, after all, let up. The Psychology Department had launched its doctoral program just the year before, and Frances decided in December that she, like her brothers, wanted to go after that advanced degree.

> Frances seems to be even more wrapped up than before the M.S. degree pressure [Bud wrote to his mother]. If it seems probable that she will get her Ph.D. if she stays one more year, we will probably stay.³⁷

The degree would not take just one year, it would take more than two. And, because of German, Bud would not be finished "by the end of the [academic] year" as he had predicted. With his studies "not going too well" (the first semester he had made straight As), his enthusiasm was once again on the wane.

> I am not over my head [he wrote to his mother], but tird [sic] of being the student, I guess. And having to do things that are down right silly just to meet the requirements.³⁸

He had for some time been working on a proposal to the National Science Foundation. The proposal, which would become his dissertation, was "mostly trying to actually solve the destruction-or-damage-of-buildings-by-earthquakes problem and I finally came up on a real, exciting idea which, if I can show that it works, will be absolutely the last word and aught to bring fame and (I hope) fortune."[39] If the National Science Foundation grant came through, he would "stay and finish up" at West Virginia University, he told his mother. Otherwise, he "could finish the research anywhere, that is, take a job and make some money."[40] His spirits lifted a bit in February as he began to dig into his research.

> I have at last begun in earnest on my research work and already I can see my way to the end. There is also great satisfaction to me in this last phase because I have at last arrived at a satisfactory way to isolate buildings from earthquake motions. It remains only to design the isolator, optimized [sic] the design, and test it. I have been building small wooden and plastic models and just last week finally hit upon the solution to the most troublesome aspect. I believe the rest will be only a matter of good engineering... It is a long row to hoe.[41]

In what had become the rare letter to Ruth, thanking her for offering to keep the girls over the summer, Frances confessed to feeling "barely human at this point."

> Appreciate the invitation to keep them again this summer [Frances wrote,] but now that they have friends here and are reaching the age where friends make a difference I think they had better stay with us. Both are going to a YWCA camp for a week. June 20 + Liza has been accepted in a special French program at the Univ. which will continue on through 9th grade and another S. school is offering typing that Pam is interested in—so sounds as if they will be well occupied. We are also involved in Bud's friends' [Jim Shafer] wine making project which requires picking millions of blackberries. Right now its rhubarb. Know you're glad Don + Tina are coming.[42]

There was the usual trip to Myrtle Beach that summer, though. "All of us had a fine time" at Irene's, Bud wrote Ruth, "but I hope we have less children next time."[43] A couple of weeks earlier, he had reported to her:

> Everything has gone smoothly so far and everyone [a total of 14] seems content, more or less, but as for me, two weeks will be sufficient. There really are too many children. I guess that after this we will be more modest in our requirements for company, although we may not. Jim Shafer, Eric (his son), Eliza and myself rented a boat and motor at Calabash and fished in Little River and Bonapart [sic] Inlet most of the day, yesterday, and caught 2 or 3 fish each plus a large crab which I managed to flip on board—causing Eliza to jump about and almost fall in. Eric and Eliza wanted to stay longer but we were being roasted by the sun so we came in at about 2 PM having started at 7 AM.[44]

At the coast he had time to read the newspapers from Charlotte, Greensboro and Raleigh. He read how the U.S. House Democrats had just outmaneuvered the Republicans on a bill to repeal part of the Taft-Hartley or Labor-Management Relations Act, passed in 1947 over President Truman's veto, but procedural coups no longer interested him as they had at Duke. He doubtless would have reflected on President Johnson's tragic decision to "Americanize" the conflict in Vietnam. He had just turned 40 and was feeling doubt, anxiety, dissatisfaction and on the cusp of a mid-life crisis.

> Why would anyone want to take part in any of it [politics]? Other than the best for money and power. But these are reason enough for most, so I've answered the question, but have not solved my own. I still at 40 years of age do not know what to do with my life. I have reached the point of being able to do many things fairly well but few really first rate. And it's time I did, I know. Frances will teach psycology [sic] and like it and make a good salary and probably so will I but who knows where! I am worried about passing the German this summer. It is the last time I am going to try it. It is pure circus—jumping through a hoop, since no one actually uses it now—everything of importance being translated. Everyone says I should join the circus, maybe they are right.[45]

A couple of weeks into the summer session Bud confessed to his mother, "I hate German and am thinking of giving up the whole Degree over it."[46] In September, he took a room in town. In a letter to his mother, written just after a visit in Charlotte to pick up the girls, he referred to Frances as "working away" preparing for "prelim[inary exam]s." He commented that "so far", he had "had lunch and dinner at 'home' but I usually walk from my fairly plesant room to a good resturant [sic] downtown for breakfast."

> I imagine this will go on until after the "prelims" [he went on], after which I plan to have some serious talks. My "prelims" will require alot of review and study and that is what I am doing now, but I must admit that I have some trouble keeping my mind on it.[47]

The post-exams talks with Frances did not resolve matters.

> Everything is still pretty much in suspension here [Bud wrote his mother]. F. thinks now that we aught to see a psycholanalyst [sic]. We have had some good talks since she has finished her exams last Saturday. But I still have no idea how things will turn out. My committee has yet to meet and decide on the German.[48]

> [A few days later, he reported] Things are slowly improving with Frances & me but we seem apart on many details (like labor and management). F. went to the psychologest [sic] last wed. and it is my tern [sic] this wed. Also whether my committee will allow me to sub. course work for the German is not decided but will be in a few days. I am so weary of this sort of obstical (?) [sic] course learning that I will be happy with a decision either way. I have refused to take the German.[49]

The committee decided to allow Bud to substitute another humanities course for German (Bud chose "The Philosophy of Science"). It may have been around this time that he joined the national organization Students for Democratic Society (SDS), which was increasingly focused on protesting the war in Vietnam. (The students of West Virginia University would not form a chapter until 1969.[50])

Irene died October 30, 1965, having been diagnosed with colon cancer just a few weeks before. She had not been feeling very well, probably for some time, and had lost weight. Bud had told his mother he thought Irene just had a virus like the one he had had "most of the summer."[51] Ruth had stayed in Mount Airy to care for Irene until she died at Forsythe Memorial Hospital in Winston-Salem, and afterward to administer her estate. During those long, lonely weeks in Mount Airy, Ruth did sometimes watch the news on Irene's television, but if anything, the exposure made her distrust the medium even more than before. Irene left everything she had to her 13 nieces and nephews, excepting Katharine's children, who had been otherwise well provided for.

In mid-November, Bud wrote to his mother that he was looking forward to Thanksgiving with the Shafers (Jim was the winemaker) and the Drakes (Tom directed the choir) and said Frances had spoken to the Unitarian Fellowship on "'Women's Role in Changing Society' or something like that." He also let his mother know they "finally broke down and got a TV." As he knew she did not approve of television, he assured her he and Frances would limit the girls' weekday access and encourage viewing of educational programming broadcast by the public station in Pittsburgh. Bud also advised her to "handle Aunt Irene's former possessions so as not to irritate anyone any more than they will be through their own efforts."[52] He let her know that they would visit as usual at Christmas, which they did. Subsequent letters follow the same vein, everyone looking forward to Christmas, choir, discussion groups, parties, settling Irene's estate and possibly going in with his brothers to buy Irene's beach house (tax value of $55,000) with no further mention of marital tensions.[53]

In February, Eliza, now 14, recorded in her diary that she wanted to "get to bed earler [sic] so I can be trusted to schedule my time and watch TV", and that she had invented a "magnabeal" using magnets and a small propeller.

> We were going to watch Man from UNCLE [spy fiction series that ran from 1964-1968] when Daddy switched the chanel [sic] and wouldn't turn it back. He does it all the time. We only get to watch it on weekends and when Daddy

> turns it on, special ocasions [*sic*] or we sneek [*sic*]. Pam started to cuss so he said we had enough TV and cut it off! How can you <u>love</u> someone who likes to toture [*sic*] people. Daddy also what you might call scorned my magnabeal. Mom didn't.[54]

The next day, she told her diary, "Daddy is mean."[55]

> Some times I feel like I live in a dictator ship [*sic*]. Daddy wants me to keep account of my allowance. I started or got ready to in Jan. but they haven't payed [*sic*] me sence [*sic*] and he expects me to keep account! When I try to tell him this he keps [*sic*] on enterupting [*sic*] me. I got a hair cut today. It looks odd. Mom talked to Daddy. He wants me to keep a book on my money. He explained nicely.[56]

Frances was rarely seen at home now, Eliza was to recall in later years. There was talk of sending her to school, but after George School in Newton, Pennsylvania, turned her down for the fall term, the matter was dropped.[57] Pamela was "doing very well with her piano" and Eliza was "doing better with her studies."[58] Except for another miscarriage, everyone was healthy, and Frances was "still hard at work on her dissertation proposal."[59]

The mill, its wanted-poster wallpaper and all its contents, burned to the ground on May 13.[60] Over the summer, there were the usual visits with family in Myrtle Beach and Charlotte. David advised Bud he thought Frances would leave him after she got her Ph.D. The thought troubled him deeply, Eliza would report years later, and fed his doubt, anxiety and dissatisfaction. To an outside observer, there may have seemed no cause for concern. His and Frances's teaching positions at West Virginia University were reasonably secure. They had hired a "1/2 time maid and cook" to take care of the "labor" issue and the girls were giving no particular trouble. The National Science Foundation had approved Bud's project (technically West Virginia University's project) subject to available funds, though it was uncertain when the funding would come through. And yet,

> At this point I really don't care [he wrote to his mother in the fall of 1966]. Teaching is now pretty much a tiresome

task and I am aiming at starting (with the proper conditions) some other preoccupations, which will have all the good qualities and none of the bad and still make money, or at least some money.[61]

Perhaps chief among those "other preoccupations" was the utopian vision of *Walden Two*. Bud had subscribed to the newsletter of an urban community called "Walden House", located in Washington, D.C., put out by Kathleen Kinkade (née Levinson, 1930-2008), who owned and lived in Walden House with her daughter Susan and second husband, George Griebe. She would later write that Bud "visited and corresponded and had a lot of sympathy with our effort to start a Walden Two community."[62] In the fall of 1966, Bud attended a conference near Ann Arbor, Michigan for utopian-minded individuals interested in forming a rural, back-to-the-land type community like Walden Two. Kinkade would describe him as having "a little bit of inherited money and a passion to do something good with it."[63] The community imagined in Skinner's *Walden Two* consisted of one thousand people sharing housing, cooking and eating facilities and child-rearing responsibilities who were, for the most part, able to grow or make what they needed. There was no money and no one worked more than half a day during the week. As noted previously, Skinner imagined this "utopia" was possible through the application of behavioral psychology early in life that scientifically conditioned individuals to develop into happy and productive members of the community. Crucially, children were housed and educated in separate quarters. Overall management of the community was vested in the "planners", trained psychologists elected by the community to fill that role.

It was in the context of the *Walden Two* vision that Kinkade was to describe Bud (using the pseudonym "Hal") as one of six, including Kinkade, George and her daughter, who were "already emotionally committed to community", who "wanted community... right then, money or no money, psychologists or or no psychologists, planning or no planning."[64] By her account, "Hal [Bud] talked to a lot of people at the [Ann Arbor] conference, discovered he was the only one there with readily available capital...and decided to put his money at the disposal of" Kinkade's group, "rather than search any further."[65] Kinkade quoted Bud as having told the group, "You kids want to farm? Well I'll buy you a farm."[66] According to Kinkade, Bud had "definitely committed himself to purchasing land for us" by January 1967, "though he would not be able to join us at first because his wife was opposed to community."[67] This account, if accurate, suggests Bud approached Frances about uprooting the family yet again to start a commune of all things while she was, in his words, "working at such a pace as not to allow for any other activities."[68] Characterizing a refusal under such circumstances as "being opposed to community" hardly seems fair.

Another preoccupation (albeit one unlikely to make any money) was flying, an interest shared with Ed Byars, whose father had died in a plane crash at the age of 38. Ed had a staggered-wing Beechcraft and several gliders that he flew competitively. Bud had said in October that he had "finally gotten around to taking lessons (3 so far) and it is great fun! My glider training comes in very handy."[69] In December, he told his mother that he was ready to "solo", and aside from Frances working all the time, "[e]verything is on a pretty even keel, except for little things like Eliza and Pamela having slight colds."

> In a few days I will know if the National Science Foundation has funded my proposal and if I pass my qualifying exams (usually oral) I will be here for almost exactly another year. Everything indicates that they will. And that I will pass the exam... Actually, I am very "cool" about this event. The money involved will be about the same either way. In any event I want to stop teaching and try somthing else, like apply all my "learning" and have it be fun too.[70]

In January, Bud wrote Ruth to thank her for letting them have some of Aunt Irene's things.

> They will be very nice when we settle in Charlotte. And settle we will after all these years, because Frances allows she is just not going to move after we leave here again. I am getting in a lot of flying during the holidays (some 10

hours solo now). As a matter of fact, it is a beautiful day right now so I'm off.[71]

[Ten days later, he wrote,] Frances is apparently overcoming all difficulties in the way of her degree. While I have become very philosophical with respect to mine.[72]

By March, the National Science Foundation funding had come through. But all was not to Bud's liking. He felt he was being made to "jump through hoops" in order to "be allowed to do my work on my NSF project."

> For example, last week I had to write a proposal and be examined orally on it to show that I could write a proposal (on a topic out of my field and in one week). The fact that I had already written one [presumably the original project proposal] and therefore had demonstrated that I could write one did not seem to matter. So after [s]leeping on it, I told Ed that I just would not do it, or to mix a metaphor, "this is the hoop that broke the camel's back." Oh well, I have almost entirely got over the PhD sickness anyway. As for vacation—things are so unsettled here. Frances may or may not have to work thru the summer on her degree. And I have no idea where I stand.[73]

Legend has it that Bud, despite being fully qualified, was not awarded a Ph.D. because he had written his dissertation in pencil and refused to have it typed. From what Bud related to his mother, it would appear that, for his Ph.D., he needed to qualify to work on (and perhaps to complete) the National Science Foundation project; he resented this requirement because he felt he had proved he qualified already, as it was after all "his" project proposal that had secured the grant. What is unclear is what the "it" was that he would not do after sleeping on it, but it *seems* like something more than just having a document typed up. One also has to wonder whether, having successfully challenged the Department's German requirement by refusing to comply with it, Bud thought the strategy might work a second time. If so, he seems to have failed to consider whether the Department had any discretion in the matter. The National Science Foundation was, after all, holding the purse strings.

There can be no denying that Bud, having "no idea where I stand", was anxious about his future generally and his marriage in particular. His feeling that "things are so unsettled here" echoes his description of his situation in September 1965, when he took a room in town. Many years after the fact, Frances would tell Eliza that she had initiated the breakup. She would also express some degree of regret that she had not given the commune idea a try and treated it as the passing phase it would turn out to be. Bud was good at solving problems, but not this sort of problem. He might have dreamed of flying away somewhere by himself, but he was working on an earthly escape—with his "Utopia friends."

> This Easter [March 26, 1967] will be quiet for us [he wrote to his mother]. Frances wants to work on her paper and I will relax I guess. I may go to Washington D.C. and meet with my Utopia friends. They are looking for a farm outside Wash. to move to and start the community. Around 8 will probably move. They are very determined. I hope they can survive![74]

Chapter 13

Leave your home behind you

The Easter letter was the last of Bud's surviving correspondence to come from Morgantown. On April 28, 1967, Bud paid $28,500 to purchase about 120 acres and farm equipment from Earnest and Willie May Jones in Louisa County, Virginia (about 35 miles southeast of where he was born), and installed his Utopia friends there, rent free for six years on the condition that the community continue each year to grow, with an option to buy at the end of the lease. When school let out, Bud drove Eliza and Pamela to Charlotte to visit for a few weeks while he helped some of the Utopia friends move from Atlanta to the farm. Shortly after they moved in, the well ran dry. Bud paid to have a new well drilled.

Bud returned the girls to Morgantown so they could begin summer school, stopping by the farm on the way. He then drove around the countryside for a few days ("the only real plesant area that I found driving my trip was Currituck County"). He told his mother that Frances was having difficulty getting her dissertation proposal accepted.

> It is a cruel game the establishment of professors play. Most of them really want the student to work on projects supported by hard cash instead of non-paying, non-supported research that F. is trying to do. Almost always their ad-

vancement demands on the amount of project money they bring to the school. Too bad!¹

By mid-July, he and Frances were dividing the furniture. Bud gave Frances a promissory note for $42,000, the money to be used for the girls' education. Frances found a house and teaching position in Albion, Michigan, and Bud moved into the beach house he now owned with his brothers to work on his rope hammock-weaving machine. While there, he wrote to Eliza.

> Dear Eliza,
> Sounds from your post card from Albion that your next house will have enough space for a change. Here at the beach I have <u>more</u> than enough, but I have set up a shope [*sic*] in the garage to make hammocks and I am really working and enjoying myself.
> Mother, Willie [her driver and cook], [Martin and Lillian's children] Charles [age 5] and Sheri [age 7] were down for a week but left last Monday. My daily food fair was much better while they were here. Actually I think that I could do a good job cooking but right now hammocks come first. I want the community to make them because they've about run out of money. Mr. Billing in California sends them $200 per month otherwise they would probably not have enough to eat, but their garden is producing now and they plan to get a cow soon. Would you like to visit there again on our way down to the beach?
> The Gibbses are down at Pawley's Island now. Mary Jo invided [*sic*] me down to dinner last night and this morning I don't feel so good. I should have known! She wanted to talk and drink not eat. I finally got some crab meat the girls fixed at midnight—never again!
> About the tape recorder—you move the red recording lever and hold it on "record" while you turn the other lever on "Forward." This locks the red lever in place.
> I haven't had enough spare cash to get me another recorder but either I use someone else's (say drop by and see your Uncle Martin in his radio store [Radio Shack]) or get another like yours or I would really like to get one that would record music better. But right now hammocks come first, because if I'm not a success I may have to get

a job—and that would be very bad & depressing. I don't mind work—just jobs.

That's about all I can think to write except that I hope you can get the tape recorder working <u>and</u> follow the rules!

Much love, Daddy[2]

It was during the visits to the farm that summer, Eliza was to recall, that she began to realize her father was not coming home. "No one ever talked to us about anything", she was to say. "It was just, 'get in the car.'" Frances and the girls moved to Albion in September, by which time Bud was staying at Twin Oaks, as the farm was now called. He took out a loan from the bank in Louisa using 70 shares of his mother's R.J. Reynolds Tobacco Company stock as collateral. He was able to persuade the community to make hammocks for income, a decision that, more than any other, would ensure the community's continued survival. He offered to cash in his veterans life insurance policy and use the money to purchase construction materials for a building that could accommodate a workshop and sleeping quarters, and the community accepted.

> The building is going pretty well [he wrote his mother in October]. The excavation and roof rafters are compleated [*sic*]. We will probably have the roof on by the end of next week if the good weather holds. Actually I am enjoying it all and consider everything from a machine design point of view—i.e. this building is a shelter machine. My main worry is that I will run out of money before it can give shelter & the "barn dwellers" can move in. I hope to have at least enough for roof, floor and outside walls![3]

> [W]hen it's all done it will be 2500 square feet of nice shelter for about $4500 which is only $1.80 per square ft. when the usual cost now-adays is around $8. The trick is, of course, that I am paying for the materials only... and I will own it to sell or otherwise if the community disbands or moves.[4]

In *A Walden Two Experiment*, Kinkade's last-woman-standing account of Twin Oaks' first five years, Kinkade would write that, even though "[a]ll the rest of us worked on it [the building]", they did not work hard enough to please Bud, who "wanted to see more dedication and less leisure" from the group.[5] As Bud put it, his "friends seem much more interested in helping me build [now that]... it's getting colder & colder in the barns where they sleep."[6] Besides wanting to get the building finished, Bud was wanting to perfect the hammock-weaving machine, find a hammock retailer, and finalize the lease agreement which, as late as December, remained unsigned. As usual, he made time to sing with a local choir (Yanceyville Christian Church) along with Kinkade, her daughter and another community member, Connie Nesmith.

Kinkade would write in her book that the community called Bud to task for trying to give orders on the construction site. Bud had evidently forgotten his advice to David that it was "social suicide to show that you think yourself superior to anyone."[7] But, to his credit, when his "authoritarian" behavior was called to his attention, "he made a genuine effort to curb his dictatorial speech and phrase things more pleasantly." The matter did not end there, however. Kinkade would refer to it as "the behavior problem that was to plague Hal [Bud] as long as he lived with us." And she was not the only one to call him on it.

> Marie [a pseudonym] felt Hal [Bud] regarded her as a nigger... His problem [Kinkade would later write] was a combination of the high-handed way he talked to everyone... and his heavy Southern accent... Hal [Bud] was castigated for saying "nigra." "But," he protested, "that's just the way I pronounce things." And it was true. I listened to his speech after that, and noticed that he consistently made final o's in a's—tobacca, potata, winda, etc. But Marie wasn't satisfied. "Any educated man can learn to say 'Negro'," she said. So Hal [Bud] learned it. It sounded odd with the rest of his speech, a Yankee word thrown into the middle of his drawl, but he made the effort, anyway.[8]

Bud would soon adopt Stokely Carmichael's preferred term, "black", which was just then coming into vogue.

Would-be members of the Twin Oaks community had to serve 90 days' probation. In January, the community accepted Bud as a member despite his flaws, though they were hardly in a position to do otherwise. Bud found an Episcopal church (St. James in Louisa), joined the choir, and for the next six months, his letters to Ruth remained fairly upbeat.

> Dear Mother,
> Not much happening here at Twin Oaks Farm now. For a while the weather was very mild and we did alot of outside work—dig [sic] a new hole for the out house and set the repaired old one over it—built a small green house for George [Griebe, pseudonym "Fred"] to start plants in etc. As to your best [underlined 4x] blanket, I would have perished in the cold (the furnace is allowed to go out—or was. but now we have learned to make it give fairly even heat all night). I'll bring them back the first passing after the cold weather, of course.
> Rudy [Nesmith, pseudonym "Brian"] keeps getting printing jobs but nothing very large. The last two were ones where he needed a paper cutter. We have a little hand paper knife but to cut two reams of $8\frac{1}{2}$" x 11' which really takes a long time. A used one will cost at least $200 and we are very short on that, as I mentioned before.
> My hammock machine is keeping me busy and I expect to have it ready for a first trial run by the end of next week. My next project is a pipe bender for the manufacture of the hammock stands. George is going to help me on this. He's also going with me to get hammock orders. We plan to make our first trip early in March.
> The synthetic rope (textured poly propolen [sic]) is really quite good for hammocks—we've just finished one and tested it. Also I weighed both the cotton & synthetic ropes and found that the cotton is about 7% more expensive!
> Hope this reaches you in Mt. Airy.
> Love, Bud[9]

If Bud wrote any letters in April, May or June, they did not survive. In July, Bud confided to his mother that "[t]hings are still very poorly run here by the planners and I am usually pretty upset."[10] At that time, the planners were Kinkade, Rudy Nesmith, and an avowed bourgeoisie-hating philosophy grad student named Scott. According to Kinkade, the planners' decisions were guided by a set of loosely worded bylaws "written largely by me [Kinkade] and passed into law [sic] by a very lazy consensus that didn't even examine them closely."[11] This "lazy consensus" made it difficult to defend the planners' decisions, especially to newcomers who might or might not have read "Walden Two and the Code [bylaws]."[12] Twin Oaks' lack of a shared vision was a continuing source of frustration for Kinkade, but it was also predictable, given how inconsistently the community advertised itself. This news bit from the *Alexandria Daily Town Talk*, for example:

> Twin Oaks advertises for converts hoping that at least 1,000 persons will want to try a way of life that promises "no rules to enforce, no personal competition, no money to be misused, and no glory or power to be gained by any single individual."[13]

The trouble with Bud, Kinkade was to write, started the following April. It was then that Bud "became deeply dissatisfied", and it became Bud "against everybody."[14] The presenting problem was the planners' refusal to conduct open meetings. An ultimatum was issued. Bud would recall it as, "either open the meetings or get off my land", Kinkade as, "either make me a planner or get off my land."[15] However, later in the book she observes, "I see that almost everything I write about him [Bud] paints him as being a community villain", and admits his primary concern was that meetings be open.

> The fact is that Hal [Bud] was and is a good person, cheerful, generous, and high-minded, and he meant nothing but good toward the Community.[16]

> It was Hal [Bud] who first said "I want to know what is going on." With hindsight [not applied until this point in the book], I can readily see that he, like any other active mind, would be interested in the details of the decision-making process. He wanted to know not only what decisions we had reached, but the reasoning that was behind them. He wanted to participate in the discussion. And we very stupidly didn't allow him to.[17]

> Were we [the planners] self-righteous? Unquestionably. We were, furthermore, self-indulgent...[18]

> [I]t is obvious... that our snobbishness was self-defeating. We had a problem with government and a problem with educating new members. We could have solved both at once if we had given up our private planners' meetings.[19]

Even though meetings were not opened (while he was there), Bud did not follow through with his ultimatum, a fact for which Kinkade would give him no credit. In her view the ultimatum was itself an unforgivable offense—the tragic result of Bud's discovering "his influence ended when his cash did", and that he (unlike she) lacked the social skills needed to "gain control of a group" or to "be happy without it."[20] Whether Kinkade understood Bud as well as she thought she did is an open question. When *A Walden Two Experiment* was published in 1973, they had known each other for six years. By that time, all the other founders, including her husband and daughter, had moved on (though her daughter would come and go). Kinkade was the only one left, and the story was hers to tell. Without question, her having lived with Bud for more than a year entitles her views to some weight. The question is, as always, how much.

Kinkade was 36 when Twin Oaks was founded; Bud was 42, the group's oldest member. She would characterize Bud as having "been raised in an upper-class family", as having "an air of being accustomed to money", and as well educated, well read, well traveled—more so than anyone else in the community.[21] Kinkade would tell *Washington Post* in 1998 that she had been raised in poverty, been sexually molested by her stepfather, and watched her family disintegrate after she reported it.[22] All her life, she told the *Post*, she had longed for a father, one "who was strict and had firm rules and expected a certain behavior from me but loved me." It is not hard to imagine the hurt Kinkade might have felt when Bud accused the planners of incompetence and factionalism, or why in her book she would keep circling back to the subject of "Hal", alternately admiring and condemning him (as well as herself, but mostly Hal), unable to come to terms with who he was or what she thought of him. And what can be said of the book's rather bizarre polemic on "competence", which claims it goes "hand in hand with intolerance", and "makes life miserable for the careless,"[23] or her assertion that her greatest regret in life was "not having been more maternal [attentive?]" to her daughter?[24] Of interest in this regard is Kinkade's characterization of Bud's response to Elliott (pseudonym "Timothy"), a four-year old whose mother had left him in the care of the community for an extended period. It seems that Rudy Nesmith, the Child Manager, who had no children of his own, did not subscribe to what behaviorists called "regulation" techniques, e.g. set bed times. Instead, he believed community members should use reinforcement and extinction techniques to reduce problem behavior, e.g. pestering the adults for attention in the evening. According to Kinkade, Bud "had no theories about behavioral engineering" and "didn't follow the arguments about reinforcement and extinction." This, she would claim, made Bud "vulnerable" in the evenings when Elliott wanted attention and Bud wanted to spend time with other adults.

> When Timothy [Elliott] said, "Tell me a story", Hal [Bud] would say, "Not right now", or "I'm busy. Maybe later." But Timothy [Elliott] soon discovered he didn't really mean it. If begged long enough, Hal [Bud] would take Timothy [Elliott] on his knees in the traditional fashion and tell him stories... Hal [Bud] could not stand to see the child standing lonely and disappointed, wanting someone to play with.[25]

So, Bud told Rudy that Elliott ought to be put to bed so he would not be a nuisance. Rudy "eventually gave in" but was "frustrated at having to resort to regulation."[26]

April also happened to be the month that Donna Hunt Edwards of Greenville, South Carolina, and her sons Kyle and Theron chose to visit Twin Oaks. Some have said that Donna and Bud met in Charlotte, but Kinkade and court documents found in Bud's papers put their meeting at Twin Oaks. Wherever they met, they got together at Twin Oaks. Kinkade was to have nothing good to say about Donna, whom she would describe as Bud's "overwhelmingly middle-class girlfriend."[27]

In June, Donna moved the children and her three bedroom trailer to Twin Oaks. Shortly thereafter, Kinkade would later recall, conflicts arose between Bud, Donna and the planners. Bud often took Donna's side, which annoyed Kinkade. The planners (if not Kinkade herself) were as much as anyone to blame for the trouble, which started with the planners' insistence that Donna's trailer was "a new Community house" that all should share.[28] The planners prevailed on that issue, but then allowed Donna to retain possession of most of the trailer for herself, Bud, and her sons. Next the planners insisted that the Child Manager should make decisions about "that bourgeois woman['s]" (Donna's) children. What this meant, in effect, was that no one, especially not the Child Manager, would be telling the boys how to behave. Rather, they would be left "largely to feel out privileges and responsibilities in community" on their own. Thus Donna continued her "whining and nagging" at seven year-old Theron to "wash his face, brush his teeth, get to bed on time, go to school, tuck in his shirt, put vegetables on his plate [etc.]", much to Kinkade's irritation.[29]

What Kinkade seemed to resent more than anything else was Bud's refusal to take his turn doing income-producing work outside the community (her husband George also refused). She never discussed his reasons for refusing, but they are easily discerned. From the community's point of view, forcing Bud and George into income-producing work would have made no practical sense, given there was a great deal of work to do on the farm, and Bud and George were its most skilled and productive workers. Kinkade herself would observe that the farm fell into neglect after they left. The other two planners had known better than to insist Bud take outside work, which also annoyed Kinkade.

At the end of the summer, Donna decided not to join the community "for mainly financial reasons."[30] Kinkade would claim they left because they "finally got tired of fighting the rest of the Community."[31] Looking for newsletter grist, Kinkade (its main contributor) asked community members for "one thing you like about the Community, and one thing you don't like." Bud's response was:

> The best thing is the close relationship between what we produce and what we consume. What I don't care for is the pedantic equalitarianism.[32]

In September, Bud wrote to his mother to let her know he and Donna would be staying at the beach house over the weekend so he could look for a job in Myrtle Beach, and that they planned to live there until what was left of "the upper farm" could be sold. (He had been in negotiations for some months.)

> After that I plan (as I think I told you) to go into the toy mfg. business. We plan to get married as soon as the N.C. divorce comes through. I know you will like her [Donna]—she is, as you would say, a "kind" person.[33]

David had recently proposed that the beach house should be sold for $70,000, and Bud was prepared to buy David and Martin out, if Martin agreed, "as soon as my land is sold." Possibly anticipating conflict between the brothers, Ruth suggested that, rather than move to Myrtle Beach, Bud might move Donna's trailer over to "the Smith farm" nearby and get a job in Charlottesville. She also suggested he try to interest Twin Oaks in "the toy business", to which he responded:

> About the toy business—I don't think you realize that this machinery and other expenses will cost at least $5,000 even to get started. And the "planners" have shown no interest in my plan to get it started. I really believe that they will fail to survive two more years.[34]

A few weeks later, Bud advised his mother that he and Donna *did* plan to move to the Smith farm, at least until the divorce was final.

> Our long range plans are still unchanged—investigate Canada next Summer with the view of settling there permenentally [*sic*]—you know my reasons. I have made some progress in finding a job near by—two custom furniture makers seem only mildly interested (I want to learn the trade for the toy mfg. venture) and a small farm machinery mfgr. that has

> no engineer, seems very interested and will let me know in a week or so. As far as your wanting to change my mind about Donna—I know that nothing you could do would do so—even tho' I respect your good intentions for my welfare. My conclusions on this matter were not "jumped at" but quite calculated and based on considerably more experience & caution than before.[35]

Ruth had yet to meet Donna and probably knew only what little Bud might have told her. When Bud and Frances eloped in Paris, she had known Frances and her family for several years. Ruth could not have hoped to do more than persuade Bud to slow down, as she had tried unsuccessfully to persuade friends of Mary Jo to slow down their wartime romances.

In December, Bud and Donna moved to Myrtle Beach with her sons and were married in a civil ceremony on December 22, 1968. Bud got a job doing machine design for an electronics and electrical components manufacturer named Aerovox. "My job is very interesting now", Bud told Ruth, "but I look forward to being my own hammock manufacturer or what not as soon as I can. i.e. I really don't like to work for someone else, as you know."[36] The first winter in Myrtle Beach was in some ways not much of an improvement on Twin Oaks—no central heating, cold showers, broken septic system, broken boiler, leaky pipes, vehicles needing repairs they could not afford, much work to do and not enough time.

> Dear Eliza,
> What are you doing with yourself? Donna, Kinch [short for Kinchloe, Kyle's nickname] Theron & I are wintering at the Beach House without a furnace! We keep the fire place in the living room going all the time. But it really isn't so bad the temp. goes down to freezing only about once a week.
> I have been wondering how you were. Do you use the canoe or is the water frozen, as I imagine it is?
> We looked at a used station wagon for the trip to Canada this summer. But I will have to make some more money before we can really look in earnest. And anyway we will probably start late in the summer so if you want, you (&

> Pam) could plan to visit with us (or as they say in the midwest) early or middle summer if you want.
> Let me hear from you. Love as ever,
> Daddy[37]

In February, Bud reported to his mother,

> My job at Aerovox goes very well. It turns out that I am very good at designing their machines and the job <u>now</u> is very absorbing—I do not like the 40 hour week 'though [*sic*]—No time to read or design <u>my</u> hammock <u>machine</u>.[38]

> We've all been to the dintest [*sic*] to the tune of $40 so far and there is still more to come, but it's money well spent. I needed only one small filling—Kinch [Kyle] eight, Theron two or so, and Donna one or two and a bridge.[39]

The dentist would eventually extract $200 from the savings intended for the scouting trip to Canada. Ruth paid the property taxes on what was left of Bud's "upper farm", helped with the electric bill, and let him borrow the station wagon. He found an Episcopal church (Trinity) and joined the choir ("I'm the only tenor"). His boss turned out to be "an Epis." and a former choir boy. ("He & I get along very well."[40]) Donna's daughter Karen, the eldest of her children, came to stay. "She is pretty—a little plump", as Bud described her to his mother, "and a 100% product of the culture of Greenville, S.C. and other such places," by which he meant no compliment.[41] In Bud's view, both Karen and Donna "suffered from 'Southern Belle Syndrome'", which was his way of saying that they "had very few personal skills and needed a man to constantly provide for" them. In the coming years, Donna's "unwillingness or inability to do her share in a communal situation" would become a "major contributing factor" in their break up.[42]

North Carolinians like to say, only half joking, that South Carolina is one the "twin towers of conceit" that border the state, the other being Virginia. Bud had left the University of Virginia partly because of its conceit (but then, having learned nothing, went to Duke). He had left Clemson partly because of its racial conceit, and now he was working for the notoriously anti-union Aerovox. In a May letter to Eliza, Bud lamented South Carolina's attitude toward Charleston's striking hospital workers.

> They want a union to represent them, the S.C. legislature says no—the late Martin Luther King's aid [sic] Rev. Abernathy says yes, and peacefully marches while the local police, National Guard etc. put them in jail & stockades. I think the <u>blacks</u> will win, I hope so too! But most every S.C. citizen hopes not.[43]

Bud had left the corporate business world for academia, and then left academia for community, and now he was back in South Carolina working for what he liked to call "a greedy corporation."

> I don't like to be a part of what I consider an exploitive [sic] system which does not exploit nature as the farmer did—but <u>people</u>! [He wrote to his mother in March] The women are paid the minimum wage ($1.60/hour). The men are the petty bosses and are allowed 2 coffee breaks per shift, Engineers (and the women and others at their level[)] do not have to punch a time clock (they are "exempt" employees). Big Deal! Every effort is made to "devide [sic] and conquer." I have been told not to fraternize with the machinists, etc.[44]

A month later, he wrote to Eliza:

> [I]t will be much better to view all this from Canada while trying to build a new culture and even maybe be part of an underground railroad for poor radicals. (I think that they will be "poor" because the establishment will be very cruel near its death).[45]

If America's "exploitive [sic] system" was one factor in Bud's wanting to move to Canada, the billions it was spending on the war in Vietnam was another, or as he told Eliza, "Canada spends more on social projects than on war!"[46]

> I notice now that almost everyone agrees that "we" should get out of Vietnam, now [Bud complained in a letter to his

> mother]. They do not say very often <u>why</u> they <u>now</u> agree with the "peacenicks" [*sic*] when they formerly were quite of the opposite opinion. Oh well, usually I do not bother to broach the subject—"don't try to reason someone <u>out</u> of an opinion they didn't get 'reasoned into'."[47]

As at Webb and in the Coast Guard and college, Bud had tried to fit in at Twin Oaks; adopting as much as he could of the required language and perspective, "pulling his weight", trying to meet expectations in order to minimize conflicts. But Twin Oaks was not an institution; it had no form, no traditions; no "praxis" or policies; and, unlike Walden Two, its planners had had no plan. It was, indeed, an experiment, and not at all a scientific one. As a scientist and engineer, not to mention an Episcopalian, Bud needed at least some degree of order. He felt deeply that a societal reordering of some sort was needed, but he was not at heart a revolutionary, or even a reformer. Still, he hoped he might find a way to make "this community thing" work.

> Even now I am torn between helping in the revolution <u>now-directly</u> or working for this community thing [he wrote to Eliza]. The average Twin Oaker really is trying to get away from the culture which has (usually) hurt them very much. My aim was and is to show how to build a really strong viable alternative culture—able to hold its own economically with the outside competitive culture and yet develope [*sic*] cultural structures making for a much better life within the community. My main idea is that a strong and happy community must have alot of "exchange" coming in from the "outside culture."[48]

Wherever Bud had been in 1945 on David's "Pendulums of Government" diagram, America's post-war consumerist excesses, violent defense of Jim Crow, and obsession with communism (McCarthy, Korea, the decision to develop the hydrogen bomb, Vietnam) had, by the summer of 1969, moved Bud further toward Henry Wallace. Canada was less of everything he had come to dislike about the U.S.—less crowded, less competitive, less afraid of cultural exchange. As the decade of the 1960s was coming to a close, Bud was again feeling inspired by a book he had read: *Fanshen: A Documentary of Revolution in A Chinese Village* by William Hinton, who had worked as a tractor technician and teacher in the north China village of Long Bow during the period of land reform.

> Along with his Chinese academic colleagues, Hinton advised the residents of Long Bow on the complicated tasks of teaching peasants to read, breaking up old feudal estates, insuring the equality of women, and replacing the old magistrates who governed the village with elected councils.[49]

Writing to his mother about the book—on which she had made a start but understandably could not "get into"—he said that reading about the people of Long Bow "gives me a little more strength to do what I have to do."

"Staying on" in Myrtle Beach would have required buying David and Martin out and doing significant maintenance work on the house, including tapping into the city's sewer system, all of which Bud could have managed, had he wanted to. Both his brothers wanted the beach house for at least a couple of weeks in the summer, and Bud promised his mother he would vacate the premises during the desired periods. In May, Donna sold her house trailer and netted about $1,000, enough to buy a station wagon ($325) for the trip to Canada. They left in late July, stopping to pick up Pamela in Albion. "My first impressions are mixed," Bud wrote in a postcard from Victoria, B.C. "Back in 2 weeks or so, if the transmission on the car holds up."[50] The transmission held up long enough to get them back to Myrtle Beach, where, after a few days' rest, Bud turned his attention to pouring a concrete floor in the garage.

Eliza, now 18, had graduated high school in June of 1969. She and Pamela, who had started going by her middle name, "Howerton", both let Bud know that they were "very unhappy with F." Bud had earlier confided in his mother that he was hearing very little from Eliza[51] and was "very anxious to hear and observe their troubles first hand."[52] Eliza was to recall this period years later as being very lonely and sad, and that after the move to

Albion, she was crying a lot, not doing well in school and under constant scrutiny for challenging the authorities. Frances, then an associate professor in the Psychology Department at Albion College, became concerned that Eliza was depressed ("underperforming") and sought medical treatment. Eliza was prescribed secobarbital, which she "hated" and "threw away." This annoyed Frances, who accused her of selling it at school (the drug was widely abused for recreational purposes in the '60s and '70s). At one point, according to Eliza, Frances had her hospitalized for two weeks for observation. Their relationship hit a low point. Over spring break, she somehow made her way to Twin Oaks. When Bud heard she was there, he telephoned.

> Eliza seemed in good spirits; she does, however, go against Frances alot, but it does seem (I phoned Pam [Howerton] too and had a long talk with her) that Frances is some what repressive. It is hard to judge, at this distance, what to think or do. I invited them both down to the Beach House after their school is out (but one at a time). They do seem to really be sad about life in general and there seems little that I can do.[53]

Eliza returned to Twin Oaks in July of 1969 and met 23-year old Lyn Magnuson, a dubious character who, according to Eliza, was looking for a place to lie low. Lyn would eventually take an apartment in downtown Baltimore. The first Sunday in September, Eliza packed a bag and left home. She landed on Lyn's doorstep and he let her stay. She got a job waiting tables at the White Spot across the street from the apartment on Maryland Avenue, opposite the burned out farmers' market and the train station. After a week passed with no word, Frances, distraught, informed Ruth, Bud and her mother that Eliza had left home for Washington D.C. and had not checked in. Ruth was in Winston-Salem looking after Maxie, her one remaining sister, who was dying in Forsyth Memorial Hospital. They had never been close, Maxie being fourteen years older.

> Dear Liza,
> I was sorry not to see you again or to hear. When I called next morning after going up to see my sister you had gone. She died last week and when I called to tell your father, he did not know where you were—Please let him hear from you—he is very concerned not to lose touch with you & it is not kind to neglect him. I'm writing now specifically to ask if you want to make your debut in Charlotte next June—(just as [Mary Jo's daughter] Irene Gibbs did this year) You will be invited if you do wish to do so. I'm sending this to Albion and have asked Pamela to foward [sic] it if you are not there. Please do let me hear—or if you write your father he will let me hear.
> Much love, as always, Grandma[54]

No one, least of all Ruth, expected Eliza would have any interest in the arcane institutions of Charlotte "society." Bud invited Eliza ("and Lyn?") to come to Myrtle Beach and "get into the hammock business with us."[55] He also tried to encourage her to use the time away from "relatives" to "feel what it is like to be 'on your own'."

> [I]t is not all together an unplesant feeling. At Webb School I was on "my own" in the service that I was away from relations, and I enjoyed it—even tho there was the problem of studies etc. My teachers related to each one of us as persons not only because the school was small [(]135 boys) but because of the trapping system (each student had to answer direct questions in class). While you are away you could investigate schools you'd like to go to. I remember the Sat. Review of Literature in its classified ad section had a few New England, small, co-ed, schools that you could write to for a start*. If you get restless in Wash. D.C. or whereever [sic], Donna & I would welcome you here—you could, if you wanted, get a job or go to the Tech Ed. Center which is like Piedmont College in Charlotte, and take somthing useful before going to college.
>
> *you could go to the Charlotte Library and do your investigation there.[56]

Eliza telephoned a few times, but long-distance phone calls were costly. Her letters from this period did not survive, and her parents' letters tended to ask the same questions over and over.

> Dear Eliza, [Bud wrote in October] (1) Did you get the money? (2) Have you found any job? (3) Are you enjoying your new freedom? (4) Why haven't you written? (5) Have you run out of money? (6) When do you plan to come down here? (7) Do you need anything? We are all fine.[57]

In mid-November, Bud and Donna drove to D.C. to see Eliza and to take part in anti-Vietnam-war demonstrations. "Donna still has Liberal leanings", Bud explained to Eliza.[58] They stopped at Twin Oaks going and coming (apparently leaving Theron there), and stayed overnight with Eliza and Lyn. On Friday all four attended the March on Death. "The march Sat was too slow", Bud reported to his mother, "we were cold and tird [sic] so we looked then left for Twin Oaks where we spent the night and picked up Theron."[59] Bud wrote a note thanking Lyn for the use of his bed, adding "Hope you both had no difficulty getting back to Baltimore."[60]

Just before Thanksgiving, Bud was laid off from Aerovox. He told his mother he thought they could get by for a few months on his unemployment insurance benefit plus $50 per week welfare assistance, perhaps calculating that they would spend Thanksgiving and Christmas with Ruth and return with provisions, which of course they did. Late December, Frances received word that Eliza had "been sick, w[as] out of a job and a few horrible other things,"[61] and sent her some money, saying she hoped she would "use it to fly to North Carolina" for Christmas and then return to Albion with her and Howerton. "I was taken straight from the hospital to the airport", Eliza was to recall years later, and from the airport to Mildred's. The holiday with Mildred was uneventful, following which Howerton took the bus to Myrtle Beach to visit her father, and was put to work making hammocks. After Howerton, it was Eliza's turn. Lyn was there when Eliza arrived in mid-January.

> Eliza seems happy and is doing her share of house and hammock work [Bud reported to his mother in early February]. All of us are doing fine, me especially since I'm "working for myself" now.[62]

Shortly thereafter, Bud wrote to Ruth to announce that Eliza and Lyn planned to marry.

> Dear Mother, Eliza and her true love Lyn Magnuson (means "son of the great one"—Swedish) are getting married here at Myrtle Beach (civil part) and having the reception at Twin Oaks this coming week end. They both plan to go to school afterwards. Lyn is interested in crafts and I've suggested Penland school [of Handicrafts in Bakersville, N.C.] which they are investigating. Frances and Pam [Howerton] are driving down to Twin Oaks, so are Lyn's folks. They seem to like each other (or better—be understanding) very well, so I am hoping for a long and happy coexistence. Frances and Pam are not getting on too well so that Pam may come on back with us after the Twin Oaks affair.[63]

This was the first of Bud's letters to mention Lyn to his mother. Ruth almost certainly knew about Lyn and the fact that Eliza was living with him in Baltimore. Frances would have told Mildred, and Mildred would have told Ruth. Ruth would not have mentioned any of it to Bud, but would have waited for Bud to speak first, because that is what she did with everyone. Visitors to Deverill never came to hear news, but to bring it, which is not to say that all news was welcome. As Ruth once said of an indiscrete acquaintance, "I can't believe he didn't care enough about my feelings to lie."

There was no service. The Valentine's Day reception at Twin Oaks, Eliza would recall, was Lyn's idea; "he said he wanted everyone there to know I was 'his'." Afterward, Bud dutifully reported to his mother on the nuptials.

> Dear Mother, Well we got Eliza's and Lyn's reception at Twin Oaks all done very well. Lyn and Eliza both made speeches. Lyn's mentioned love alot, I remember. And

> Eliza's (they were supposed to explain why they got married) speech was long and ended after many reasons with the reason that getting married was neat. Frances had contributed a large cake and myself alot of wines, so after the speeches a good time was had by all.[64]

A good time, however, was not had by all. Asked about the decision to marry, Eliza would recall that, shortly after she arrived in January, Donna had persuaded Bud and Lyn that Lyn should marry Eliza for the sake of appearances, for fear Ruth would find out about the living arrangement (Eliza and Lyn sharing a room) and blame Bud for allowing it—and not just blame, "disinherit." Where Donna got this idea is anyone's guess, but, Eliza would recall, she was adamant. Lyn she remembered as "an opportunist." Together, "they bullied me into it." As for why she did not stand up for herself, say what she wanted: "It never occurred to me. No one ever asked."

Lyn's mother and 17-year-old sister had taken the bus from Detroit to Myrtle Beach, so, had not stopped at Twin Oaks for the reception, for which Lyn had made no advance arrangements. Consequently, "they [the Twin Oaks community] probably felt it was an invasion," Eliza would recall years later. As for her long "speech", "I didn't know what to say—I couldn't say I was being shot-gunned", all she could think was "Oh my God, I'm not here, my body is here but I am not here." Frances, who had never before met Lyn, was apparently the only one to have realized something was very wrong, or at least the only one to have said anything about it. "[I]t was not just your behavior that upset me", Frances would write to Lyn in response to his letter of apology, "it was the whole dissociated mass with hostility underlying it all."[65] It was that "[n]o body seemed to care about anybody," or be able to express any positive emotions.

Bud's failure to sense his daughter's distress during this period, to say nothing of "the whole dissociated mass", is perhaps less perplexing if one considers that his social development had been almost exclusively male-oriented—an all boys' boarding school, the all-male Coast Guard, the male-dominated fields of math and engineering. In those days everyone, not just men, was expected to suppress emotions and "get along." To say Bud lacked empathy (which he clearly did) is too easy. Though it is perhaps a less-than-satisfactory explanation, Bud may have said it best in 1962, when referring to a disagreement that had occurred at Deverill over the holidays.

> I feel sad about leaving as we did [he wrote to his mother] and I agree that relations will never be the same exactly again but as far as I am concerned I have been blessed with a poor memory about most details and retain mostly a broad feeling which details do not upset.[66]

As Bud suspected she might, Howerton returned with him and the others to Myrtle Beach from Twin Oaks. ("She seems happy with us. I hope she is not too intolerant of the high school here and is not kicked out."[67]) His community now had eight members (Bud, Donna, Karen, Kinch, Theron, Eliza, Lyn and Howerton), making hammocks and attending weekly Mao-style sessions of criticism and self-criticism. Bud seemed to enjoy these "stormy", *Fanshen*-inspired sessions. "Everyone 'gets emotional'—except me[,] and Pam [Howerton] and Eliza get emotional at me because I don't get emotional."[68] Those who "pulled their weight" were rewarded with voting rights. The hammock business was growing.

> The hammock business is doing better, now that the new rope has been delivered, last evening. We've finished two complete hammocks and alot of parts. I may settle for just one size of hammock this season selling for $26.95 and being just a little smaller than Pawley's $30.00 medium size one. They are brown rope and unpainted cedar in color and look real nice to everyone here, but who knows wheather [sic] they'll sell.[69]

The Myrtle Beach community was turning out three to four hammocks a day, netting ten dollars a hammock at a labor rate of two dollars an hour. "The quota...is 5 hours for [each of] the 4 of us while the children are in school." The goal was to make and sell 500-600 a season. Bud, concerned that his savings would not be enough to cover the cost of the rope, asked his mother if there were any household furnishings that could be sold.

> I hate to have to consider it, but the things down here which I could sell...would they bring in much? Actually we have enough money coming in from child support and unemployment to pay for living expenses. But we need rope now! Probably about $1000 in order to make 5 or 6 thousand by August or Sept. So please let me know which items and about how much they should sell for.[70]

Ruth's niece, Nancy Susan Reynolds Bagley (1910-1985), bought a large cupboard for $1,000. The proceeds rightly should have been apportioned between all owners, but may have been treated as an advance against Bud's share. Bud's extended occupation of the beach house had by this time become a point of contention with his brothers, although there was little they could do about it without Ruth's cooperation, and Bud of the poor memory had other things to think about.

> Donna and I have started singing in the Presperterian [sic] Chior [Bud wrote to his mother in mid-March]. Last week two nice ladies came "calling" and wanted to know our intentions, I guess. Anyway I asked them if Prespertiarns [sic] did not beleave [sic] in predestination—"oh yes, that's fundamental to our religion." Then Donna ask [sic] what predestination ment [sic] to them and they said they did not know but that the Sunday school had a book which explained all about it, and the minister had explained to them very clearly too. We did not say anything to make them feel bad, but I am always supprised at what "religion" does to people's thinking.[71]

Aerovox had been bought out and the new plant manager was Bud's former boss; Bud thought he might get his job back—if he wanted it. He and Donna planned a Charlotte-Penland-Twin Oaks trip for spring break with Theron, Eliza and Lyn, whom Ruth had yet to meet. "Howerton [age 17] wants to stay [at Myrtle Beach. Carol,] a friend from Albion[,] is coming down. Kinch [age 15] is going to stay with a friend" in Florida, he informed his mother.[72] Howerton, he told her, was "slowly settling down in school"[73] though she had told Frances she was "hating school,"[74] and failing all her courses.[75]

> [T]hree big parties [occurred] while Bud and Donna were gone [Susannah informed her mother and siblings, based on information from Frances, who had it from Carol]. Everyone was drunk and drinking cheap wine. Boys were running around in their under-shorts and some of the girls were in their underwear. Pamela [Howerton] and Carol tried to lock themselves in one of the upstairs bedrooms but the door was kicked in. Everyone was throwing buckets of water all over the place. There seems to have been right much damage. Bud and Donna came home earlier than expected and walked in on the last party. Kinch is supposed to pay for the damage. Bud was very mad at first but later calmed down.[76]

Bud's letter to his mother of the same date made no mention of the incident, even though it discussed Kinch at length.

> The only other news is that Kinch is about to quit school—he has not been studying at all for some time and complains about almost everything—I feel sorry for him, but he is the cause of most of his troubles. He would like to be told what to do (study go to school on time, etc.[)] because then he would not have to make himself do these things but he wants to get paid for following orders like his friends (or those he identifies with) are, whoes [sic] "pay" is a snappy car of their own and money for dates and clothes. Our attitude turns him off—and his attitude turns us off so there seem [sic] to be nothing to be done! He is not dull, just the opposite so I guess he'll do all right if he can be happy in terms of the U.S. culture i.e. happiness is the feeling you get when you consume the products (cokes, autos, girls) which make profits. And what is happiness to me? It is not to feel like a stranger in a strange land! It's the opposite of this.[77]

One may assume Bud meant by "stranger in a strange land" to refer to Moses ("And she bore *him* a son. He called his name Gershom, for he said, 'I have been a stranger in a strange land.'" Exodus 2:22, *King James Bible*) and not the far more complicated "Man from Mars" character portrayed in the science fiction novel, *Stranger in a Strange Land* by Robert Heinlein, published in 1961, though it is possible he had both in mind.

Penland School of Handicrafts, which Eliza and Lyn were now planning to attend in August for "about $700 for both"[78] was founded in 1929 by Lucy Morgan, a teacher at the Appalachian Industrial School who was determined to help local women make money weaving (foot power floor looms, not the hobby stuff).[79] Though the school had been expanding since 1962 under a new director, instruction in 1970 was still limited to summer sessions.

> We met and were shown around some by a glass artist who was on a Mary Babcock scholarship [Bud wrote to his mother]. It's way up in the hills somewhat run down and hogpog [sic] but it will be fun for Lynn and Eliza and they will learn alot.[80]

Mary Reynolds Babcock (1908-1953) was Katharine's eldest daughter. Her younger sister, Nancy Susan, the one who had bought the cupboard, had recently invited everyone to a multi-day, multi-venue (the homestead in Critz, Virginia, "Reynolda" in Winston-Salem, and "Tanglewood" in Clemmons) reunion of the descendants of her grandfather, Hardin William Reynolds (1810-1892) and grandmother Nancy Jane Cox (1825-1903), for whom cousin Nancy was (presumably) named. How the Lucases came to be invited probably had more to do with the fact that cousin Nancy was quite fond of her aunt Ruth than with the fact that Ruth and Katharine's grandmother, Mary Catherine Cox (1818-1893) was Nancy Jane's sister—the remotest of connections to Hardin Reynolds. The reunion was to take place in June, and everyone including Bud was looking forward to it.

Kinch did go to Florida, and when he did not return, Bud thought he might take a job in construction there (he would end up finishing school in Greenville). "We are getting along fine considering how many of us are here,"[81] Bud wrote to his mother who visited in May, along with her usual country ham. The pendency of an upzoning petition before the Myrtle Beach City Council was the only impediment to the sale of the beach house. Bud followed the petition's progress closely, hoping it would pass and increase the value of the property, though he missed the hearing "because Donna and I had promised to take on a sewing class for poor black women."⁸² Hammock sales picked up with the summer season, "[b]ut we still are a long way towards 'getting our money back'." Lyn took an apartment in town, where he hoped to make better money selling bead necklaces. Bud told his mother that he and Eliza had both decided to move, but Eliza recalled it as, "one day he was just gone." Eliza drifted between the beach house and Lyn's apartment for a while before returning to Charlotte to stay with Mildred and attend Central Piedmont Community College. She did not go to Penland and did not live with Lyn after that summer.

> Dear Eliza, [Bud wrote a year or so after she had returned to Charlotte] Thanks for the post card. We really aught to keep in touch since we'll be so far apart when we move to Canada. As for actually being ready to go, we are moving slowly + packing things, buying truck & trailer (we've put money down on both and are just waiting for the house to be sold)...Grandma Lucas tells me you are going to [Central] Piedmont [Community College]... The learning process should be satisfying (if not fun) and aught always to be related to social practice and needs. I haven't heard from Pam (Howerton)...Maybe I should write. She needs to experience more real struggle and thereby become stronger of conviction and character... the push with all middle class is to isolate ourselves from the struggle and seek an easy place. I hope to struggle, but not in the Nazi like U.S.A. bent on robbing the world and thereby asking for destruction. My struggle will be with getting a community of people to do their own work, feed themselves, and rule themselves, and also to grow fast enough so that no one need be turned away who will work with us. Basically this is what the Chinese Communist [sic] did in their Northern Salviets [sic]. They learned how to struggle on a small scale first.⁸³

By "Chinese Communists" Bud probably had in mind the 1945-1948 land-reform campaign in Long Bow described in *Fanshen*, and not the Jiangxi-Fujian Soviet established 1931-1934 by Mao Zedong and Zhu De, but both involved organizing peasants. Did Bud truly see himself as a potential organizer of Western "peasants"? Was he really trying to overcome the temptation to isolate himself from "the struggle" and "seek an easy place"? Or was he perhaps just trying to inspire his daughter(s) to reject middle-class comforts and education unrelated to "social practice and needs", to "struggle" to make a better world? Such advice, if it may be called advice, was common enough in '60s and '70s, though even then it was not necessarily the sort of advice one would expect to come from a well-educated parent with marketable skills and ample financial resources. Wayne Seward, the doctor for the Vernon, B.C. area where Bud and Donna would eventually settle, found Donna to be "idealistic,"[84] which is to say her thinking was lofty, focused on ideas and not terribly grounded–certainly not what Irene and Mary Jo would call "earthy." Donna's influence may have led Bud to believe he needed to counterbalance the advice his daughters were then getting from Frances (make a budget, go to school, get a job, become financially independent) even though he did not at all disagree with it. Not surprisingly, the advice was ignored.

The Twin Oaks community closed its third year without renewing its lease-option to purchase. Bud and Donna visited in July and found the farm "as run down as we remembered."[85] Rudy Nesmith and Kathleen Kinkade were away, visiting another community. Susan Kinkade was a planner now, along with two new members. Bud and Donna talked with Earnest Jones, the farmer who had sold Bud the property. Jones reported that the community had allowed several cows and the horse to starve to death over the winter and was generally doing a poor job maintaining the pastures, fencing and crop land. Despite this, Bud and Donna beneficently agreed, based on the planners' assurances that conditions would be improved, to give Twin Oaks another three-year lease on the same terms as before. On the return trip via Highway 181, they spent "the evening and night with the Lucas clan."

> I did not see [Ted's elder son] Jimmy because he was teaching night school but saw [his sister] Sarah whom I had not seen since I'd worked for Uncle Ted years ago. We finally got away at about 11 AM after [Uncle] Rod showed us his leaf "operation."[86]

In September, Howerton returned to Albion High School and Bud sold the remainder of the upper farm for $110,000 (it would be sold a year later for $163,000). The beach house sold a couple of months after that for around $77,000. Both transactions involved complicated financing arrangements and very little cash, but their completion freed Bud for migration to Canada. By Christmas Eve, Bud, Donna and Theron were on the road, having made it as far as California.

> Dear Mother, Here it is Christmas eve! And we are in Sequoia Nat. Forest. Yesterday we put on chains and climbed these snowy mountains and saw the biggest trees I've ever seen all covered with snow. Oranges are being harvested in the Valleys here so we sent you some, but they probably won't get to you 'till [sic] after Christmas. We plan to head North again as soon as these huge Blue birds [probably Western Scrub Jays] finish our leftover grits. Merry Christmas, Bud[87]

They spent about a month in a trailer park in Nanaimo on Vancouver Island, waiting for their immigration papers to come through, and looking at area farms which were going for about $1,000 an acre.

> You might wonder [Bud wrote to Eliza,] how well the three of us get along in a twenty foot trailer that you can hook up to a car and go here and there. Well, since we arrived (Jan.) the sun has not come out except for about 10 minutes this morning. The rest of the time it has been a drizzle or snow, which means we three have been inside for over a week except for the very important absence of Theron (off to school) and also occasional trips to town and farm hunting. Yet with all this "togetherness" we still are "getting along"! Theron has called two meetings so that he could let his feelings be known at the "gate", which probably helped things too.[88]

> My search for a good chior here has not been successful, none has any basses. The United Church here is the largest denomination (seems like a combo of Buddist [sic], Methodist & Presbetrarin [sic]). They have the chior facing

> the people as per the Pres & Bab. in the U.S. The Anglican church is a carbon copy of the Episcopal Church U.S.A. but their chior has no bass and one weak tenor. Too bad. I hope I'll find things better inland. The enclosed clipping shows what unemployment feels like to the unemployed. Many people in the U.S. can [sic] express themselves well enough to write such a letter, but most people here are pretty well educated and seem to me alot more knowledgable [sic] than people in the U.S. especially the South. Too bad![89]

After moving north and inland several hundred miles, they thought they had found a farm.

> The owners are letting us camp on the place 'till all the legal and other details are settled. The farm is located near Cherryville (which consists of Fran's General Store and 3 homes) which is 18 miles east of Lumby (a town about 1/2 the size of Louisa) The nearest large town is Vernon about 35 miles west. The size of the farm is 135 acres about 80 of which are cleared. It's approx. square, fronts on a gravel road winding up a valley. The rest is woods which rise up a 1000 ft hill. There are springs in the woods one of which furnishes water by gravity to the house. Almost everyone around here builds there [sic] own homes. This one is crudely but well constructed out of local wood. It is a 3 bdrm [sic] split level with a good bacement [sic], no paint, split cedar shingles, fiberglass insulation, and a wood furnace made from an old oil drum that seems to keep the house quite warm. Also there is a bathroom with all the fixtures new & working. There is also a new barn which a contractor built. It has a concrete floor 40' x 30', hay loft, and oval roof of tin. There is also a sturdy 30' x 70' chicken house. There are less than a dozen farms in the valey [sic]. The hills are all government land leased to the lumber companies. The soil looks very rich with few rocks. All in all it looks perfect. The price is the cheapest we've seen (about the same as Twin Oaks) [$31,000] and we've put [$5,000] money down. So if there are no "hitches" this is where we'll be for a while. The trees are a beautiful white birch, a tall cedar with other evergreens that I don't recognize. Theron goes to a new elementary school (4 rooms) down

the road about 3 miles. The teachers are young and helpful and Theron is actually enjoying himself (as he did not in Virginia and South Carolina). We are to go into town (Vernon) Sat and sign papers with Mr. Foisy (the owner) & then he has about 5 weeks to move to his other farm before we "take possession." So when Vera comes up to take over the garden directions and the snow melts (unless there is another cold spell it should be gone in a week) and we get a few kitchen appliances etc, then we should be on our way towards building the ideal (tolerable) culture, or at least a good life.[90]

Vera Fisher had read Bud's advertisement in the Guardian newspaper and visited Bud and Donna while they were in Myrtle Beach. Bud described her to his mother as "a 57-year old former 1930+ escapee from Germany who lived in New York City and had two sons who were 'SDSers'."

> [S]he would make an excellent member of our B.C. community esp. as the manager of cookery, which she has done for summer camps cooking for 150 with one helper.[91]

Vera and her husband John would visit the Cherryville farm that summer, and Vera would put in three gardens "almost by herself,"[92] as well as contributing $500. She did not, however, join Bud's community. "We are", Bud would explain to his mother, "too far 'out of it'" for Vera.[93] Bud spent the weeks before the Foisys were to move out thawing the trailer's pipes, looking half-heartedly for a "chior", and writing letters.

> Glad to hear Eliza has found a chior [he wrote to his mother]. Vernon has most of the name brand churches but is 40 miles [away] over not too good roads (they develop many bumps from frost heaves). Lumby is about 18 miles away but has only a "mission" type Anglican church with 9:15 services only. But I really haven't checked their chior yet. It may be o.k. I'll try them next Sunday, If I can get up that early...
>
> Mr. Foisy has tried to make a go of the farm as a full time occupation, but recently had to have his gall blater

> [*sic*] removed and so has decided to give up farming for some sort of lighter work. He's in his 30's, 3 children, works at odd jobs in the lumber industry, has a color TV, sporty car, but no kitchen sink, wood furnace to heat the house, wringer type washing machine, good looking clothes, etc.—striving to meet the demands of the TV culture but only partly able to do so with the externals, like the poor whites and blacks—very sad to me.[94]

Both Eliza (in Charlotte) and Howerton (in Albion) had been looking for work, but not having much luck. The U.S. unemployment rate was hovering around six percent, higher were "discouraged job-seekers" to be included, and economists were referring to the job market as "stagnant." Bud helpfully advised them that youth everywhere were simply less able to compete in the modern economy.

> Due to recent advances in Science and technology [he wrote to Eliza], it is no longer necessary for anyone to compete to have enough... This fact is the main "contradiction" of the world today and the youth everywhere in "competition" systems will suffer more than those more able to compete (voters, skild [*sic*] workers, productive property owners, agents of the competitive system). The people who have made progress in freeing themselves from these competitive systems (Algeria, Egypt, Cuba, China, Russia, etc.) have been whole nations of people. Afterwards the struggle has been inside the nation between competing groups (producers and non-producers). The basic theory on which I base our efforts towards making a community is that a better life results if one lives and works among producers than among producers and nonproducers (those able to produce and yet do not) and their agents (police[,] "salesmen", "managers", etc.).[95]

1970 was "the most inflationary year since the Korean War", United Press International reported in 1971, the year that then-President Nixon cut the last threads tying the U.S. dollar to gold. These were the years that the Depression-era fear of debt that Frances and Bud had felt so keenly in the '50s and '60s finally lost its grip on the economy, freeing U.S. households and government to fuel it by consumption and spending. Despite Bud's sometime reputation among family as "the communist" and his nominal support for popular revolutions (Algeria 1954-1962, Egypt 1952, Cuba 1953-1959, China 1949, Russia 1917), he was not a communist as that term is generally understood. He was not particularly interested in questions of wealth ownership and distribution (mere "struggles inside the nation"), and he was generally tolerant of willful "nonproducers", despite admitting they make life less-than-better for the "producers." It was "too bad", he would write to his mother in 1973, that "Martin was pushed out of David's pipe outfit [Lucas Concrete Products, Inc.]" after a couple of nonproductive years. Bud's world was one of abundance, not scarcity; it was "[t]he economic system that pits people against one another", he insisted, claiming that there was "really enough for everyone", whether they "produced" or not. To Bud, there was always enough.[96]

> We are slowly meeting our neighbors [Bud reported to his mother]. Most are loggers or farmers or a combination of both. There is a Mr. Workington, who makes cedar shingles (shakes) by hand for a living. A Mr. Adcock who makes honey for a living, both live across the road. Then there is a relative of Mr. Foisy down the road who sells eggs off his farm. Everyone has built their own house and uses wood to heat, with a few exceptions. Then there are the Holmans who live in a 2 bedroom house, twenty of them, about 3 or 4 families on 10 acres of rocky soil, who raise rabbits for a living. They migrated from the cold midwest of Canada, as many have done who live in this area.[97]

Bud's financial situation during this period was, in his words, "o.k." The payments on the new farm would be $240 a month until he could pay down the balance with the proceeds from the sale of the upper farm and the beach house. Cash in hand was around $3,000 (about $19,000 in 2021) after "spending on the basics for the house and farm", including chickens and milk goats. The goats were given names such as Rosa Luxemburg, Felix Greene, and Lysistrata. They put 50 acres in oats on shares and rented the trailer to the Warrens ("our new friends who have the helth [*sic*] food store in Vernon") until Canada's laws would allow its sale. Ruth gave Bud cash for his birthday, as she usually did. She also packed up and sent Bud by "motor freight" all his tools, books and other belongings, including his drill press and grinder which, after several letters back and forth and an exhaustive search, were finally located in the feed room of the barn. Bud's thanks was, for him, effusive. "I know getting all those boxes off was a chore and I really appreciate your efforts", he wrote.[98]

Having been unable to find a choir to his liking, Bud borrowed movies from the local office of the National Film Board and started holding movie-nights for the neighbors, followed by "a few songs."[99] The B.C. summers were, he was learning first hand, dry and often hot. The oats did not produce enough grain to warrant combining and were baled for hay. He sprained or strained or otherwise injured his lower back (as he had done picking beans at Twin Oaks) and was unable to walk for three days. He thought at first it might be due to his forgetting to take his vitamins (it would be Bud's generation that would popularize the fear of vitamin deficiency[100]) but, in the end, he had to admit that, at age 46, his crate-slinging days were over. ("I guess I'll just have to get use [*sic*] to taking my back into consideration."[101]) Eliza and Howerton, who had given some indication early in the season that they might come up for a visit, had not been in touch. He was disappointed. "They both seem to be pretty sloppy along those lines", he complained to his mother.[102]

The rain came at the end of September. Bud, who had grown a beard while bedridden, continued working on farm- and home-improvement projects, fencing in the goats, putting in flooring and glass windows, burying the line from the spring, and laying in enough wood to last the winter.

> [T]he house is heated very well by an old oil drum turned sideways along with a sort of radiator in the flue pipe with a small electric fan to force the air through the radiator [he wrote to his mother]. About 4 green logs last all night if the damper is shut off. And the wood is got for the sawing.[103]

Bud was spared having to make furniture by the Warrens, who let them borrow beds, chests of drawers, a table and chairs. Ruth sent additional chairs and a couple of bales of rugs. Canada disallowed Bud's using the tools Ruth had sent to make hammocks and toys for sale for the first year after their arrival, but after the winter weather set in, Bud was ready to make a start. "One rocking boat and one see saw, so far," he wrote to Ruth in late November.[104] The holidays were shared with neighbors, "food and little presents for the children... movies, sing[ing] songs etc." Ruth was concerned about Eliza, who had been living mostly with her and some with Mildred, while working for Dr. Hechenbleikner in the botanical garden at the University of North Carolina at Charlotte. Ruth thought she would be happier living nearer Bud, and he promised to write to Eliza and suggest she begin planning to come up for a visit.

The Isaacsons, a couple with four children, moved their trailer to the farm for about two weeks, thinking they might form a community with Bud, Donna and Theron. It was agreed that the children would work for the community for two and a half hours per week, but the parents would not agree to have the community decide what work the children should do. So, the Isaacsons did not join, and Bud began redesigning the wood stove.

> I used a heavy oil drum like the old furnace. Bud [sic] I made it stand up right and load from the top. I made a tin lid slide over the entire top, but it warps with the heat and is not air tight as it should be. I ordered the thermostatic air inlet control from the Ashley stove dealer in Vancouver and attached it to the drum, which makes the draft flow just enough to keep the fire all night. So that is the improvement I was after. I now don't have to build a fire every morning, just throw on some wood and open the draft. It cost $40 for parts. The Ashley stove of the same size sells here for over $200 and has thinner guage [sic] metal so won't last as long.[105]

Other machine design projects included work on his rope-making machine and attaching a motor drive to his hand grinder so he could grind his own corn, because "[t]he corn meal up here is awful."[106] He would have done better to get in touch with his uncle Rod, who, being something of a local historian, was writing about how "country folks" made corn meal for a book he would have printed the next year.

> In my youth we were still clearing land by hand with axes and mattocks. The old "Heal Tap" variety of white corn, which was hard and flinty in texture was the favorite variety for corn meal but not for horses and hogs as it was too hard... Country folks, to get their corn meal, would put one of the younger boys on a horse and throw a sack of shelled corn on behind. A bushel was the usual amount. If they thought the sack would come untied, a half bushel was tied in the bottom of the sack and rocks put on the other end. Should it come untied the rocks would fall out and the corn fall to the ground tied in the bottom of the sack. On arriving at the mill the good miller would take the corn and the boy off the horse, do the grinding for [the price of] one gallon out of the bushel. The [remaining] meal and the lad were placed back on the horse for his trip back home. In our part of the country there were two water-powered stone grinding mills. One was at Childress owned by Mrs. Watts Palmer and one at Snowville, owned by Mr. Glenn Summers [whose daughter Eloise aka "Weasie" married Uncle Ted.][107]

Still hoping to grow "Workshare", as the farm was now called, Bud and Donna gave a talk to a group of about 50 at "a small college" and placed another ad in the *Guardian*.[108] They bought a used tractor and put the local children to work making hammocks for two dollars an hour. That summer, they would sell "about 70" at $20 apiece wholesale through two outlets, and another 20 at $26 apiece retail. Also that summer, Eliza and Howerton would visit.

When Howerton let Ruth know she planned to hitchhike to Lumby to visit her father, Ruth bought the sisters two non-refundable bus tickets. The visit went well enough for Eliza to decide she wanted to give British Columbia a try.

> Eliza left yesterday on the bus for Charlotte via Albion [Bud wrote his mother]. We enjoyed her visit, but she does

not seem to care much about whether or not anyone worries about her activities. I took her by to talk with the people at Vernon College (2 year college housed in old WW2 Army base here) and she was impressed enough to want to give it a try this fall. However, she wanted to have her car up here too so that is why she is on her way back to Charlotte. Classes start Sept 5th so I hope she makes it back in time.[109]

Eliza did make it back on time, but without a car. She took a room in Vernon to avoid a weekday commute. "She spent the weekend here [at the farm] and we had a plesant time."[110] That fall, Bud and Ruth were both busy protesting government action: Bud, the logging of the Crown land above Workshare, and Ruth, the annexation of Deverill by the City of Charlotte. They would both lose. "[T]he harvest came to about 500 bushels or 10 tons" of barley, Bud wrote his mother, commenting that it was less than it should have been because "I did not plant but about 50 lbs per acre when I should have put in 100/lbs per acre" and that it "seems like I go madly from one job to the next and never getting much done."[111] Concrete was laid for a carport and front walk. A local man came by Workshare and gave Bud fifty dollars to make him one of his thermostat-controlled oil drum stoves. Bud wrote to his mother saying, "Think I'll make two and have one on hand when someone else comes by."[112] Knowing she was concerned about Eliza, Bud tried to reassure her.

> Eliza seems to be happy now. She uses this old pickup truck we bought from a friend near here for $150. She's getting it fixed up mostly at her expense so the money arrangement has been o.k. I think she has decided to try and become a "landed immigrant" like us, but I don't know for sure.[113] [Eliza was not allowed to attend school under the terms of her visa and, being over 21 years of age, could not be sponsored by her father.]
>
> Eliza and her new boyfriend Gary [Lomax] came out last week end. She seems happy and we all like Gary alot. I hope she does not get sent back to the U.S. against her will by the immigration people. I went with her to a nice lawyer

> (a Mr. Allen) who is looking after our interest in buying the farm. He is doing what he can, but Eliza hasn't told me (phoned) what's developed.[114]
>
> Eliza and her best friend Gary Lomax were out last week. They seem happy and we enjoyed them alot. He seems more kindly, helpful, and stable than Lyn.[115]
>
> We see Eliza about once a week in Vernon when we go to get supplies. She seems to like Vernon and has found friends, whom we like (those that we've met).[116]
>
> Eliza seems fairly happy, but she has not "settled" down to say getting a job or going back to school. But I think she's moving in that direction now. At any rate she seems relaxed and happy when she comes out here or when we see her in Vernon.[117]

Eliza would later recall being told that, to avoid trouble with the authorities, she should "marry her boyfriend—that's how Lomax became my sponsor." The arrangement served its purpose well enough until Lomax was arrested on drug charges. Bud dutifully visited him in prison and allowed him to stay at Workshare until he became openly involved with another woman. Eliza would recall Bud's "kicking him out" as one of the few times she remembered anyone being "in my corner." Eliza and Lomax would stay married—but not together—for another 15 years. There is nothing in the surviving correspondence to indicate Bud ever let his mother know Eliza had remarried.

The hammock business picked up a good bit that summer, but, despite efforts, Bud and Donna were unable to expand the Workshare community. As reported to his mother,

> We had various people visit us who were interested in becoming members possibly but right now we've only a young couple with 7 mos. child. We think there will be others soon. So far each prospect has required alot of time and energy—most, we find, have pretty bad "hang ups"—like they would be doing us a favor if they joined! ... Just this minute the husband of the couple who are here banged open

the back door grabbed wife by hair telling he[r] she had to go with him (she wants to stay here) and with rifel [sic] in other hand threatens Donna and I not to interfear [sic]. As soon as they leave the house we call the RCMP [Royal Canadian Mounted Police]. I hope Lyn (the wife) sticks up for her self when they are found.[118]

We've had three couples come by to look us over then leave recently. The basic reason, I suspect, is that there is alot of work to be done and (for middle class types) proportionally less return for this work. For working class type we would yield about the right labor vs. fruits of labor ratio, I suspect. Anyway there are a few such working class types on their way up for a visit so we shall see. Right now we have only one visitor, Garry Black, from Arlington Va. His father is with a stock brokerage firm and he has just graduated from V[irginia] M[ilitary] I[nstitute]. Right now Donna and I have got him thinking about the whys of Watergate, Vietnam, dollar devaluation, etc. He has also become very good at making hammocks... That couple that I mentioned in my last letter—the RCMP finally found them that evening, walking along the road some 4 miles from here. They came by and said she had changed her mind and wanted to go with him after all.[119]

The summer of 1973, Bud represented "the Vernon area" at the national convention of the New Democratic Party in Vancouver (founded in 1961 by the Co-operative Commonwealth Federation and the Canadian Labor Congress).

The NDP is a "Democratic Socialist" type party. They now hold power in 3 of 10 provinces. We spent 2 days debating and voting on various resolutions and listening to various party leaders make speeches. It was a good way to find out "where people are at" up here. The class bias of the NDP is small business and bureaucratic labor. They claim to be champions of the people against big business, but very few wage earners were delegates because few could take the time off (3 work days) nor afford the expense (probably some $125 average). These people are especially sensitive to those of their own class in other countries.[120]

A very few letters written after this point survived. The community at Twin Oaks started making payments on the farm that summer, at the expiration of the second 3-year rent-free lease period; $193 per month for 25 years. In October 1974, Gene Smith, Ruth's last living sibling, died. In April 1975, Mary Jo attempted to establish aristocratic *bona fides* (never easy in a country with no aristocratic tradition) by applying for membership in the National Society of the Colonial Dames of America in North Carolina by submitting documentary proof of her descent from Capt. Anthony Savage, a justice of the peace and "High Sheriff" for Gloucester County, Virginia *circa* 1660. (Possibly her application was inspired by the discovery among Maxie's papers of her 1913 application to the same organization, proving eligibility in right of descent from Colonel James Taylor, member of the House of Burgesses for Kings and Queens County, Virginia *circa* 1702.) David and Mary Lou's eldest, Katharine Anne, married her best boyfriend Sidney Randolph Monk of Charlotte. There was a large reception at Deverill, and Bud and Donna visited around this time. When Bud wrote to Ruth to let her know they "got home o.k.", he told her "[e]verything was fine except home was pretty dirty as we expected, because our bachelor house keeper never learned to use a broom etc.", suggesting that Workshare had not grown significantly.[121] Bud did continue trying to expand, but, as at Twin Oaks, people would come, stay awhile, then leave. Eliza was still in Vernon, taking the occasional class and working odd jobs to make ends meet. Theron went to live with Charles and Betty Cooper in Kaslo to attend high school there. He had lost interest in school recently, and his attendance had suffered. Eliza was to recall Theron's being very lonely at Workshare, with no one to talk to or trying to engage him, and that Bud and Donna expected him to feed the animals and milk the goats before and after school, which made the days very long indeed. It was around this time that Donna, now 44, learned she was pregnant.

Chapter 14

Stranger in a strange land

Donya Karla (for Karl Marx, later spelled Carla) Lucas was born at the hospital in Vernon with no complications about a month after Bud's 51st birthday. Donya was soon "sleeping thru' the night", Bud reported to his mother, "and has no problems that we know of."[1] Donna, however, was suffering from prolonged exposure to the Lucas empathy gap. It was not entirely Bud's fault. As David was to describe their upbringing in 2000:

> Then [in the 1930s], most of us were part of a much simpler and less diverse culture. There were certainly differences in economic situations, but the cultural differences were less distinct and were bridged by established protocols and good manners. We were not as conscious of feelings as now. Many of us (here, I must acknowledge to myself as well as you, that I am White, Southern, very secure economic status, old family, farm raised, from a relatively large family, etc.—this is a viewpoint that, most likely, colors my remembrances and my thinking) did not have to feel before acting much less did we feel before thinking. We knew who we were and were not self conscious. We did not do much feeling.[2]

Donna of Greenville, South Carolina, was very different. Donna put feelings first, and pushed Bud to do the same. She wanted him to "get in touch" with his feelings so he could better relate to her feelings. This conflict (which the pregnancy did not create but did exacerbate) had led them to the study of "TA" or Transactional Analysis, a psychoanalytic theory developed in the 1950s by Eric Berne that was popularized with the 1964 publication of the book *Games People Play: the Psychology of Human Relationships*, followed in 1969 by *I'm OK—You're OK: A Practical Guide to Transactional Analysis* by Thomas A. Harris, MD, followed in 1974 by *Scripts People Live* by Berne's pupil, Claude Steiner. Bud read all three, and "TA" language and concepts began to appear in his writings in a manner that suggests he was at last beginning to grok (a term coined by Heinlein and popularized by *Stranger in Strange Land*) that he lacked a certain emotional intelligence. This realization may have caused him to overestimate Donna's abilities in this area (consider that he "corrected" a court report quoting their family counselor as saying "I would see Donna as being more labile emotionally" by insert "re-" before the word "labile"[3]).

It had been toward the end of the pregnancy that the marriage began to fall apart. That was when, according to Donna, Bud became "irritable and authoritarian." Friends would later say that Donna made "wholly unrealistic emotional demands of Bud" after Donya was born, and speculate she might have been suffering from some form of postpartum depression.[4] In fairness to Bud, he had had little to no prior experience dealing with emotionally disturbed individuals whom he could not simply avoid. He had been through miscarriages, pregnancies, childbirth and childcare with Frances and probably thought he knew what Donna expected of him emotionally. Obviously, he was wrong about that, and it is quite possible he became maladaptively "irritable and authoritarian" after Donya was born. But, it is also possible that Donna expected a degree of "support" that she knew, or should have known, he was unwilling or unable to provide, and she could not or would not adjust her expectations. A person not in touch with his feelings might find such a situation tolerable; Bud did not, and he let Donna know. Separation meant Workshare would have to be sold, and Bud at least would have to find someplace else to live.

Figure 14.1: Bud and Donya

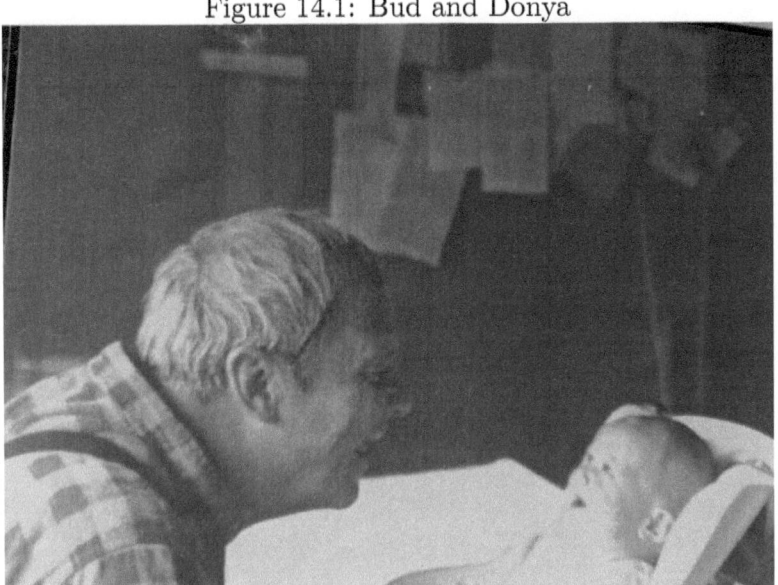

Several members of a Belgian community calling itself "Genesis" visited Workshare and expressed interest in buying the farm, along with the hammock and heater "industries." In April 1978, Donna and Donya flew south to visit her parents in Florida, and Bud planned to pick them up in Greenville. He started a journal, which he kept on and off for the next several years. Bud's friend Terry Durocher rode south with him as far as Windsor, Ontario. They stopped in the Slocan Valley to visit Stonetree, a housing cooperative. Some had suggested Workshare might be turned into a cooperative, and Bud was thinking about it. ("Felt that such co[-]ops have many problems but less than a community since they demand less 'togetherness', but still seem to allow members to move better from where they are to more intimacy."[5]) He also wanted to check out the Vallican Whole School. ("Donya would really like it!") He was thinking of moving to the Slocan Valley. He thought Donna might want to continue at Workshare with Genesis, or possibly move to Vernon. On the fifth day of the trip, he dropped Terry at his parents' house in Windsor, noting in his journal,

> Suddenly leaving Terry in Winsor [sic] and being by myself feels lonely—especially when I knock on 405 E. Erie St Albion [Frances's house] and no one home. Is Donna feeling lonely now too? People really need each other, but they (and I) will except [sic] substitutes (food, games [in the TA sense of the word], movies etc). Detroit paper headlines "Bomb decision upsets many" referring to Carter's decision to defer production of Neutron Bomb.[6]

Saturday, he drove all night to Mount Airy, where he got a room at the Starlite Motel.

> What a sad empty feeling Mt. Airy gives me! [he wrote in his journal] Aunt Irene's house gone forever so too North Main School etc. I cried at both places... Old memories of Irene, Lidia [sic], Minny & being molded by my 1st grade experience all flooded my mind... Saw also Gertrude Smith [distant cousin] and had a plesant chat. She seems to have some trouble remembering things, but was warm and offered to put me up for the nite. Also saw Edwin Strother Smith (cousin) in a Motel room. ("cheaper than rattleing [sic] around in a house"). He seems depressed to the point that he cannot relate too well, also smokes (drinks) and really seems bent on destroying himself (slowly) So sad! Mary Madison [Strother's sister] gone with family to Bahamas and all other contacts scattered to the winds.[7]

Monday he was "off to Charlotte and Mother." His next journal entry began the following Saturday as he prepared to drive his mother into town to visit with Mary Jo and the rest of the Gibbs family.

> I'm all dressed up to go out to dinner with Mother at Mildred's (Wallace's mother). —I'm back, DISCOURAGED. Enjoyed singing some with [Mary Jo's daughter] Irene [age 18], but was usually unsatisfied with low level of INTIMACY. Mary Jo is impossible! So were others. Is it me? Can't seem to get past pastimes + games. With so little love, how do people survive?[8]

A week later, Bud drove to the Greenville-Spartanburg airport to meet Donna and Donya, coming back from Florida. "Donya hugged me for a long time with no words—very moving", he wrote in his journal. He left Donna the Toyota, and took the bus back to Charlotte. A week after that, he took the bus to Greenville, and drove both of them back to Deverill.

> Up tight talk most of the trip. Tried to make no loose agreement ... But as we were talking (right after we had arrived at Mother's) I could tell that all would fail... I said that I did not want to stay together any longer.[9]

Donna told Bud she planned to return to Workshare but wanted to attend Kinch's graduation at the end of the month. Bud wanted to get back—with Donya—which Donna resisted by various means, delaying their return a couple of weeks. Bud and Donya flew back to B.C. mid-May, and Donna followed a month later. In the interim, Bud did some more work on the possibility of turning Workshare into a co-op, but found there were too many issues for his time frame. A week or so after Donna returned to Workshare, she moved out without saying where she was going, leaving Donya with Bud. Bud decided to fly back to Charlotte with Donya. While they were gone, Donna obtained an *ex parte* interim custody order in Vernon and then flew to Charlotte. "Donna showed up July 7th—much tension", Bud told his journal. For reasons not explained in the journal, he and Donna then decided to take Donya on a road trip across North Carolina, Virginia and Maryland, to look at communes. Finding them all "either too poor to care for Donya or too rich to care," Donna returned to Greenville with Donya.[10] "What to do now?" Bud asked his journal.

Ruth advised Bud to let Donna make the first move "re what to do about Workshare[,] Donya[,] etc.", and Bud agreed.[11] But Donna was more of a feinter than a mover. She persuaded a Unitarian minister she knew in Greenville to call Bud and tell him she wanted full custody of Donya, all of Workshare, three years of Twin Oaks payments, plus child support. Frustrated that Donna was not honoring her agreement to share custody, and needing to check on the sale of Workshare, Bud flew back to B.C. and Donna followed a few days later. Bud's lawyer Bill Wagner negotiated the terms of the sale to Genesis, consisting of a downpayment of $10,000 each to Bud and Donna, plus $430 per month each for 20 years, Donna and Donya to stay on as Genesis Workshare members. In addition, Donna would receive the Twin Oaks payments as child support. The last of the sale papers was signed on August 11.

> How do I feel about this? [Bud wrote in his journal] (1) good at the prospect of getting away from Depressing vibes of D. & of seeing new people. (2) good at the prospect of having the folks from Belgium carry on the things started at Workshare. (3) bad at the prospect of not seeing Donya as much.[12]

Bud stayed for a few weeks at Workshare in order to show the Belgians how to make hammocks, thermostats and stoves. Mid-September, he wrote in his journal,

> Still at Genesis Workshare Community. After packing things away (so to Eliza's place in Vernon) I'll be leaving. Donna left with Donya 12 Sept (?) for Greenville via Tronto [sic], where she planned to visit Alternatives to Alienation. I said I'll contact her in about a month. Maby she'll be willing to come to some sort of agreement about Donya. Anyway I plan to relax on the trip down and at mother's.[13]

> Said good by's [sic] to Eliza and Belgium [sic] friends at Genesis Workshare (Norbert Martens, Antoine, Bree, Cheri, Fredrick, Eddie, Sishka, Ellie. Urged Eliza to visit Theron [at University of British Columbia] (in her Toyota) and possibly come down to Charlotte Xmas. Felt sad leaving Workshare, but also releaved [sic] that the Belgiums [sic] will carry on. Told Eliza I thought Donna & I separating left me with many things to do but Donna with out anyone to try to change (except, as Eliza pointed out, Donya).[14]

Along the way, Bud stopped in Albion to visit Frances and Howerton. "Howie" was working for the Albion Historical Society. He told her he was going to try and start a workers co-op and she

Stranger in a strange land 245

"seemed interested."[15] He also started looking for a used sheet-metal machine and visited, or tried to visit, a couple of communes.

> Arrived yesterday at Mother's—Slept in old room which excited many old memories. I could easly [sic] fall into automated life here so I must make plans for a more autonomus [sic] one. Also such factors as Eliza, Donya, & Howerton complicate matters.[16]

Bud wintered at Deverill, building drum wood heaters, trying to convince Twin Oaks to join a workers co-op, and visiting communes. Martin, who was by then going by "Zach" (his first name was Zachary), had separated from Lillian and was living at Deverill with Bud's 16 year-old godson Charles. "Charles gets out of school this Thursday", Ruth confided to Bud, "I dread it until he can get settled in a job—I wish he would/could go to summer school/camp with tutoring—he is so far behind."[17] Mary Jo's youngest daughter Diana Gibbs was also living at Deverill. Diana was working for a bank, and Zach (Martin) for a staffing agency called Manpower. This mix of relatives would not have suited some, but it suited Bud. He was even able to persuade Martin to help from time to time with his heaters. Some of the cousins started referring to the pair as "Uncle Dud" and "Uncle Slack."

Bud had Donya for two weeks in December, two weeks in January, and ten days in March while Donna attended a consciousness-raising retreat at the Cornucopia Institute in St. Mary, Kentucky. Back at Workshare, a number of the Belgians had been ordered to leave Canada after they failed to heed the immigration authorities' order not to work. Only the group's leader, Norbert Martens, who was away when the farm was raided, was allowed to return.

Donna sent Bud two letters and a poem titled, "I Just Go on Loving You." In replying, Bud used terms from Steiner's book, *Scripts People Live*, to convey his belief they were stuck in what Steiner called "the banal scripting of powerlessness", also known as "The Rescue Game."

> I feel that the line "I know that I can't change your life" is the opposite of our case history. So it occurred to me that

> you can keep on loving me because, in a sense the Rescuer can "love" the Victem [*sic*]. And for a while the (one down) Victem can love the Rescuer. When the Victim finds out, however, that "I want to be what I want to be", then this love is lost, even tho' the Rescuer may still want to "love" the Victem and renew the old relationship.[18]

The news of the partial meltdown at the Three Mile Island nuclear facility in Pennsylvania got Bud's attention. He wrote in his journal: "N.C. being peppered with [nuclear] plants. Maybe B.C. really the best place to be at this stage in history, esp. for Donya."[19] Mary Denny died, and he and Ruth attended the funeral in Red Springs. By Easter, he was "anxious to be off to B.C."

> This Easter "re-birth" time I'm thinking about my plans for the future. Donna & I will have been separated for about a year now (since May 7, 1978). Every feeling of wanting to reconcile is defeated by a feeling of distrust of her. Her basic feeling for me as a person is nil; as someone to be used and manipulated.[20]

Bud made the 2,800 mile trip in five days of hard driving. Donna and Donya were at Workshare when he arrived on a Monday. Evidently, and notwithstanding Bud's Easter reflections, their months-long separation had so eased tensions that Bud and Donna planned to go to Argenta the following weekend to see if they liked the land co-op there. "If so," he wrote in his journal, he planned "to build two cabins and raise Donya and maybe get back together!"[21] The next entry states that the Argenta trip was "fairly successful", and that "Donna plans to try 3 months trial period." They even went to see a counselor in Winlaw, Betha Phaigh.

> She [Betha] tried to help us, and did some, esp. to show that Donna had laid a heavy "You didn't fill my needs during Donya's arrival" trip on me, which Donna said she saw, but did not act like it as soon as we left and were driving back to Workshare.[22]

A letter from Theron in May advised Bud, in the language of transactional analysis, to "try for simple Child-Child exchanges" with Donna. What Theron was probably trying to suggest is that Bud should aim for simple, honest, "I feel" statements—that he should not try right off the bat to negotiate custody, visitation, finances, etc. As his journal attests, Bud agreed with this advice as far as it went. The problem was, however, that the goal of transactional analysis is for participants to relate Adult-Adult, which would have required a higher degree of motivation, discipline and self-awareness than Donna was then capable of.

After a couple of weeks of "trying to work things out", Bud staying with the Coopers (the couple that Theron had lived with while in high school) and Donna and Donya in their trailer at the co-op, Bud confessed to his journal: "I think Donna still wants me to 'live up to her expectations'."

> She thinks I should be a loving father and provide a home for Donya. I usually visit out at the Coop. to see Donya & also to see if there are any warm feelings toward Donna. There are some, but not enough to live together again, aparently [sic]. However, my love for Donya grows stronger. I still feel one-down from Donna because she assumes the last word for Donya's care and nursing.[23]

> [The next day he wrote,] So last nite I asked Donna for equality with respect to raising Donya. This morning she refused on the grounds that I deserted her during pregnancy! So how can I relate to Donna and Donya under this stigma. Probably the best approach will be to volunter [sic] to keep Donya on occasion, not making a threesom [sic] any more as I've been trying to do since April 23rd [the day after he arrived at Workshare].[24]

Genesis had by this time defaulted on the purchase agreement. Donna urged foreclosure, hoping to "get the farm back", but interest was accruing on the debt, and Bud felt Norbert was doing his best to sell the farm. A farmer from Manitoba and his family were interested, but not if Donna was to continue as a member. "[T]oo much controversy (or words like that)."[25] Bud did his best to deal with these setbacks.

> How to reconcile all that I do want with what I don't want! I do want: (1) to be near Donya & help raise (2) keep immigrant status in Canada (3) make heaters, get P.P.L. [private pilot license] get devorce [sic] start coop, buy plane, date, etc. I do not want to: (a) send Donya to crummy school (b) wait around for $ [from sale of Workshare] much longer (c) spend $ foolishly (e) [sic] buy expensive property again soon.[26]

Bud feared Donna might decide to leave Canada to live near family in the U.S. He wanted to share in Donya's upbringing, and this would make it harder for him to preserve his landed immigrant status. Despite his "strong desire to go ahead with my life and certainly not depend on what others do if it can be avoided," all his plans hinged on where Donna would decide to live.[27] He would need to improve his financial situation. Where should he set up heater production? In B.C. with the Coopers, or in Charlotte with David? Should he resume flying lessons and get his private pilot's license (assuming Donna did move to the U.S. and he stayed in Canada for half the year)? Complicating matters were the long lines and panic buying of diesel fuel and gasoline that spring and summer, the result of a decline in oil production during the Iranian Revolution. How should he factor the potential for fuel shortages into his planning?

Unable to make any progress with Donna on his request for "regular periods of sharing Donya's care", Bud finally came to accept that Donna was "not interested in finding solutions." "However", Bud told his journal, "I think that since she does not want 100% care of Donya, she will eventually agree to regular periods of sharing Donya's care."[28] He made the "heavy decision" to leave the area for North Carolina and said his goodbyes to Eliza and all his friends. He thought Donna might follow him as she had before, but he was not sure, as she refused to tell him her plans.

> Told Donya I was going to see Grandma Lucas and would like her to visit me there when her mother agreed. She (of course) wanted to come then. How I hate leaving her!... It's hard to leave (maybe forever) these people who you've known so long. But the people in Charlotte too are dear to my

heart (some of them more so than others) so I'll not suffer a total loss. I'm esp. anxious to see Mother again & Martin etc.[29]

He again made the trip in five days. It was uneventful except for two speeding tickets. He was by now "broke" and needing income-producing work. "I start tomorrow!", he told his journal.[30] David gave him some work at the Lucas Company at seven dollars an hour.

Ruth and Diana were glad to see him. Ruth had let him know he was greatly missed at the Lucas family reunion in July, that Ford's sons (Sam and Davis) in particular had asked after him, that it had been wonderful to see the place looking so beautiful and the trip over had been delightful, only three hours now that the New River bridge was up. In other news, she told him that, after a weeks-long trial in the federal court in Richmond, Nancy Susan's son Smith Bagley had been acquitted of fraud charges, that Martin (Ruth rarely remembered to call him "Zach") was still working for Manpower three days a week, that Charles was working for a lawn care service and refusing to get his learner's permit, and that Diana was working for a textile mill (computer mostly), and planning to move to New York City in the fall.[31] Ailsie's sister Lois had been in poor condition but Ruth had arranged to get her in to see John Ransom for a check up, and now a nurse was visiting twice a week. They both really needed to be in a nursing home, but they did not want to go. "You know they have no relations at all", she told Bud, "and I feel very responsible." Not long after, Ruth would move Ailsie and Lois to Deverill where they would live out the remainder of their lives.

Donna used what was left of her $10,000 from the Workshare sale to go to Hawaii for the winter, taking Donya with her. While she was away, Norbert Martens called Bud to say he could now pay the entire balance due. Bud continued trying to sell his stoves and working for David. Hoping to improve his social life, he started going to Parents Without Partners meetings with Zach (Martin). At one such meeting, he led a discussion of transactional analysis. "Everyone said I did a good job", Bud wrote in his journal, "Met a Nancy Kiefer... we have [ ] good P[arent]-P[arent] transactions so far."[32] In February, Donna flew into Greenville with Donya, and Bud drove down to pick her up. He had arranged to have Donna served with a summons and complaint for divorce. "I hope she does not want alimony & signs," Bud told his journal.[33] She did sign, and then returned to B.C. with Donya. Bud stayed until the judgment of divorce was entered. While he was in town having the Toyota serviced for the trip back, he ran into Howerton.

> She "says" she wants to join a Buhidist [sic] group somewhere (probably just talk). In so many words she said that my relationship with both Frances & Donna were not Adult-Adult, but mainly Child (me)—Parent/Adult. Maybe! I[t] sure it has been hard to cooperate with Donna these last few years.[34]

Donna, who had begun using as her last name "Workshare" or "Share", rented a two bedroom unit at the Tumbleweeds Apartments in Vernon and filed an action for custody and child support in a lump sum of $50,000. Bud was not surprised, but he still hoped to share custody and have the Twin Oaks checks earmarked for Donya's expenses. "So", he told the journal, "I'd better get a real good lawyer right off."[35] In August, Donna moved to Salmon Arm, having invested $20,000 in the purchase of a house in order to create the New World Family Co-op with two parters, Peggy Novosel and Ira Zbarsky. Bud bought a camper and joined the Stonetree co-op as a provisional member. He also rented shop space in Castlegar. After trips to Calgary and Spokane for tools and equipment, he was ready to start making heaters. Calling his new business Castlegar Stove Works, he had by December made "some 15 or so heaters" and was preparing to make 20 more smaller ones.[36] In January, Donna allowed Bud to take Donya to North Carolina. They drove south by way of Eastwind, a descendant of Twin Oaks organized in 1974 by Kathleen Kinkade that was situated on 160 acres in the Ozarks at Tecumseh, Missouri. "They don't seem interested in anything except having a good time (which is ok but not what I'm after now)", Bud told the journal.[37]

While Bud and Donya were in North Carolina, Donna was asked to leave the New World Family Co-op for reasons that had implications for her fitness as a parent. She then purchased a camper truck and moved back to Vernon for a time. Bud, on his return to the area in April, learned that Donna had left the co-op and something of the reasons. Concerned about her mental stability, he thought he should keep Donya with him. He contacted his lawyer John Maguire and was advised to hold on to Donya, but before they could get to court, Donna called in the Royal Canadian Mounted Police to force Donya's return. It was around this time that Bud began staying at Donna's former co-op, which Peggy and Ira had renamed "Branch Flower Co-op", after the road on which it was located. With Lucas v. Lucas on the docket for a May hearing, Bud diligently gathered witness statements, met with court personnel and his lawyer, and prepared for the court date. Against all odds, he was awarded interim custody.

From that point forward, Donna's refusal to cooperate with Bud would grow increasingly pathological, such that every aspect of daily life would become a potential source of controversy. In one instance, and there were many, Donya was prescribed a course of penicillin for what appeared to be strep throat. Bud, who was then caring for Donya, gave the initial doses, but Donna refused to administer the medication or let Donya stay with Bud until the course was completed, insisting instead that Reiki (a form of spiritual healing) could cure Donya's illness. With the help of the court's family counselor, a compromise was agreed whereby Donya would stay in Donna's care for a couple of days and then be checked out by Donya's doctor. If penicillin was still indicated, Donya would go with Bud who would administer the medication since Donna would not. When, after a couple of days with Donna, the doctor recommended that the penicillin be continued, Donna reneged on the agreement.

> As we left, Dr. Williams, I asked Donna to help Donya understand the need for her to come with me and to make her transfer as smooth as possible. Donna made no attempt to do this. While getting Donya's clothes in Donna's camper, parked nearby, Donya said "pinicillin [sic] is not good for you." Donna then said "I'm not going to pressure her if she does not want to go with you. Since I did not want

to force Donya to come with me, I left after saying good by to Donya and hugging her. I recall Donya saying during the above conversation 'I love mother more than I love you.'" My reply was "that's o.k. as long as you love me too," And she said she did. I do not have any confidence in Donna's Riki [sic] method of healing (a sort of laying on of hands). I fear for Donya's health. Dr. Williams mentioned that rhumatic [sic] fever could result if Donya's throat is not treated properly. [Donya did not contract rheumatic fever.][38]

In July, Donna bought a used mobile home and put it on a lot she had purchased in a swampy area on the lake shore of Little White Lake, the one north of Tappen on the Trans Canada Highway, a half-hour drive from Salmon Arm. She started attending weekly meditation and stress reduction classes and joined the Seven Circle Society in Salmon Arm, a group described in court records as interested in growth and healing. She had, over the past year or so, become a follower of Ruth Montgomery, a respected journalist who later in life gained a reputation as a psychic. Among her New Age writings were *Companions Along the Way* (Penguin, 1974)("An extraordinary account, dictated from the other side, of Group Karma and incarnations shared with the world-famous medium, Arthur Ford") and *Strangers Among Us* (Penguin, 1979) ("You may know a walk-in. You may even be one. They are high-minded entities permitted to take over the bodies of human beings who wish to depart this life. Their mission is to lead us into an astonishing new age"). Donna was not, it should be noted, the only Lucas to cultivate an interest in things paranormal; Bud's aunt Josephine, who would decease later that year, wrote and self-published a couple of books on UFOs and space-age mysteries. The court would rely on Montgomery's *Strangers Among Us* to put Donna's beliefs in some kind of context.

> Montgomery feels that the world is quickly headed to a terrible end [the court report reads]. Generally it would appear that the general view regarding reincarnation is that people will come back to earth in different bodies over and over again to make amends for wrongs in previous lives in

which they are presently living as well as lay the foundation for a more secure and happy future. Basically, it would appear to be a case of having to do it again until you get it right. Montgomery's book expands on this notion to some extent in that she feels that people do not have to be necessarily reincarnated through the birth process, but can "walk in" to an existing body when the host has given up on life and has decided to "walk out." One of the reasons for conducting a "regression" would be to determine who an individual was in a previous life so as to "understand our motives better" and "avert another holocaust" as expressed by Mrs. Lucas. Mrs. Lucas stated that she has determined that she had been gassed at Aushwitz [sic] and that Mrs. Wilkinson [a friend with similar interests and beliefs] had in a previous life been Adolf Eichman. Mrs. Lucas...feels that "she is one of the chosen 5 survivors to prevent another holocaust."[39]

Donya, her mother apparently had come to believe, was her spiritual guide, a very advanced being who had come to teach and help her, who knew Bud would one day turn against her and would show Bud how to "love."[40] Donna believed not merely that she was able to perform regressions, but that she was obligated to do so by her care and concern for the individual involved. It was partly for conducting a regression either on, or in the presence of, 13 year-old Judy Miller (the daughter of a guest at Donna's co-op) that she had been asked to leave (the child had been very upset by the experience and run to the neighbor's house, "scared to death").

> [According to the court report], Mrs. Krick [the neighbor] stated that she [Judy] was so scared that she wouldn't go back to the house to get her clothes, and that she had to stay up all night with her because she couldn't calm her enough to go to sleep. Mrs. Krick stated that Judy told her that Mrs. Lucas and Mrs. Wilkinson had advised her that there were two spirits trying to take over her body, one good and one bad. They allegedly advised Judy that she had died of stomach cancer in a previous life and that she would do so again if she didn't allow the positive spirit to take over control. Mrs. Krick stated that Donna subsequently

discussed this situation with her, and admitted that "she had conducted a regression on Judy Miller."[41]

This incident almost certainly figured in the court's April decision to award custody to Bud, pending its final determination. That Donna, knowing she would have to be back in court for that, chose to attempt a regression on another young person the following year, is significant. The young person was 19-year-old Rod Pringle, a "diagnosed schizophrenic" whom Donna apparently believed was a reincarnated Nazi. Donna had promised Rod's mother she would not "under any circumstances" discuss her belief with him.[42] The incident occurred while the Pringles were vacationing in Hawaii; Donna had agreed to look after Rod and his 20 year-old sister at their house in Vernon while they were away.

> [According to the court report] Rod stated that though he was "wary" of Mrs. Lucas from previous experience [she and his mother were friends], he tried to "do everything to accommodate her." He stated that the first two or three days went without significant incident, but then Mrs. Lucas raised the issue regarding the possibility that he may be in fact a reincarnated Nazi. Rod stated she became increasingly persistent and was "always at me to talk about dead Nazis." He stated that she wanted him to read "a book she was writing about dead Nazis", and at one point refused to give him the allowance money his parents had left in her custody unless he would sit down and "talk for a couple of hours about it." Rod's birthday arrived during this period and after baking him a cake which he stated he very much appreciated, she began to ask him questions about his natural mother. Rod stated that he had been adopted at a very early age and Mrs. Lucas zeroed in on this area making statements to the effect of "shouldn't you be thinking about your natural mother on a day like this" and other similar kinds of statements. Rod stated that this interrogation in combination with the "Nazi reincarnation routine" got him so upset that he "freaked out" and had to run out of the house "just to get away."[43]

Rod's description of Donna's behavior resonates with descriptions in Bud's journal. The impression is of someone who is quiet but can be intensely intrusive and demanding; someone lacking in self-awareness, who cannot honor her agreements or hold herself accountable. Bud's accounts of his interactions with Donna were not included in the court report because, there being no witnesses other than Donya, the family court counselor who wrote the court report, Blair Peden, was unable to confirm them. Among Peden's concerns, aside from Donna's metaphysics, were that Donna had come to believe that children should be not disciplined or taught table manners, but should be allowed to "do their own thing", even if it meant their not going to school (or not spending time with their father), and that doctors are not needed to treat illness or injury, because she herself possessed the power to heal. Of particular concern to Peden was Donna's "continuing and unabated pattern of alienating friends and turning them into conspirators against her in her own mind."

> Mrs. Lucas appears to use her considerable empathy and compassion like a baseball bat wherein her sincere motivation to help turns into a weapon and an offensive force in many instances. If Mrs. Lucas is going to continue on this road of alienation and broken relationships, it would appear likely that, were Donya in her custody, she would, by osmosis, become one half of the "us" in a "them against us situation."[44]

So it was that, on May 28, 1982, after a two-day trial, the court ordered that Bud be given full custody of Donya, now nearly six years old. Donna was to be allowed "restricted access... in the presence of Petitioner or other adult designated by the Petitioner at a place designated by the Petitioner."[45]

> In Vernon Court Judge Arkell's Decision was a Victory for me [Bud wrote in his journal]. Donna burst out crying. I have custody with no "tertioral" [sic] restrictions. Donna has access at my discresion [sic] and in my presence. Maguire [his lawyer] advised my having a witness during these supervised access periods. I am feeling better all the time![46]

Restricting Donna's access was Judge Arkell's idea. Peden had considered recommending it, but he told the court in his report that he hesitated "to go that far, given the apparent significant bond between Donya and her mother, as well as Donya's apparent preference to live with her mother."[47] Bud knew that Donna was certain to resist supervision every way she could, but for now, he was ready to think about other things. On his birthday, he told his journal,

> May 31, 1982: I'm 57 now...I feel good. Donya and I are leaving these parts (Branchflower Co-op). Donya got her shots today and must say good by to [her teacher] Mrs. Gardiner and Salmon Arm West School. Then we're off to Vernon + Eliza's for a few weeks.[48]

Chapter 15

New beginnings and new shoots

Bud paid his legal bills (Maguire charged $4,111.41, including a 25% discount given Bud's "limited means"—about $12,400 in 2021), and took Donya back to North Carolina via San Francisco to pick up Howerton who had moved there. Once they were settled at Deverill, they went to visit Nancy Keifer, the woman Bud had met at Parents Without Partners. They had become friends. Nancy had visited in B.C., and Bud had begun thinking of her as being in his future, along with Donya. Eliza was to say of Nancy that she was "the warmest, kindest, most common-sensical of all the women in his life, but she wouldn't marry him." Eliza suspected part of the reason may have been that "Bud was trying to get her to play the stepmom role which she did not want." She also suspected Nancy was receiving alimony payments that would cease if she were to remarry.

In July, Maguire let Bud know Donna's action for maintenance had been dismissed and sent Bud a bill for $1,179.29, which he promptly paid. Shortly thereafter, Bud heard from Twin Oaks that Donna had asked to have the monthly payments sent to her instead of him, even though she had agreed many times that the money should be spent for Donya's welfare. Thus denied a vacation from his lawyers, Bud set John Nagle to work sorting things out with Twin Oaks. In September, he flew back B.C. hoping to make 32 stoves by mid-October and return to Charlotte. He still hoped to arrange things so that Donya could go to the Vallican Whole School in the Slocan Valley. "It somewhat depends on whether Donya likes N.C. school [the one built on the upper farm], how things go w[ith] Grandma, how Nancy feels, how the politics of the world goes."[1] Bud of course had his mother, at 84, looking after Donya while he was away, doing her best to teach her a few table manners. This test or trial or experiment apparently went well enough for Bud and Donya to continue living with "Grandma" for the next several years. Summers were spent in B.C. with Eliza. Bud and Nancy eventually would rent one side of a duplex off of Park Road where they lived for several years along with Donya.

The living arrangement was a challenge for both Donya and Ruth, but more so for Ruth, who still had Ailsie to look after, as well as Charles, and later Zach (Martin), after his second marriage failed. And she had David breathing down her neck to make provisions for the disposition of her estate, mainly the land. He had begun in March to survey and map a "development plan" for the homestead that carved it into 20 lots for distribution to Saint Timothy's (a splinter of the Episcopal Church that appealed to Ruth because they did not use the new 1979 *Book of Common Prayer* or women priests), her children, and any grandchildren who had the means and desire to build and live on the property, which only a few did. It was probably the gift of ten acres she wanted to make to Saint Timothy's that was uppermost in her mind that summer. David was paid $5,000 for his work, in advance, about what she and Charles had paid for the property in 1935, less the 35 acres sold to Susannah and Jim in 1957.

Property development is always complicated, and David's 1982 plan would go through many modifications. In addition to all the usual issues, the homestead was subject to certain restrictions as to subdivision size (no less than three acres) and use (agricultural and single family residential). They had seemed like a good idea when she proposed them in 1957 (before Vatican II), but they complicated the gift to Saint Timothy's. It all worked out eventually, and Ruth got an Episcopalesque Church within walking distance of Deverill, which pleased Bud. The next year, Ruth gave the mill's remains and the one-half acre they sat on to the county to be part of the fledgling greenway system. The rest of the land along the creek (about 28 acres) she gave to David and Zach (Martin) (wives and offspring included to maximize gift tax exemptions), who then sold it to the county. She gave David the 12 acres off Piney Grove Road, between the creek and the Hewsons' eastern boundary, which he then sold to the Barksdales, the Rays, the Randles, and Orrie Graves, who built houses and became neighbors.

That was the fall, October to be precise, that Uncle Rod died. He is remembered in the family as a benefactor who believed in the power of an education, and as a local historian in the Little River Valley. A bit of Rod's Little River Valley history, known to the grandchildren as "the stagecoach", lived for many years in the garage at Deverill. As he told the story, it was

> [w]hile passing through the village of Hiwassi [sic] [that] we saw in a shed a beautiful horse-drawn coach. It had two seats enclosed that faced each other and a driver's seat on top. Sometime later Ralph [Palmer] and I went back and traded for the coach and hauled it home on a truck. We fixed it up and had it looking like new. Ralph's father, Mr. Watt Palmer, had a team of fine white horses and a set of white breast harness. There was an old friend named Tete Anderson who became our coachman. We would dress him up and put a high silk hat on his head. He sat on the high outside driver's seat and coached us around.[2]

The boys would drive along the Little River Road, visiting neighbors, singing and talking, and every now and then discreetly sipping a little of Rod's home-brewed beer (this was during Prohibition, 1920-1933). When it came time for Ralph and Rod to leave home, they sold the coach to Charles, and that is how it ended up at Deverill in the garage.[3]

The summer of 1983, Bud, Nancy and Donya returned to B.C. by way of San Francisco, to visit Howerton. As they drove north to Eliza's, they visited communes along the route. Donya was many years later to recall these summers with Eliza fondly, especially after the birth of Eliza's son Galen-Maia Webb Lucas Milner (later shortened to Webb Lucas).

> July 24, 1986
> Dear Mother,
> We have been gone almost 5 weeks now. It seems like much longer, but I don't know why. Maybe it's because of the complex everyday round of cleaning, laundry, meals, dishes, shoping [sic], ocassionaly [sic] looking after Webb, and if time permits fixing the Toyota, Truck & making heaters.
> I hope all is going well with you & Martin. Here it's been plesantly mild with ocassional [sic] rain to keep things green. I hear it has been dry in N.C. & S.C. and hot. I guess things are not too comfortable for you.
> Donya seems to enjoy looking after Webb (who is now 18 mos.) She claims he has a vocabulary of 38 words but I can distinguish only half dozen or so. We all went to see <u>As You Like It</u> at a rural theater community near here, and Webb got up on the in-the-round outdoor stage before the play started and did a cute little dance, which he enjoyed more than anyone.
> Donya's reading seems to be improving. We read about an hour most mornings out of the Grimm's Fairy Tale book. The cherry season is about over but the large apricot tree gives basketfulls [sic] now. So we are "pigging out" on them. Webb has about a dozen for breakfast.
> Eliza seems to enjoy looking after Webb and not to mind Donya and me too much. I'm reading a very interesting book— The Origin of Consciousness in the Breakdown of the Bicameral Mind by J. Jaynes, a Princeton Psychologist. I'll tell all when I get back.
> Have they started on the house yet?
> Much love—Bud[4]

"The house", another of Ruth's projects, she was to call "Deverill Minor." The so-called Roaring 1980s had both put some extra money in her pocket, and made her look for ways to reduce her tax liability. Whether she ever really intended to live there or just said she did to qualify for the home mortgage interest deduction is a matter of speculation. What she *said* was that she wanted a smaller version of Deverill with "handicap-accessible" bathrooms, bedroom on the first floor, etc., in which she might live out her remaining years. She built it about 250 feet north of the main house on the mill road. After the house was finished, she moved Zach's (Martin's) daughter Sherry and her family into it. That summer was perhaps the last Bud and Donya spent in B.C.

> Dear Grandma,
> Webb has really grown. He is saying hole [*sic*] sentences now. Every one thinks he is a girl. We call him Webb.
> The new house Eliza moved to is nice. It is yellow on the outside. In side the wall is baby blew [*sic*]. It has lots of windows. The house is one in a half [*sic*] story high. It has fore [*sic*] bed rooms, one bathroom and a kitchen.
> Hope it's not to [*sic*] hot down their [*sic*] because it's cold up here!
> Bud, Mom and I whent [*sic*] on a boat ride on Little White Lake for fathers day! I payed [*sic*] for the boat ride. Webb is tow in [*sic*] half years old today. Webb can count to 5!!! Bud [*sic*] cold is getting better very slowley [*sic*]. He is going to see a doctor today. When we whear [*sic*] going to visit my mother we saw a big pipe lening [*sic*] over the aera [*sic*] becide [*sic*] the road purd [*sic*] out a hole [*sic*] lot of water. Bud drove the car under it for a car wash. We love you, and we miss you.
> Love, Donya[5]

The image of a happy family on a Fathers Day boat ride notwithstanding, for Bud, encounters with Donna never stopped being the unpleasant, "uptight" experiences they had become, and she did everything she could to pressure him into allowing Donya to stay with her unsupervised, resulting in numerous lengthy scenes and standoffs. The toll on Bud, Eliza would later recall, was cumulative. The summer of 1987 "there was a big fight", and when Bud returned with Donya to Eliza's house, "he looked really bad." Eliza thought that he might have had a heart attack. Ruth's heart had also begun to give out, prompting her doctor to implant a pacemaker for which she was something less than grateful. Bud would eventually have to have bypass surgery.

Bess, Charles's last remaining sibling, died in May of 1988. When Ruth turned 90 in October of that year, David, impelled by "duty, tradition and self-interest" sought to enlist the aid of his siblings in getting her to settle her affairs in a more financially advantageous manner than she had in her will. He helpfully laid out the "things and facts and considerations" requiring attention in a dot-matrix machine-printed paper memo, and gave everyone a copy. In pertinent part:

> RSL 90 AND ALONE AND DECLINING
>
> RSL HAS NOT MADE SPECIFIC PROVISION FOR CARE IN FUTURE
>
> RSL HAS SUFFICIENT MEANS
>
> RSL HAS NOT APPROPRIATELY PROTECTED HER MEANS
>
> RSL HAS NOT DEVELOPED A CADRE OF COMPETENT SERVANTS
>
> RSL HAS A MIND SET PRECLUDING HIRING OF QUALITY SERVANTS
>
> RSL DESIRES TO REMAIN IN PRESENT RESIDENT [*sic*]
>
> RSL IS CAPRECIOUS [*sic*] AND IS DIFFICULT TO REPRESENT
>
> RSL CONSIDERS HER AFFAIRS HER BUSINESS
>
> RSL HAS EXPRESSED DESIRE TO TREAT HER CHILDREN EQUALLY AS SHE SEE [*sic*] IT AND PREFERS TO TREAT ONE ON ONE (THIS IS SINCERE * * THIS IS NOT MY WAY)
>
> RSL HAS RESPONDED IN RECENT YEARS TO A MORE OPEN TREATMENT OF HER AFFAIRS
>
> RSL HAS EXPRESSED WILLINGNESS TO SELL LAND AND RESIDENCE

Ruth was not exactly "alone"; Zach (Martin) was still living with her, and Sherry and her family were living next door in

Deverill Minor. Moreover, she appeared to be in good health, which is not to suggest there was no need to make contingency plans. But Ruth's "personal needs", as the memo put it, were not David's primary focus. Nor was he concerned with the trust set up by her sister Katharine. By its terms, that was to be distributed to Ruth's children upon her death. As detailed in David's memo, his mother planned to leave what acreage remained to David (a small, land-locked parcel adjacent to those he had already sold), Mary Jo (about 18 acres) and Martin (about 14 acres, plus a life estate in Deverill Minor with the remainder to his children). Deverill and about 22 acres ("the homestead") she planned to leave to all five children. David had what he thought was a better idea.

David thought his mother should "swap" the two Deverills and her remaining land for other, income-producing, land in what was known as a "1031 exchange" (1031 referred to the controlling section of U.S. Internal Revenue Code), which allowed long-term property owners to defer capital gains tax obligations. His idea was that she would sell everything to the county, who he said was interested, and keep a life estate. (If he had in mind what income-producing property she might then buy, he did not identify it in the memo, but he estimated the annual income on such property would be 8%.) Her apparent lack of interest in doing this is presumably what he meant by "RSL has not appropriately protected her means." Thinking she might agree to "having the children act in consert [sic] to receive the gift and make the swap", he proposed that the five of them do what the Rea family had done with the land off Highway 51, and form a Title S corporation "to receive and handle the land from their parents." But, the Lucases being Lucases and not Reas, David's plan went nowhere.

The next year, Ruth had a mild stroke from which she was determined to and did recover, however, it was decided she needed someone to look after her (Zach (Martin) was to remarry in January), so in December 1989, Mary Jo's daughter Diana returned to Charlotte from New York to stay at Deverill. Ruth was ambivalent about the arrangement, but acquiesced. That same month, Donna reignited the controversy over the Twin Oaks payments by filing suit and seeking back payments from 1981 with interest, an amount in excess of $10,000. The thing dragged on as such things do, until one day the following May, when Bud came home from Sedgefield school with Donya to find Donna sitting in their living room.

> I was for calling the police & having Donna escorted out but relented [Bud recounted to his journal]. The next houer [*sic*] or so Donna managed to get everyone up tight. Finally Nancy helped us get some things to think about agreeing on. (1) Bud would send Donna the Twin Oaks checks from now on. (2) Donna would not ask for my other monies. (3) If Donya wants to, she would visit her mother once each year. Donya would decide on how long. (4) Donna & Bud would split the cost of the transportation to be p[]-based here in USA or wherever cheaper. I agreed to 1, 3, & 4. Donna agreed to think it over. I gave her a copy of the proposals when she left on the 15th... during the living room talks with Donna [while Nancy and Donya sat in the dining room], she admitted that she had agreed that the T.O. moneys should go to whomever had custody of Donya but only if we shared custody equally. She said she needed the money now for her support. She also said she probably could get some sort of support from the B.C. gov't but had no intention of doing so.[6]

Bud wrote that journal entry shortly after dropping Donna at the bus station. He also made a note that Donna had left a letter for Donya telling her, among other things, that Donya was the reincarnation of Queen Elizabeth who enjoyed seeing people hanged. As for Bud's settlement offer, Donna waited six weeks to respond, by which time Bud was no longer interested in settling. The outcome of the court case is not known, but she probably fared no better than she would have had she accepted Bud's offer. That summer, Theron invited Donya to B.C. for a visit and sent her a plane ticket. During that visit, Donya saw her mother for the last or nearly last time. The next year, Donya was sent off to Gunston School, in Centreville, Maryland, and Bud moved back to Deverill to live with Ruth and Diana.

New beginnings and new shoots

It was in these last years before Ruth's death that Bud attended Sunday evening socials at the author's house on Studley Road, one of several hundred built on Bud's upper farm. Bud seemed to enjoy these gatherings and invariably had everyone singing toward the end of the evening, after they had tired of arguing. It was during one of those socials that Ruth finally gave up the ghost. She was 94. Her death was not unexpected; she was at home and had been heavily sedated for days, organs failing one by one, until her heart gave out. Martin's daughter Sherry, a devout Christian of the fundamentalist variety, insisted that the body be embalmed and the casket open. Otherwise, the wishes of the deceased that her pacemaker be removed and her body buried next to her husband in accordance with the Order for the Burial of the Dead (1928 BCP), were respected. The service was graveside and included her favorite hymn, "Eternal Father! Strong to Save."

The house was filled with flowers, guests were served pimento cheese and vegetable sandwiches, cheese straws and smoked turkey, and there was an open bar. Thankfully, there were no scenes and no memorable unpleasantness. Bud and Diana continued on at the house for a time. At the end of the year, Bud bought a house and outbuilding on a heavily wooded lot in Woodberry Forest. Then, in February, after executing a prenuptial agreement, he married Christina Davie Hedrick of Charlotte, a slight woman with curly dyed red hair who looked vaguely like Nancy.

Wachovia took four years to settle Ruth's estate. The delay was due to a number of factors, including Wachovia's accepting without criticism and submitting as part of the 90-day inventory an appraisal of the real estate that was double the valuation obtained in 1988, such that the estate had insufficient cash to cover the estate tax. A question thus arose whether or not the bank should sell some or all of the real estate, or try to obtain a lower evaluation with a new appraisal and hope that the Internal Revenue Service would not challenge it. Proceeding slowly on the first front, the bank credulously accepted David's renewed assertion that a sale to the county was a viable course, and delayed moving on the second front until it proved not to be, basically wasting a year. Another factor was the remote possibility that the estate might incur additional tax liability in excess of $2 million should the IRS decide the trust should be included in the estate, which basically tacked on another, "wait-and-see", year.

The uncertainty over the estate debts did not preclude the sale of the property, but there were other complications, e.g. the need for the bank and Martin to designate which three-acres should make up the Deveril Minor parcel, and for the bank to resolve Deverill Minor's access issues (well and road) which had been exacerbated by flaws in the 1986 deed used to obtain its building and occupancy permits. The siblings eventually bought out Martin's share of Deverill for $120,000, Martin relinquished his life estate to his children, Sherry bought out Charles, and Bud transferred his interest in Deverill to Christina (he would, at her request, later transfer to her the house in Woodberry Forest as well). With David still determined to sell the property to the county for a park and threatening to force a judicial sale, Sherry finally got a lawyer and petitioned to reopen the estate to resolve the access issues, which took another couple of years, during which time David filed suit for partition, which resulted in the property being put up for auction. Had Wachovia not tried to administer the estate out of the Winston-Salem office, or had more capable trust officers in Charlotte, or had Ruth asked someone other than David to provide the survey plat for the 1986 deed to Deverill Minor, or had Wachovia's legal counsel been a firm other than that belonging to Ruth's very old friend and counselor Jimmy Craighill, or had David not been so hell bent on selling the property to the county, many problems could have been avoided or resolved sooner and with less expense. In the end, the property almost went to the county through a company called American Property Development Company, LLC, which planned to buy and swap it for surplus county property. But Susannah, anticipating a lawsuit over the deed restrictions if the county deal went through, thwarted the plan by filing an upset bid and purchasing the property herself. Deverill was then marketed as an estate and sold at a profit through Sotheby's, a course David had from the beginning stubbornly resisted for reasons known only to him.

New beginnings and new shoots

Bud attended the meetings between the bank and the heirs, held at Deverill in the upstairs drawing room, but he seemed uninterested. He would pick up a book and begin reading, or he would pretend to read, while others did the talking. Working in Deverill's garage "shop" with Martin, making stoves and hammocks and hanging out at farmers markets, had been very pleasant for him, and he would miss it. Maybe his thoughts were drifting further back, to all the Christmas mornings in that room, or to the days spent shooting and fishing, sailing Bobbie across the mill pond, riding to Matthews on horseback over unpaved roads. All the issues preventing the settlement of the estate were but details, soon to be forgotten. Details that could not, as Bud would say, disturb the mostly broad feeling associated with Deverill.

Chapter 16

Thus the tale ended

Less is known about the last third of Bud's life than one might wish. None of his letters or journals, if there were any, survived, and factual details are sketchy. He set up shop for the last time in the garage of the house in Woodberry Forest. He got to know the neighbors. He found a cafeteria he liked nearby, and the farmers market, and there was a place in Matthews where he and Christina regularly went for breakfast. He did all the grocery shopping and most of the cooking. He worked some for David's son Paul, doing machine design for Paul's molded concrete business for ten dollars an hour, but he stopped when Paul started trying to boss him around. He made a point to visit his sisters and David (Martin was in Florida) when he could.

After graduating from Gunston, Donya enrolled in the University of North Carolina at Charlotte and lived with Bud and Christina until Bud helped her buy a condominium. Later, they helped her buy a couple of houses, presumably so she might live off the rental income. Mary Jo died in September 2002. The funeral was held at Christ Episcopal Church in Myers Park. Ten months later, Martin died. He was only 67, but in poor health. His daughter Sherry arranged for a funeral in Charlotte at her church (Providence Road Church of Christ) and burial in the family cemetery in Mount Airy.

The year Martin died, Bud and Frances helped Eliza buy a townhouse in Vernon. Eliza and Pamela (who by this time had reverted to her first name), then working as a librarian for the City University of New York in Queens, stayed in touch with Bud, mostly by phone. Pamela visited Bud and Christina at least annually, taking the train because she would not fly. Eliza and Webb visited when they could, but less often. In the winter of 2006, Frances's health began to deteriorate markedly. Her brothers, then Pamela, then Eliza took turns staying with her in Albion until she died a couple of days after her 79th birthday. She left everything she had to Pamela and Webb per Eliza's request, in consideration of US-Canadian tax laws and exchange rates.

After Donya finished her studies at UNCC in 2007, she bought a house in High Point, got married and moved there to start a family and pursue a second Master of Arts at University of North Carolina at Greensboro. That was the year Bud and Christina joined the "Socrates Cafe", a weekly discussion group that met at the Ben Craig Center at University Research Park. Bud's financial situation up until this time had been "o.k." Eliza was to recall, until he found $45,000 "missing" from his bank account. He and Eliza both suspected Christina, who Bud said had started going through his papers. In early 2008, Bud consulted an estate attorney because he had misplaced the original of his prenuptial agreement with Christina and was concerned about its enforceability. The attorney confirmed that his will, which, consistent with the prenup, left Christina only the house in Woodberry Forest, with all else going to Donya, was vulnerable unless he could locate the original. He told the attorney he did not want to ask Christina if she knew where the original was located, and he did not want the attorney's advice letter mailed to the house. In 2009, Bud gave Donya full power of attorney, naming Pamela as successor in the event Donya was incapacitated. Pamela had at some point offered to move to Charlotte and take care of Bud and Christina in exchange for the house after their deaths, but they were not interested. They were in fact, Eliza was to recall Pamela saying, rather rude and hurtful in rejecting the offer. It seems they planned to move in with Donya, in anticipation of which Donya used some of Bud's money to fix up her house in High Point. The rest, according to Donya, her husband lost in "daytrading." Together, Bud and Christina had a little over $2,000 a month in Social Security income.

David died in 2010. There was no funeral service, worship in many previously observant Charlotte families having been replaced by secular gatherings or sometimes nothing at all. In 2012, Eliza moved from Canada to Bloomington, Indiana, to be near Webb and his wife. The last time she visited Bud and Christina, she could tell that it was not safe for them to be alone. Bud had seemed tired and confused in the afternoons, but when Eliza made him meals (for which she had to buy groceries) and ate with him, he seemed to get better. He and Christina moved into an apartment for a few months after a big storm dropped a tree through the roof and crushed, among other things, the Kortheuer portrait. Bud, in particular found the experience very disorienting. It was after that, Eliza would recall, that Bud would complain about no one taking him to the grocery store and not having enough to eat.

When Susannah died in 2016, Bud was 90. The plan to move in with Donya never materialized. Donya attempted to involve local social services in developing a care plan of some sort, but Christina was adamantly opposed to what she saw as outside interference. Eliza later described Bud as being "completely isolated." Things got to where Bud would say almost nothing to Eliza on the phone if Christina was around, but "would have lots to say when she was not." Finally, in 2018, Bud's need for surgery to repair a hernia gave Donya an opening. Exercising her power of attorney, she moved him into a post-op rehab facility near her, and from there to a nursing facility where he died after a fall, just a few weeks after his 93rd birthday. Donya held a memorial gathering for family at her house in High Point. There was no obituary.

Chapter 17

Looking backward

It is a shame that more is not known about Bud's later life and that so few of his papers from that period survived. The inevitable impression is one of a mind that was rather less active than it may in fact have been, of one suffering in relative isolation, no building projects and no one to argue with. According to Eliza, he did worry some about death, not dying so much, but "not knowing what to expect." She thought he was not in the end an atheist, though "he might have been an agnostic." Many if not most lives, especially those lived to such an old age as Bud was able to reach, close in circumstances less than ideal, but one hopes to have it said that death came with mind intact and loving friends and family at the bedside. If this cannot be said confidently of Bud, it is well to remember that, in the first instance, before Belamy, before the Bruderhof and before Skinner, utopia for Bud was cornbread, and that during the war, in the weeks before the Normandy landing, as he contemplated the possibility of his own death, it was cornbread he dreamt of. Bud seemed to understand at an early age that we all die alone.

Despite coming from a loving family, Bud suffered amongst his nearest and dearest the general prejudice against the (double) expatriate (from the South as well as the country), and was made to pay for thinking he could do better, for having divorced and (twice!) remarried, and for having had a child in his dotage (though he was no older than Ruth's father had been when she was born). "Uncle Dud" was the failed communist and prodigal son who abandoned his family, hijacked the beach house, cheated at welfare, and absconded to Canada only to limp home to Mother when reality finally hit. His own children were hardly more charitable, though Eliza and Pamela agreed they were "lucky compared to most people" in their upbringing. None of the criticism phased Bud. In 1972, in response to an article titled "Children to the Communal", Bud wrote to his mother that he thought he had had "the best possible up bringing" because there were "all sorts of people for me to 'relate' to—Menny, Lidya, Elonza, Molly, Irene, Charlie, etc. just to name a few", adding on the back of the envelope, "I forgot about Willie! & Leonard & the Blacks etc."[1] His journal echoed these sentiments.

Eliza felt that Bud had a vision to recreate "the friendly village" that her mother shared. (The image of "The Friendly Village" came from a tableware pattern of the same name made in England by the Johnson Brothers that was among the several sets of Ruth's china.) Given their many compatibilities, it seems they might have succeeded had they stayed married. Bud did seem to learn from his mistakes, e.g., recognizing the importance of feelings and shouldering more of what he had grown up thinking of as "women's work." No one knows exactly why Bud and Frances parted ways. Safe to say, however, that the boy who signed on for nine more months of sea duty, rather than give up his rating, did not abandon his family and doctorate to start a commune. Walden Two was not Bud's vision for the friendly village, and Twin Oaks was even less so. And while he hoped the founders would fulfill their vision, he repeatedly expressed doubt they would succeed, and he was fully prepared to repossess the farm if they did not. The fact is, had Father Chapman not driven Bud and Frances to the Unitarians, had the Unitarians not introduced them to the Bruderhof, had Frances not given Bud *Walden Two*, and had Irene's money not come to him just when it did, Bud might never have sired the summer camp for misfits and lost souls that was Twin Oaks. But he did not just give Twin Oaks life. At least as important as the land, the new well, and the buildings were to the endeavor, it was his pragmatism, his ingenuity, his foresight and understanding of the community's need for a reliable, income-producing industry generally, and hammock-weaving in particular, that gave Twin Oaks the potential for longevity. Without Bud's contributions, Twin Oaks very probably would not have had the "financial backbone" it needed to outlive all its contemporaries.[2]

Trite though it is to say, starting over at 40—leaving one's spouse and children, career, community of friends and even one's country, building a new life, all take considerable courage and not a little confidence. It would have been very easy to retreat to Deverill for a while. He still had the upper farm, he could have raised cows or crops and supplemented his income with almost any kind of job that suited him. Eliza was to recall Bud saying that he moved to Canada because he got tired of being told to "love or leave it" whenever he talked about racial discrimination or the war, particularly in South Carolina, and that he had been encouraged by the candidacy of Dave Barrett (NDP) to replace the B.C. premier W.A.C. Bennett (Social Credit Party). Given that he was planning as early as October 1968 to move to Canada, just as he and Donna were preparing to marry, the decisions were almost certainly linked. Was Donna worried her sons might be drafted? President Nixon had promised to end the draft, but maybe she was. Nearly 240,000 Americans emigrated to Canada between 1966 and 1975, perhaps as many as half due to the war. If he moved because he did not like feeling complicit in "mass murder, the leadership, the 'wall of silence'" and did not want to be a "victim of competition in its ultimate form—nuclear war", it may well have been because Donna was amplifying those messages. In the end, it was Donna who gave up her U.S. citizenship, not Bud.

A few years after he returned from Canada, Bud paid Susannah a visit, as he did from time to time. She was still living in the house on the knoll above the pond (long since silted up) in the middle of the 35 acres just south of Bud's upper farm that she and Jim had purchased in 1957. Upon being seated with a cool drink in his hand, he opened the conversation by asking her what she had done lately to justify her existence. His question was, no doubt, intended to be mildly provoking, and Susannah rose to the bait by showing irritation, as little sisters can be counted on to do, and asking rhetorically why she or anyone should have to justify their existence. Bud just laughed. "[A] man with wife and babies to be fed, clothed, and sheltered can't spend too much time contemplating about whether he is 'above all being true to himself'", Mary Jo had told him, not considering the possibility that the wife might turn out to be the idealist, or even a bit loony. The irony of Donna's being a driving force behind Bud's desire to pursue "this community thing" (if indeed she was) was that Workshare simply could not expand with her there. Nor were he and Donya likely to find a suitable community someplace else if Donna was in the picture. Once Donna was out of the picture, Bud basically stopped looking. He remained interested in communities as a place to market his stoves and hammocks, but the grander vision just seemed to shrink quietly back to that of the friendly village. Bud knew his primary duty was to Donya.

Leaving it to Donna to raise Donya would have been much the easier course for him to take. Donya had said she wanted to live with her mother. There would have been no stigma; Canada Justice Department statistics from 1994-1995 show that courts placed close to 80% of children under age 12 in the mother's custody. The percentage was probably even higher in 1980. He could have lived nearby and visited often, much more often than he had visited Eliza and Pamela, but of course they were older, and they had Frances. Donya did not have Frances, and Bud was afraid, with reason, of what might happen to Donya if raised by her mother. Going against Donna as he did meant participating in the worst kind of conflict imaginable between two people who supposedly used to love each other; personal, pointless, painful and protracted—just the sort of conflict he was the least equipped to handle well. That he would sign up for it, see it as his duty, and see it through to the end, is a measure of his character.

Bud was not a genius, and did not seriously consider himself to be one. Though his reading and letter writing doubtless sharpened his consciousness (to use Van Wyck Brooks's phrase) of the world around him, he was by his own estimation of only average intelligence.[3] Had he been willing to work merely for money, he might have been less of a nomad in those early years. But, there being in his temperament at least as much of the artist or writer as there was of the engineer, he lacked the "passion for money" so necessary to success in a competitive economy. Paraphrasing William James, one might say of Bud that he preferred to pay his way by what he was and did, and not by what he had. "The passion for money," Oliver Allston had told him, "is like the magnetic mountain in *The Arabian Nights* that drew all the metal out of the ships and sent them to the bottom."[4] Bud's metal was his active intellect, and he knew it. One cannot help admire his refusing to become "set in his ways" and wanting to keep his "fancy free", as he put it in a letter to his mother after seeing *Devotion*, starring Olivia DeHavilland and Ida Lupino as the Brontë sisters,

> The aurthors [sic] were sisters + also geniuses (it said so in the movie) so I came back inspired at how wonderful it must be to be a real genius + to put your thoughts + feelings into words. I have considered this idea a long time—that a writer is only good when he can make the reader visulize + experience or better re-visulize + re-experience because he is only putting into words what you have already become acquainted with. Therefore a person with limited experience has only a limited enjoyment from great books. Older people should enjoy good reading more than younger on the whole except for the fact that some older people become so fixed in their ideas + opinions + everything else.

> When I was one + twenty,
> I heard a wise man say,
> Give crowns + pounds + guineas,
> But not your heart away
> Give pearls away + rubies,
> But keep your fancy free.
> But I am one + twenty,
> No use to talk to me.[5]

> The third from the last line is the only one that has anything to do with what I am talking about. It's a good poem anyway.[6]

And what did he want of those around him? To belong and to think. Bud's basic attitude was that anyone, regardless of age or experience, should be willing to examine cherished beliefs. Good conversation depended on it, and good conversation, or the perpetual hope of it, was to Bud almost better than cornbread.

Appendix

Figure 1: Deverill Floor Plan

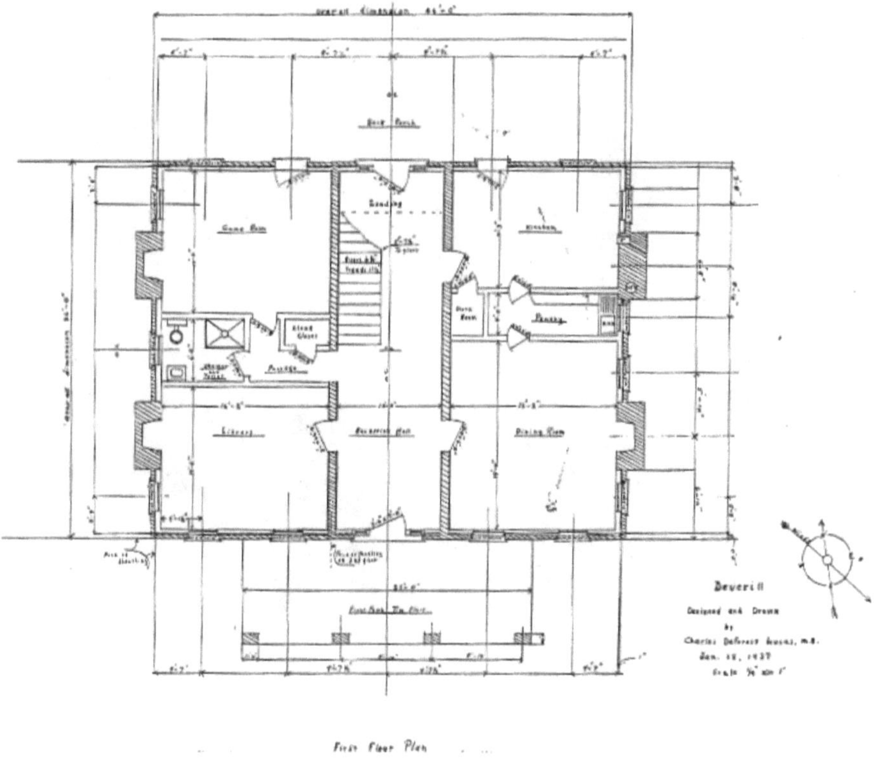

Figure 2: Martin at the Lucas mill

Figure 3: Deverill, Rear View

Figure 4: Lucas driveway, c. 1945

Figure 5: Coast Guard training boat, courtesy St. Augustine Lighthouse & Maritime Museum digital collection (https://www.staugustinelighthouse.org)

Figure 6: USS *Bayfield* loading LCVs off Utah Beach, 6 June 1944 (U.S. Navy photo 80-G-252391)

Figure 7: The Pendulums of Government

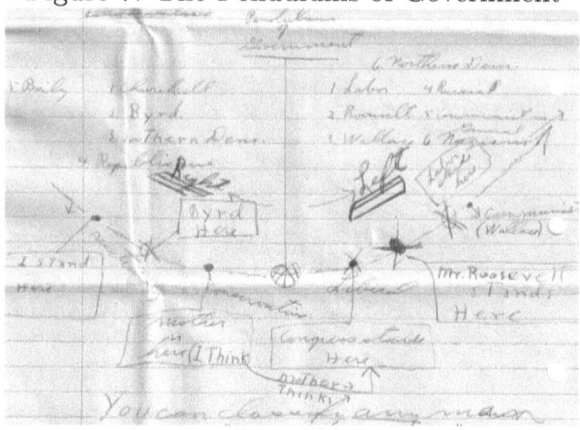

Figure 8: Battle stations

Figure 9: Don Dunne, Deverill, Christmas 1945

Figure 10: Mary Jo and Bud 1946

Figure 11: Bandaged Bud

Figure 12: Thanksgiving 1947, Mount Airy (from left: Don, Bud, Irene, Susannah, Ruth, Zach (sipping), David)

Figure 13: Donna and Bud

Bob's own design for a hammock-weaving machine has a manually operated shuttle.

Figure 14: Bud and Nancy

Figure 15: Bud and Christina

Figure 16: Bud

Notes

Chapter 1. The land of lost content

[1]Lucas, Bud to Ruth Lucas, 16 September 1943, DCL Collection, Lucas Family Papers

[2]Lucas, Bud, Journal, 9 April 1978, DCL Collection, L.F.P.

Chapter 2. Newcomers

[1]Research has shown that, following Emancipation, racial intermingling persisted 20 years or more in cities such as Atlanta, Houston, Charleston, Louisville and Charlotte. For more, see Thomas Hanchett, *Sorting Out the New South City*, 2d Ed. (Chapel Hill: University of North Carolina Press, 2020), Ch. 5

[2]Lucas, David to "Misty", 28 March 2000, DCL Collection, Other Documents, L.F.P.

[3]"Death in the Midst of Life", *Charlotte Observer*, 15 March 1939

Chapter 3. The equal dealings of providence

[1]Lucas, Bud to David Lucas, 11 January 1941, DCL Collection, L.F.P.

[2]Lucas, Bud to Ruth Lucas, 10 February 1941, DCL Collection, L.F.P.

[3]Lucas, Bud to Ruth Lucas, 5 May 1941, DCL Collection, L.F.P.

[4]George Gallup, "Majority Opposes U.S. Convoy at Present", *Richmond Times-Dispatch*, 23 April 1941

[5]Lucas, Bud to Ruth Lucas, 23 October 1945, DCL Collection, L.F.P.

[6]Lucas, Bud to Ruth Lucas, 20 October 1942, DCL Collection, L.F.P.

[7]Lucas, Ruth to Bud Lucas, 22 October 1942, DCL Collection, L.F.P.

[8]Smith to Bud Lucas, 28 October 1942, DCL Collection, L.F.P.

Chapter 4. A soldier is the lad for me

[1] Lucas, Mary Jo to Bud Lucas, 7 December 1942, DCL Collection, L.F.P.
[2] Lucas, Mary Jo to Bud Lucas, 14 October 1943, DCL Collection, L.F.P.
[3] Lucas, Mary Jo to Bud Lucas, 30 September 1943, DCL Collection, L.F.P.
[4] Lucas, Mary Jo to Bud Lucas, 18 November 1943, DCL Collection, L.F.P.
[5] Lucas, Mary Jo to Bud Lucas, 14 October 1943, DCL Collection, L.F.P.
[6] Smith to Bud Lucas, 23 April 1944, DCL Collection, L.F.P.
[7] Lucas, Mary Jo to Bud Lucas, 11 March 1944, DCL Collection, L.F.P.
[8] Lucas, Ruth to Bud Lucas, 31 May 1944, DCL Collection, L.F.P.
[9] Lucas, Mary Jo to Bud Lucas, 22 June 1944, DCL Collection, L.F.P.
[10] Lucas, Ruth to Bud Lucas, 25 August 1944, DCL Collection, L.F.P.
[11] Lucas, Mary Jo to Bud Lucas, 21 September 1944, DCL Collection, L.F.P.
[12] Lucas, Mary Jo to Bud Lucas, 22 December 1943, DCL Collection, L.F.P.
[13] Lucas, Mary Jo to Bud Lucas, 21 September 1944, DCL Collection, L.F.P.
[14] Lucas, Mary Jo to Bud Lucas, 29 November 1944, DCL Collection, L.F.P.
[15] Lucas, Ruth to Bud Lucas, 12 December 1945, DCL Collection, L.F.P.
[16] Lucas, Mary Jo to Bud Lucas, 31 October 1945, DCL Collection, L.F.P.
[17] Lucas, Mary Jo to Bud Lucas, 28 May 1945, DCL Collection, L.F.P.
[18] Lucas, Bud to Mary Jo Lucas, 19 November 1945, DCL Collection, L.F.P.
[19] Lucas, Mary Jo to Bud Lucas, 28 May 1945, DCL Collection, L.F.P.

Chapter 5. Choose now while you can

[1] "Hitler sent German U-boat carrying secret agents to terrorise New York during World War Two (but it got wedged off Long Island)", *Daily Mail*, 5 April 2011
[2] Lucas, Ruth to Bud Lucas, 17 October 1944, DCL Collection, L.F.P.
[3] Lucas, Ruth to Bud Lucas, 19 June 1945, DCL Collection, L.F.P.
[4] Lucas, Bud to Ruth Lucas, 27 October 1943, DCL Collection, L.F.P.
[5] Lucas, Bud to Ruth Lucas, 27 November 1944, DCL Collection, L.F.P.
[6] Lucas, David to Bud Lucas, 9 October 1945, DCL Collection, L.F.P.
[7] Lucas, Bud to Ruth Lucas, 17 October 1966, DCL Collection, L.F.P.
[8] Lucas, Bud to Ruth Lucas, 19 September 1943, DCL Collection, L.F.P.
[9] Lucas, Bud to Ruth Lucas, 2 November 1943, DCL Collection, L.F.P.
[10] *See* War Department Pamphlet No. 21-1 "When You Are Overseas"
[11] Harrison, G. A. (1951). *Cross-Channel Attack* (PDF) at 119 et seq. United States Army in World War II: The European Theater of Operations. Washington, DC: Office of the Chief of Military History, Department of the Army. OCLC 606012173.
[12] Lucas, Bud to Ruth Lucas, 17 November 1943, DCL Collection, L.F.P.
[13] Lucas, Bud to Ruth Lucas, 28 May 1945, DCL Collection, L.F.P.
[14] Lucas, Mary Jo to Bud Lucas, 5 April 1944, DCL Collection, L.F.P.
[15] Paul Fussell, *Wartime* (New York: Oxford University Press 1989), 78
[16] Lucas, David to Bud Lucas, 8 October 1943, DCL Collection, L.F.P.
[17] Lucas, David to Bud Lucas, 1 November 1943, DCL Collection, L.F.P.

[18]Lucas, David to Bud Lucas, 13 November 1943, DCL Collection, L.F.P.
[19]Lucas, David to Bud Lucas, 15 February 1944, DCL Collection, L.F.P.
[20]Lucas, Ruth to Bud Lucas, 23 March 1943, DCL Collection, L.F.P.
[21]Lucas, David to Bud Lucas, 15 February 1944, DCL Collection, L.F.P.
[22]Lucas, Mary Jo to Bud Lucas, 14 October 1943, DCL Collection, L.F.P.
[23]Lucas, David to Bud Lucas, 28 March 1944, DCL Collection, L.F.P.
[24]Lucas, Ruth to Bud Lucas, 27 February 1944, DCL Collection, L.F.P.
[25]Lucas, Ruth to Bud Lucas, 27 August 1945, DCL Collection, L.F.P.

Chapter 6. Tales of the stormy sea

[1]*See* Nigel Lewis, *Exercise Tiger: The Dramatic True Story of a Hidden Tragedy of World War II* (New York: Prentice-Hall Press, 1990). For a fuller understanding of the Allies' strategic use of deception generally and its role in Tiger, see Nigel Lewis, *The Cover Plan Conspiracy: The British and Exercise Tiger, 1944* (Kindle e-book, 2017)
[2]Lewis, 1990, at 43
[3]Lewis, 2017, Ch. 23
[4]Lewis, 1990, at 253
[5]Lucas, Ruth to Bud Lucas, 22 June 1944, DCL Collection, L.F.P.
[6]Roderick L. Lucas, *A Valley and Its People*, (self-pub, c. 1973), 15-17
[7]Lucas at 18
[8]J. Ekrable, "Matthews Lad Piloted Boat For Invasion", *Charlotte News*, 22 June 1944
[9]"Cornbread Spells Utopia for This Coast Guardsman, Charles DeForest Lucas is Getting It After Close Calls Off Normandy Coast During Invasion", *Charlotte Observer*, 30 September 1944
[10]Lucas, Bud to Ruth Lucas, 27 November 1944, DCL Collection, L.F.P.
[11]Lucas, Bud to Don Dunne, 1 March 1944, DCL Collection, L.F.P.
[12]Lucas, Ruth to Bud Lucas, 22 June 1944, DCL Collection, L.F.P.
[13]Lucas, Ruth to Bud Lucas, 18 July 1944, DCL Collection, L.F.P.
[14]Lucas, Ruth to Bud Lucas, 19 September 1944, DCL Collection, L.F.P.
[15]Rosenbaum to Bud Lucas, 16 September 1944, DCL Collection, L.F.P.
[16]Lucas, Ruth to Bud Lucas, 7 November 1944, DCL Collection, L.F.P.
[17]"Foreign News: Five Crises", *Time*, 11 December 1944
[18]Lucas, Ruth to Bud Lucas, 13 December 1944, DCL Collection, L.F.P.
[19]Lucas, Bud to Ruth Lucas, 19 December 1944, DCL Collection, L.F.P.
[20]Lucas, Bud to Ruth Lucas, 19 December 1944, DCL Collection, L.F.P.
[21]See "International: Democracy", *Time*, 18 December 1944
[22]Lucas, Ruth to Bud Lucas, 2 January 1945, DCL Collection, L.F.P.
[23]Lucas, Bud to Ruth Lucas, 18 January 1944, DCL Collection, L.F.P.
[24]Lucas, Bud to Ruth Lucas, 12 December 1944, DCL Collection, L.F.P.
[25]Sullivan to Bud Lucas, 4 December 1944, DCL Collection, L.F.P.
[26]Lucas, Bud to Ruth Lucas, 22 December 1944, DCL Collection, L.F.P.
[27]Lucas, Bud to Ruth Lucas, 27 December 1944, DCL Collection, L.F.P.

[28] "LCVP Plan" by Fred the Oyster licensed under the CC BY-SA 4.0 license
[29] Lucas, Bud to Ruth Lucas, 16 December 1944, DCL Collection, L.F.P.
[30] "Coast Guard School Opens", *Wyandotte News Herald*, 19 April 1945
[31] Lucas, Bud to Ruth Lucas, 30 November 1944, DCL Collection, L.F.P.

Chapter 7. We bawled church anthems in choro

[1] Lucas, Bud to Ruth Lucas, 1 January 1945, DCL Collection, L.F.P.
[2] Lucas, Bud to Ruth Lucas, 5 January 1945, DCL Collection, L.F.P.
[3] Lucas, Bud to Ruth Lucas, 6 January 1945, DCL Collection, L.F.P.
[4] Lucas, Bud to Ruth Lucas, 7 January 1945, DCL Collection, L.F.P.
[5] Lucas, Bud to Ruth Lucas, 7 January 1945, DCL Collection, L.F.P.
[6] Lucas, Bud to Ruth Lucas, 16 January 1945, DCL Collection, L.F.P.
[7] Lucas, Bud to Ruth Lucas, 7 December 1944, DCL Collection, L.F.P.
[8] Lucas, Ruth to Bud Lucas, 18 January 1945, DCL Collection, L.F.P.
[9] Lucas, Ruth to Bud Lucas, 17 December 1944, DCL Collection, L.F.P.
[10] Lucas, Bud to Ruth Lucas, 25 May 1945, DCL Collection, L.F.P.
[11] Lucas, Ruth to Bud Lucas, 4 June 1945, DCL Collection, L.F.P.
[12] Lucas, Ruth to Bud Lucas, 24 January 1945, DCL Collection, L.F.P.
[13] Lucas, Bud to Ruth Lucas, 24 January 1945, DCL Collection, L.F.P.
[14] Lucas, David to Bud Lucas, 31 January 1945, DCL Collection, L.F.P.
[15] Lucas, David to Bud Lucas, 31 January 1945, DCL Collection, L.F.P.
[16] Lucas, Bud to David Lucas, 12 February 1945, DCL Collection, L.F.P.
[17] Carsten Fries, "Battle of Iwo Jima 19 February-26 March 1945", Historical Summary, *Naval History and Heritage Command*, February 2020
[18] H. C. Hewson, Confidential Journal, Vol 14, 22 November 1954
[19] Fussell at 153
[20] Lucas, Bud to Ruth Lucas, 16 July 1945, DCL Collection, L.F.P.
[21] Lucas, Bud to Ruth Lucas, 10 March 1945, DCL Collection, L.F.P.
[22] Lucas, David to Bud Lucas, 22 March 1945, DCL Collection, L.F.P.
[23] Raymond A. Mann, "Bayfield", Ship History, *Naval History and Heritage Command*, 28 February 2006
[24] Lucas, Ruth to Bud Lucas, 15 February 1945, DCL Collection, L.F.P.
[25] Lucas, Ruth to Bud Lucas, 26 February 1945, DCL Collection, L.F.P.
[26] Lucas, Bud to Ruth Lucas, 19 February 1945, DCL Collection, L.F.P.
[27] Lucas, Ruth to Bud Lucas, 14 March 1945, DCL Collection, L.F.P.
[28] Lucas, Ruth to Bud Lucas, 30 March 1945, DCL Collection, L.F.P.
[29] Lucas, Bud to Ruth Lucas, 3 May 1945, DCL Collection, L.F.P.
[30] Lucas, David to Bud Lucas, 18 April 1945, DCL Collection, L.F.P..
[31] Lucas, David to Bud Lucas, 10 December 1944, DCL Collection, L.F.P.
[32] *See* "The Congress: 'I think we are cowardly'", *Time*, 19 March 1945
[33] Lucas, Bud to David Lucas, 22 April 1945, DCL Collection, L.F.P.
[34] Lucas, Bud to Ruth Lucas, 17 March 1945, DCL Collection, L.F.P.
[35] Lucas, Bud to Ruth Lucas, 19 August 1945, DCL Collection, L.F.P.
[36] Lucas, Bud to Ruth Lucas, 20 March 1945, DCL Collection, L.F.P.

[37] "A Matter of Opinion", *Time*, 16 April 1945 at 32
[38] Lucas, Ruth to Bud Lucas, 8 May 1945, DCL Collection, L.F.P.
[39] Lucas, Ruth to Bud Lucas, 8 May 1945, DCL Collection, L.F.P.
[40] Lucas, Ruth to Bud Lucas, 27 May 1945, DCL Collection, L.F.P.
[41] Lucas, Ruth to Bud Lucas, 22 February 1944, DCL Collection, L.F.P.
[42] Lucas, Bud to Ruth Lucas, 15 February 1945, DCL Collection, L.F.P.
[43] Lucas, Ruth to Bud Lucas, 11 March 1945, DCL Collection, L.F.P.
[44] Lucas, Bud to Ruth Lucas, 16 December 1945, DCL Collection, L.F.P.
[45] Lucas, Bud to Ruth Lucas, 27 May 1945, DCL Collection, L.F.P.
[46] Lucas, Ruth to Bud Lucas, 30 April 1945, DCL Collection, L.F.P.
[47] *See* "Foreign News", *Time*, 30 April 1945
[48] Lucas, Bud to Ruth Lucas, 10 May 1945, DCL Collection, L.F.P.
[49] Lucas, Bud to Ruth Lucas, 4 March 1945, DCL Collection, L.F.P.
[50] Lucas, Ruth to Bud Lucas, 19 September 1944, DCL Collection, L.F.P.
[51] Lucas, Bud to David Lucas, 28 May 1945, DCL Collection, L.F.P.
[52] Lucas, Bud to David Lucas, 16 May 1945, DCL Collection, L.F.P.
[53] Lucas, Bud to David Lucas, 18 May 1945, DCL Collection, L.F.P.
[54] Lucas, Bud to Ruth Lucas, 12 May 1945, DCL Collection, L.F.P.
[55] Lucas, Bud to Ruth Lucas, 12 May 1945, DCL Collection, L.F.P.
[56] Lucas, Bud to Ruth Lucas, 18 May 1945, DCL Collection, L.F.P.
[57] Lucas, Bud to Ruth Lucas, 25 May 1945, DCL Collection, L.F.P.
[58] Lucas, Ruth to Bud Lucas, 27 May 1945, DCL Collection, L.F.P.
[59] Lucas, Bud to Ruth Lucas, 1 June 1945, DCL Collection, L.F.P.
[60] Mann, n.23
[61] Lucas, Bud to Ruth Lucas, 4 June 1945, DCL Collection, L.F.P.
[62] R. Mulford, "Meet the Old-Timers: Osmond Barringer Had Many 'Firsts'", *Charlotte Observer*, 30 September 1951
[63] Lucas, David to Bud Lucas, 7 June 1945, DCL Collection, L.F.P.
[64] Lucas, David to Bud Lucas, 7 June 1945, DCL Collection, L.F.P.
[65] Lucas, Bud to David Lucas, 16 May 1945, DCL Collection, L.F.P.
[66] Lucas, Ruth to Bud Lucas, 17 February 1946, DCL Collection, L.F.P.
[67] Lucas, Bud to Ruth Lucas, 1 June 1945, DCL Collection, L.F.P.
[68] Lucas, Ruth to Bud Lucas, 5 June 1945, DCL Collection, L.F.P.
[69] Lucas, Ruth to Bud Lucas, 17 February 1946, DCL Collection, L.F.P.
[70] Lucas, David to Bud Lucas, 7 June 1945, DCL Collection, L.F.P.
[71] Lucas, Bud to Ruth Lucas, 21 June 1945, DCL Collection, L.F.P.
[72] Lucas, Bud to Ruth Lucas, 1 July 1945, DCL Collection, L.F.P.
[73] Lucas, Bud to Ruth Lucas, 1 July 1945, DCL Collection, L.F.P.
[74] Lucas, Bud to Ruth Lucas, 8 July 1945, DCL Collection, L.F.P.
[75] Lucas, Bud to Ruth Lucas, 8 July 1945, DCL Collection, L.F.P.
[76] Lucas, Bud to Ruth Lucas, 11 July 1945, DCL Collection, L.F.P.
[77] Lucas, Bud to Ruth Lucas, 16 July 1945, DCL Collection, L.F.P.
[78] Lucas, Bud to David Lucas, 30 August 1945, DCL Collection, L.F.P.
[79] Lucas, Bud to David Lucas, 30 August 1945, DCL Collection, L.F.P.
[80] Mckay to Bud Lucas, 4 September 1945, DCL Collection, L.F.P.

⁸¹Lucas, Bud to David Lucas, 6 September 1945, DCL Collection, L.F.P.
⁸²Lucas, Bud to David Lucas, 30 August 1945, DCL Collection L.F.P.
⁸³Lucas, Bud to Ruth Lucas, 1 September 1945, DCL Collection, L.F.P.

Chapter 8. Rush to the fireside

¹Collin Makamson, "'Home Alive By '45': Operation Magic Carpet", *NationalWW2Museum.org*, website of the The National WWII Museum, New Orleans
²Lucas, Bud to Ruth Lucas, 4 September 1945, DCL Collection, L.F.P.
³Lucas, Bud to Ruth Lucas, 11 September 1945, DCL Collection, L.F.P.
⁴Lucas, Bud to Ruth Lucas, 6 September 1945, DCL Collection, L.F.P.
⁵Lucas, Bud to Ruth Lucas, 27 August 1945, DCL Collection, L.F.P.
⁶Lucas, Bud to Ruth Lucas, 10 September 1945, DCL Collection, L.F.P.
⁷Lucas, Bud to David Lucas, 6 September 1945, DCL Collection, L.F.P.
⁸Lucas, David to Bud Lucas, 24 October 1945, DCL Collection, L.F.P.
⁹Lucas, David to Bud Lucas, 13 November 1945, DCL Collection, L.F.P.
¹⁰Lucas, Bud to Ruth Lucas, 10 December 1945, DCL Collection, L.F.P.
¹¹"A True Pioneer", *Charlotte Observer*, 10 March 1968
¹²*See* Ronnie W. Faulkner, "Fusion Politics", *NorthCarolinahistory.org: An Online Encyclopedia*, North Carolina History Project, accessed 23 July 2022 and John V. Orth and Paul Martin Newby, *The Oxford Commentary on the North Carolina State Constitution*, (New York, NY: Oxford University Press, 2012)
¹³"Mecklenburg County Is Ready", *Charlotte Observer*, 1 August 1900, at 5
¹⁴Hanchett, Ch. 5
¹⁵*See* Albion W. Tourgée, *A Fool's Errand, By One of the Fools*, (Cambridge, Mass.: Belknap Press, 1961)(written 1879)
¹⁶McElvain to Bud Lucas, 8 October 1945, DCL Collection, L.F.P.
¹⁷Lucas, David to Bud Lucas, 18 February 1946, DCL Collection, L.F.P.
¹⁸Lucas, Bud to David Lucas, 26 February 1946, DCL Collection, L.F.P.
¹⁹Lucas, Bud to Ruth Lucas, 12 October 1945, DCL Collection, L.F.P.
²⁰Van Wyck Brooks, *The Opinions of Oliver Allston* (New York: E.P. Dutton & Co., Inc., 1941), 62
²¹Brooks at 82
²²Brooks at 16
²³Brooks at 136
²⁴Brooks at 128
²⁵Brooks at 129
²⁶Lucas, Bud to Ruth Lucas, 23 September 1945, DCL Collection, L.F.P.
²⁷Lucas, Bud to Ruth Lucas, 25 September 1945, DCL Collection, L.F.P.
²⁸Dunne to Ruth Lucas, 23 January 1945, CDH Collection, L.F.P.
²⁹Dunne to Ruth Lucas, 5 July 1945, CDH Collection, L.F.P.
³⁰Lucas, Ruth to Don Dunne, 25 August 1945, DCL Collection, L.F.P.

[31] Lucas, Ruth, to Bud Lucas, 12 October 1945, DCL Collection, L.F.P.
[32] Lucas, David to Bud Lucas, 9 October 1945, DCL Collection, L.F.P.
[33] Lucas, David to Bud Lucas, 19 October 1945, DCL Collection, L.F.P.
[34] Lucas, Bud to Ruth Lucas, 17 October 1945, DCL Collection, L.F.P.
[35] Lucas, Bud to Ruth Lucas, 17 October 1945, DCL Collection, L.F.P.
[36] Lucas, Bud to Ruth Lucas, 18 October 1945, DCL Collection, L.F.P.
[37] *See* "Address Before a Joint Session of the Congress on Universal Military Training" The American Presidency Project, *www.presidency.ucsb.edu*, 23 October 1945
[38] Lucas, Bud to David Lucas, 27 October 1945, DCL Collection, L.F.P.
[39] Lucas, Ruth to Bud Lucas, 29 October 1945, DCL Collection, L.F.P.
[40] Lucas, Bud to Ruth Lucas, 23 October 1945, DCL Collection, L.F.P.
[41] Lucas, Mary Jo to Bud Lucas, 31 October 1945, DCL Collection, L.F.P.
[42] McKay to Bud Lucas, 2 November 1945, DCL Collection, L.F.P.
[43] McKay to Bud Lucas, 27 October 1945, DCL Collection, L.F.P.
[44] McKay to Bud Lucas, 8 November 1945, DCL Collection, L.F.P.
[45] McKay to Bud Lucas, 13 December 1945, DCL Collection, L.F.P.
[46] *See* Cody Melcher and Michael Goldfield, "The Failure of Labor Unionism in the US South", *Oxford Research Encyclopedia of American History*, published online 22 November 2019 at OxfordRE.com/American History
[47] *See* Jacquelyn Dowd Hall *et al, Like a Family*, (Chapel Hill: University of North Carolina Press, 2012)
[48] "Mills Are Closed By Strike Pickets", *Charlotte Observer*, 4 September 1934
[49] Hall at 326
[50] "Shelby Excited as Zero Hour Draws Near", *Charlotte Observer*, 1 September 1934
[51] "Charlotte to Be Headquarters for N.C. Strikes", *Charlotte Observer*, 3 September 1934
[52] "Mills Are Closed By Strike Pickets", *Charlotte Observer*, 4 September 1934
[53] "Shelby Squads Busy", *Charlotte Observer*, 8 September 1934
[54] "Flying Squadrons Force More Mill Closings", *Charlotte Observer*, 6 September 1934
[55] "Textile Peace Plan Rejected", *Charlotte Observer*, 11 September 1934
[56] Lucas, Bud to Ruth Lucas, 5 November 1945, DCL Collection, L.F.P.
[57] Lucas, Bud to David Lucas, 13 November 1945, DCL Collection, L.F.P.
[58] Lucas, David to Bud Lucas, 13 November 1945, DCL Collection, L.F.P.
[59] Lucas, Bud to David Lucas, 23 November 1945, DCL Collection, L.F.P.
[60] Lucas, Bud to David Lucas, 23 October 1945, DCL Collection, L.F.P.
[61] Lucas, Bud to Ruth Lucas, 19 November 1945, DCL Collection, L.F.P.
[62] "Typhoon's Rage Told By Two Survivors", *Charlotte Observer*, 22 October 1945
[63] Lucas, Ruth to Bud Lucas, 21 November 1945, DCL Collection, L.F.P.
[64] Lucas, Bud to Ruth Lucas, 22 November 1945, DCL Collection, L.F.P.

⁶⁵Lucas, Bud to Ruth Lucas, 23 November 1945, DCL Collection, L.F.P.
⁶⁶Lucas, Bud to Ruth Lucas, 30 October 1945, DCL Collection, L.F.P.
⁶⁷Lucas, Bud to Ruth Lucas, 23 November 1945, DCL Collection, L.F.P., note verse XXIII of the *Rubáiyát* of Omar Khayyam, translated by Edward FitzGerald: Ah, make the most of what we yet may spend,/Before we too into the Dust Descend;/Dust into Dust, and under Dust, to lie,/Sans Wine, sans Song, sans Singer and...sans End!
⁶⁸Lucas, Bud to Ruth Lucas, 22 November 1945, DCL Collection, L.F.P.
⁶⁹Lucas, Bud to Ruth Lucas, 8 December 1945, DCL Collection, L.F.P.
⁷⁰Lucas, Bud to Ruth Lucas, 8 December 1945, DCL Collection, L.F.P.
⁷¹Lucas, Bud to Ruth Lucas, 8 December 1945, DCL Collection, L.F.P.
⁷²Lucas, Ruth to Bud Lucas, 12 December 1945, DCL Collection, L.F.P.
⁷³Lucas, Ruth to Bud Lucas, 12 December 1945, DCL Collection, L.F.P.
⁷⁴Lucas, Bud to Ruth Lucas, 10 December 1945, DCL Collection, L.F.P.
⁷⁵*See* Sam Perkins, "Why WWII Soldiers Mutinied After V-J Day", *www.history.com*, accessed 13 August 2020
⁷⁶Lucas, Bud to Ruth Lucas, 24 December 1945, DCL Collection, L.F.P.
⁷⁷Lucas, Ruth to Bud Lucas, 12 December 1945, DCL Collection, L.F.P.
⁷⁸Lucas, Martin to Bud Lucas, 10 December 1945, DCL Collection, L.F.P.
⁷⁹Lucas, Ruth to Bud Lucas, 12 December 1945, DCL Collection, L.F.P.
⁸⁰Lucas, Susannah to Bud Lucas, 11 December 1945, DCL Collection, L.F.P.
⁸¹Lucas, Ruth to Bud Lucas, 9 November 1945, DCL Collection, L.F.P.
⁸²Lucas, Mary Jo to Bud Lucas, 19 February 1946, DCL Collection, L.F.P.
⁸³Lucas, Ruth to David Lucas, 22 December 1945, DCL Collection, L.F.P.
⁸⁴Lucas, David to Bud Lucas, 24 December 1945, DCL Collection, L.F.P.
⁸⁵Lucas, Martin to Bud Lucas, 15 December 1945, DCL Collection, L.F.P.
⁸⁶Lucas, Ruth to Bud Lucas, 17 December 1945, DCL Collection, L.F.P.
⁸⁷Lucas, Ruth to Bud Lucas, 27 December 1945, DCL Collection, L.F.P.
⁸⁸Lucas, Ruth to Bud Lucas, 30 December 1945, DCL Collection, L.F.P.
⁸⁹John Dos Passos, *The Big Money: Volume 3 of the U.S.A. Trilogy*, (Boston, New York: Houghton Mifflin, 1936) Kindle e-book, 79
⁹⁰Lucas, Bud to David Lucas, 3 January 1946, DCL Collection, L.F.P.. Of the importance of being able to spell Veblen wrote: "As felicitous an instance of futile classicism as can well be found, outside of the Far East, is the conventional spelling of the English language. A breach of the proprieties in spelling is extremely annoying and will discredit any writer in the eyes of all persons who are possessed of a developed sense of the true and beautiful. English orthography satisfies all the requirements of the canons of reputability under the law of conspicuous waste. It is archaic, cumbrous, and ineffective; its acquisition consumes much time and effort, failure to acquire it is easy of detection. Therefore it is the first and readiest test of reputability in learning, and conformity to its ritual is indispensable to a blameless scholastic life." Veblen, Kindle e-book, Loc 4962
⁹¹Lucas, Bud to David Lucas, 16 January 1946, DCL Collection, L.F.P.

[92] Lucas, David to Bud Lucas, 18 January 1946, DCL Collection, L.F.P.
[93] Lucas, David to Bud Lucas, 18 January 1946, DCL Collection, L.F.P.
[94] Lucas, Ruth to David Lucas, 21 February 1946, DCL Collection, L.F.P.
[95] Lucas, Bud to Ruth Lucas, 20 January 1946, DCL Collection, L.F.P.
[96] Lucas, Ruth to Bud Lucas, 7 January 1946, DCL Collection, L.F.P.
[97] Lucas, Ruth to David Lucas, 22 January 1946, DCL Collection, L.F.P.
[98] Lucas, Ruth to Bud Lucas, 13 January 1946, DCL Collection, L.F.P.
[99] Lucas, Bud to Ruth Lucas, 8 Feburary 1946, DCL Collection, L.F.P.
[100] Lucas, Ruth to Bud Lucas, 13 Feburary 1946, DCL Collection, L.F.P.
[101] Lucas, Bud to Ruth Lucas, 14 February 1946, DCL Collection, L.F.P.
[102] Lucas, Bud to Ruth Lucas, 14 February 1946, DCL Collection, L.F.P.
[103] Lucas, Bud to Ruth Lucas, 18 February 1946, DCL Collection, L.F.P.
[104] Lucas, Bud to Ruth Lucas, 28 February 1946, DCL Collection, L.F.P.
[105] Lucas, Bud to Ruth Lucas, 28 February 1946, DCL Collection, L.F.P.

Chapter 9. Come you home a hero

[1] Sullivan to Bud Lucas, 13 March 1946, DCL Collection, L.F.P.
[2] Lucas, Bud to David Lucas, 30 June 1946, DCL Collection, L.F.P.
[3] Lucas, Bud to David Lucas, 14 March 1946, DCL Collection, L.F.P.
[4] Lucas, Ruth to Bud Lucas, 11 June 1945, DCL Collection, L.F.P.
[5] Lucas, Ruth to Bud Lucas, 15 April 1944, DCL Collection, L.F.P.
[6] Lucas, Ruth to Bud Lucas, 18 June 1945, DCL Collection, L.F.P.
[7] Lucas, Mary Jo to Bud Lucas, 11 June 1945, DCL Collection, L.F.P.
[8] Lucas, Ruth to Bud Lucas, 19 June 1945, DCL Collection, L.F.P.
[9] Lucas, Ruth to Bud Lucas, 13 June 1945, DCL Collection, L.F.P.
[10] Lucas, Ruth to Bud Lucas, 29 March 1946, DCL Collection, L.F.P.
[11] Dunne to Ruth Lucas, 4 May 1946, CDH Collection, L.F.P.
[12] Lucas, Bud to Ruth Lucas, 2 April 1946, DCL Collection, L.F.P.
[13] Lucas, Bud to Ruth Lucas, 9 June 1946, DCL Collection, L.F.P.
[14] Lucas, Bud to David Lucas, 8 April 1946, DCL Collection, L.F.P.
[15] Lucas, David to "Misty", 29 March 2000, DCL Collection, Other Documents, L.F.P.
[16] Lucas, David to Bud Lucas, 18 April 1945, DCL Collection, L.F.P.
[17] Lucas, Bud to Ruth Lucas, 8 January 1971, DCL Collection, L.F.P.
[18] Lucas, Bud to Ruth Lucas, 24 April 1945, DCL Collection, L.F.P.
[19] David Halberstam, *The Fifties*, (New York: Villard/Random House, 1993), 133
[20] Halberstam at 132
[21] Dunne to Ruth Lucas, 1 October 1946, DCL Collection, L.F.P.
[22] Dunne to Ruth Lucas, 11 October 1946, CDH Collection, L.F.P.
[23] Dunne to Ruth Lucas, 16 October 1946, CDH Collection, L.F.P.
[24] Dunne to Ruth Lucas, 10 December 1946, CDH Collection, L.F.P.
[25] Lucas, Bud to Ruth Lucas, 5 November 1946, DCL Collection, L.F.P.
[26] Dunne to Ruth Lucas, 1 October 1946, DCL Collection, L.F.P.

[27] Dunne to Ruth Lucas, 11 October 1946, CDH Collection, L.F.P.
[28] Dunne to Ruth Lucas, 29 October 1946, CDH Collection, L.F.P.
[29] Dunne to Ruth Lucas, 16 October 1946, CDH Collection, L.F.P.
[30] Lucas, Mary Jo to Ruth Lucas, enclosed in a letter from Dunne to Ruth Lucas, 10 December 1946, CDH Collection, L.F.P.
[31] Dunne to Ruth Lucas, 11 January 1947, CDH Collection, L.F.P.
[32] Dunne to Ruth Lucas, 4 February 1947, DCL Collection, L.F.P.
[33] Dunne to Ruth Lucas, 17 November 1946, CDH Collection, L.F.P.
[34] Dunne to Ruth Lucas, 11 January 1947, CDH Collection, L.F.P.
[35] Dunne to Ruth Lucas, 18 March 1947, CDH Collection, L.F.P.
[36] Dunne to Ruth Lucas, 23 March 1947, CDH Collection, L.F.P.
[37] Lucas, Bud to Ruth Lucas, 29 March 1947, DCL Collection, L.F.P.
[38] Dunne to Ruth Lucas, 13 April 1947, CDH Collection, L.F.P.
[39] Lucas, David to Ruth Lucas, 23 March 1947, DCL Collection, L.F.P.
[40] Lucas, David to Ruth Lucas, 21 February 1947, DCL Collection, L.F.P.
[41] Dunne to Ruth Lucas, 24 February 1947, CDH Collection, L.F.P.
[42] Dunne to Ruth Lucas, 18 March 1947, CDH Collection, L.F.P.
[43] Dunne to Ruth Lucas, 29 October 1946, CDH Collection, L.F.P.
[44] Dunne to Ruth Lucas, 24 February 1947, CDH Collection, L.F.P.
[45] Dunne to Ruth Lucas, 29 October 1946, CDH Collection, L.F.P.
[46] Lucas, Bud to Ruth Lucas, 29 March 1947, DCL Collection, L.F.P.
[47] Lucas, Bud to Ruth Lucas, 3 May 1947, DCL Collection, L.F.P.
[48] Lucas, Bud to Ruth Lucas, 3 May 1947, DCL Collection, L.F.P.
[49] Dunne to Ruth Lucas, 4 May 1947, CDH Collection, L.F.P.
[50] Dunne to Ruth Lucas, 24 September 1947, CDH Collection, L.F.P.
[51] Lucas, Bud to Ruth Lucas, 16 February 1948, DCL Collection, L.F.P.
[52] Lucas, Bud to Ruth Lucas, 7 February 1948, DCL Collection, L.F.P.
[53] Lucas, Bud to Ruth Lucas, 25 October 1948, DCL Collection, L.F.P.
[54] Lucas, Bud to Ruth Lucas, 20 February 1948, DCL Collection, L.F.P.
[55] Lucas, Bud to Ruth Lucas, 1 December 1948, DCL Collection, L.F.P.
[56] Lucas, Bud to Ruth Lucas, 10 November 1947, DCL Collection, L.F.P.
[57] Lucas, Bud to Ruth Lucas, 27 February 1948, DCL Collection, L.F.P.
[58] Lucas, Bud to Ruth Lucas, 27 February 1948, DCL Collection, L.F.P.
[59] Lucas, Bud to Ruth Lucas, 22 September 1948, DCL Collection, L.F.P.
[60] Lucas, Bud to Ruth Lucas, 23 April 1948, DCL Collection, L.F.P.
[61] Lucas, Bud to Ruth Lucas, 22 September 1948, DCL Collection, L.F.P.
[62] Lucas, Bud to Ruth Lucas, 11 May 1948, DCL Collection, L.F.P.
[63] Lucas, Bud to Ruth Lucas, 22 September 1948, DCL Collection, L.F.P.
[64] Lucas, Bud to Ruth Lucas, 26 February 1949, DCL Collection, L.F.P.
[65] Lucas, Bud to Ruth Lucas, 4 October 1948, DCL Collection, L.F.P.
[66] Lucas, Bud to Ruth Lucas, 4 October 1948, DCL Collection, L.F.P.
[67] Dunne to Ruth Lucas, 15 December 1948, CDH Collection, L.F.P.
[68] Lucas, Bud to Ruth Lucas, 2 February 1949, DCL Collection, L.F.P.
[69] Lucas, Bud to Ruth Lucas, 26 February 1949, DCL Collection, L.F.P.
[70] Previously, sessions were held in the fall, at the end of the first semester.

[71]Lucas, Bud to Ruth Lucas, 5 May 1949, DCL Collection, L.F.P.
[72]"University Administration's Views On Student Assembly In Raleigh Presented By Dr. Graham", *Greensboro Daily News*, 9 December 1945
[73]"University Delegates Resent Poor Coverage Of Student Legislature", *Greensboro Daily News*, 10 December 1945
[74]"Racial Issue Figures Prominently in Action Canceling Annual Student Legislature Meet", *Greensboro Daily News*, 11 November 1947
[75]Lucas, Bud to Ruth Lucas, 10 May 1949, DCL Collection, L.F.P.
[76]"Student Meet Is Concluded, 12th Annual North Carolina Legislative Assembly Ends at Raleigh", *Charlotte Observer*, 16 May 1949
[77]Lucas, Bud to Ruth Lucas, 16 May 1949, DCL Collection, L.F.P.

Chapter 10. May I squire you round the meads

[1]Lucas, Bud to Ruth Lucas, 24 September 1949, DCL Collection, L.F.P.
[2]Lucas, Bud to Ruth Lucas, 10 November 1949, DCL Collection, L.F.P.
[3]Lucas, Bud to Ruth Lucas, 9 December 1949, DCL Collection, L.F.P.
[4]Lucas, Bud to Ruth Lucas, 8 February 1950, DCL Collection, L.F.P.
[5]Lucas, Bud to Ruth Lucas, 27 February 1950, DCL Collection, L.F.P.
[6]Howerton to Ruth Lucas, 21 June 1950, DCL Collection, L.F.P.
[7]Lucas, Bud to Ruth Lucas, 29 June 1950, DCL Collection, L.F.P.
[8]Lucas, Bud to Ruth Lucas, 10 July 1950, DCL Collection, L.F.P.
[9]Dunne to Bud Lucas, 11 July 1950, CDH Collection, L.F.P.
[10]Lucas, Bud to Ruth Lucas, 16 July 1950, DCL Collection, L.F.P.
[11]Lucas, Bud to Ruth Lucas, 22 July 1950, DCL Collection, L.F.P.
[12]Lucas, Ruth to Don Dunne, 3 August 1950, DCL Collection, L.F.P.
[13]Lucas, Bud to Ruth Lucas, 6 August 1950, DCL Collection, L.F.P.
[14]Lucas, Bud to Ruth Lucas, 8 August 1950, DCL Collection, L.F.P.
[15]Lucas, Bud to Ruth Lucas, 9 August 1950, DCL Collection, L.F.P.
[16]Dunne to Ruth Lucas, 19 August 1950, CDH Collection, L.F.P.
[17]Dunne to Ruth Lucas, 2 May 1950, CDH Collection, L.F.P.
[18]Dunne to Ruth Lucas, 25 September 1950, CDH Collection, L.F.P.
[19]Romano, to Ruth Lucas, 30 April 1951, CDH Collection, L.F.P.
[20]Dunne to Ruth Lucas, 28 October 1951, CDH Collection, L.F.P.
[21]Dunne to Ruth Lucas, 7 April 1952, CDH Collection, L.F.P.
[22]Lucas, Frances to Ruth Lucas, 9 January 1951, DCL Collection, L.F.P.
[23]Lucas, Bud to Ruth Lucas, 9 August 1951, DCL Collection, L.F.P.
[24]Denny to Bud Lucas, 1 June 1945, DCL Collection, L.F.P.
[25]Lucas, Bud to Ruth Lucas, 15 December 1950, DCL Collection, L.F.P.
[26]Lucas, Bud to Ruth Lucas, 15 December 1950, DCL Collection, L.F.P.
[27]Lucas, Frances to Ruth Lucas, 12 March 1951, DCL Collection, L.F.P.
[28]Lucas, David to "Misty", 29 March 2000, DCL Collection, Other Documents, L.F.P.
[29]Lucas, Frances to Ruth Lucas, 12 March 1951, DCL Collection, L.F.P.
[30]Lucas, Bud to Ruth Lucas, 9 January 1951, DCL Collection, L.F.P.

[31] Lucas, Bud to Ruth Lucas, 22 April 1951, DCL Collection, L.F.P.
[32] Clemson University, "The Bobbin and Beaker Vol. 5 No. 1", (1947) *Bobbin and Beaker*, 148
[33] Lucas, Bud to Ruth Lucas, 7 July 1951, DCL Collection, L.F.P.
[34] Lucas, Frances to Ruth Lucas, 14 July 1951, DCL Collection, L.F.P.
[35] Lucas, Bud to Ruth Lucas, 7 July 1951, DCL Collection, L.F.P.
[36] Lucas, Frances to Ruth Lucas, 16 August 1951, DCL Collection, L.F.P.
[37] Lucas, Bud to Ruth Lucas, 10 September 1951, DCL Collection, L.F.P.
[38] Lucas, Bud to Ruth Lucas, 9 January 1951, DCL Collection, L.F.P.
[39] A. Kirschenfeld, "They Laughed til it Hurt: A History of Humor Magazines at Duke", *Duke Magazine*, 1 August 2011
[40] Kirschenfeld, n. 39
[41] Lucas, Frances to Ruth Lucas, 20 August 1951, DCL Collection, L.F.P.
[42] Lucas, Frances to Ruth Lucas, 16 August 1951, DCL Collection, L.F.P.

Chapter 11. My love is true and all for you

[1] Halberstam at 588
[2] Lucas, Bud to Ruth Lucas, 5 February 1952, DCL Collection, L.F.P.
[3] Lucas, Bud to Ruth Lucas, 24 September 1951, DCL Collection, L.F.P.
[4] Lucas, Bud to Ruth Lucas, 1 September 1945, DCL Collection, L.F.P.
[5] Lucas, Frances to Ruth Lucas, 30 November 1951, DCL Collection, L.F.P.
[6] Lucas, Bud to Ruth Lucas, 17 February 1952, DCL Collection, L.F.P.
[7] Lucas, Frances to Ruth Lucas, 6 March 1952, DCL Collection, L.F.P.
[8] Lucas, Bud to Ruth Lucas, 15 March 1952, DCL Collection, L.F.P.
[9] Lucas, Bud to Ruth Lucas, 15 March 1952, DCL Collection, L.F.P.
[10] Lucas, Bud to Ruth Lucas, 16 April 1952, DCL Collection, L.F.P.
[11] Lucas, Bud to Ruth Lucas, 16 April 1952, DCL Collection, L.F.P.
[12] Lucas, Bud to Ruth Lucas, 14 May 1953, DCL Collection, L.F.P.
[13] Lucas, David to "Misty", 30 March 2000, DCL Collection, Other Documents, L.F.P.
[14] Lucas, Bud to Ruth Lucas, 24 April 1954, DCL Collection, L.F.P.
[15] Lucas, Bud to Ruth Lucas, 20 April 1955, DCL Collection, L.F.P.
[16] Lucas, Bud to Ruth Lucas, 5 May 1954, DCL Collection, L.F.P.
[17] Lucas, Bud to Ruth Lucas, 22 June 1954, DCL Collection, L.F.P.
[18] Lucas, Bud to Ruth Lucas, 24 April 1954, DCL Collection, L.F.P.
[19] Lucas, Bud to Ruth Lucas, 5 May 1954, DCL Collection, L.F.P.
[20] Lucas, Frances to Ruth Lucas, 20 October 1954, DCL Collection, L.F.P.
[21] Lucas, Frances to Eliza Lucas, 20 October 1969, DCL Collection, L.F.P.
[22] Lucas, Bud to Ruth Lucas, 22 June 1954, DCL Collection, L.F.P.
[23] Lucas, Bud to Ruth Lucas, 22 June 1954, DCL Collection, L.F.P.
[24] Lucas, Frances to Ruth Lucas, 30 January 1955, DCL Collection, L.F.P.
[25] Lucas, Frances to Ruth Lucas, 24 February 1955, DCL Collection, L.F.P.
[26] Lucas, Frances to Ruth Lucas, 30 March 1955, DCL Collection, L.F.P.
[27] Halberstam at 59

[28] Lucas, Frances to Ruth Lucas, 7 May 1955, DCL Collection, L.F.P.
[29] Lucas, Frances to Ruth Lucas, 25 April 1955, DCL Collection, L.F.P.
[30] Lucas, Bud to Ruth Lucas, 20 April 1955, DCL Collection, L.F.P.
[31] Lucas, Frances to Ruth Lucas, 25 April 1955, DCL Collection, L.F.P.
[32] Lucas, Frances to Ruth Lucas, 7 May 1955, DCL Collection, L.F.P.
[33] "Clark is Dropped for Vatican Post", *Charlotte Observer*, 14 January 1952
[34] *Brown v. the Board of Education of Topeka, Kansas*, 347 U.S. 483 (1954)
[35] *Charlotte Park and Recreation Com'n v. Barringer*, 242 N.C. 311, 88 S.E.2d 114 (1955)
[36] Lucas, Frances to Ruth Lucas, 7 March 1956, DCL Collection, L.F.P.
[37] Lucas, Bud to Ruth Lucas, 3 March 1957, DCL Collection, L.F.P.
[38] "History of CMS", *Charlotte Mecklenburg Schools*, https://www.cmsk12.org/Page/1047, accessed 29 May 2022
[39] "Negro Boys Sentenced For Kissing White Girl", *Dallas Morning News*, 24 November 1958
[40] "Three Local Schools Integrated", *Charlotte Observer*, 5 September 1957
[41] Lucas, Bud to Ruth Lucas, 6 June 1959, DCL Collection, L.F.P.
[42] Lucas, Bud to Ruth Lucas, 11 April 1959, DCL Collection, L.F.P.
[43] U.S. Army records show Byars enlisted 29 April 1946 as a private with four years of college and served at Fort Jackson, S.C., reportedly in the Signal Corps
[44] Lucas, Frances to Ruth Lucas, 19 September 1961, DCL Collection, L.F.P.
[45] Lucas, Bud to Ruth Lucas, 6 September 1961, DCL Collection, L.F.P.
[46] Lucas, Bud to Ruth Lucas, 19 September 1961, DCL Collection, L.F.P.
[47] Dunne to Ruth Lucas, 22 August 1962, CDH Collection, L.F.P.
[48] Lucas, Frances to Ruth Lucas, 31 October 1961, DCL Collection, L.F.P.
[49] Lucas, Bud to Ruth Lucas, 1 January 1962, DCL Collection, L.F.P.
[50] Lucas, Bud to Ruth Lucas, 12 February 1962, DCL Collection, L.F.P.
[51] "Bishop Says Political Influence Caused Mollegen's Withdrawal" and "HUAC Files Contain Six Entries On Dr. Mollegen", *News & Courier*, 4 February 1962
[52] *News & Courier*, 15 February 1962
[53] Lucas, Bud to Ruth Lucas, 15 May 1962, DCL Collection, L.F.P.
[54] Lucas, Bud to Ruth Lucas, 3 June 1962, DCL Collection, L.F.P.
[55] Lucas, Bud to Ruth Lucas, 25 June 1962, DCL Collection, L.F.P.
[56] Lucas, Eliza to Ruth Lucas, 30 June 1962, DCL Collection, L.F.P.

Chapter 12. Why must true lovers sigh?

[1] Lucas, Bud to Ruth Lucas, 20 July 1962, DCL Collection, L.F.P.
[2] Lucas, Bud to Ruth Lucas, 20 July 1962, DCL Collection, L.F.P.
[3] Lucas, Bud to Ruth Lucas, 31 July 1962, DCL Collection, L.F.P.
[4] Lucas, Bud to Ruth Lucas, 29 August 1962, DCL Collection, L.F.P.
[5] Lucas, Bud to Ruth Lucas, 27 August 1962, DCL Collection, L.F.P.
[6] Lucas, Bud to Ruth Lucas, 14 September 1962, DCL Collection, L.F.P.
[7] Lucas, Bud to Ruth Lucas, 1 October 1962, DCL Collection, L.F.P.

[8] Lucas, Bud to Ruth Lucas, 16 October 1962, DCL Collection, L.F.P.
[9] Lucas, Bud to Ruth Lucas, 5 November 1962, DCL Collection, L.F.P.
[10] Lucas, Bud to Ruth Lucas, 27 January 1963, DCL Collection, L.F.P.
[11] Lucas, Bud to Ruth Lucas, 27 January 1963, DCL Collection, L.F.P.
[12] Lucas, Bud to Ruth Lucas, 14 March 1963, DCL Collection, L.F.P.
[13] Lucas, Bud to Ruth Lucas, 25 March 1963, DCL Collection, L.F.P.
[14] Lucas, Bud to Ruth Lucas, 1 April 1963, DCL Collection, L.F.P.
[15] Lucas, Bud to Ruth Lucas, 29 July 1963, DCL Collection, L.F.P.
[16] Halberstam at 594
[17] Lucas, Bud to Ruth Lucas, 13 October 1963, DCL Collection, L.F.P.
[18] Lucas, Bud to Ruth Lucas, 24 October 1964, DCL Collection, L.F.P.
[19] Lucas, Bud to Ruth Lucas, 5 January 1964, DCL Collection, L.F.P.
[20] Lucas, Bud to Ruth Lucas, 5 January 1964, DCL Collection, L.F.P.
[21] Lucas, Bud to Ruth Lucas, 10 February 1964, DCL Collection, L.F.P.
[22] Lucas, Bud to Ruth Lucas, 14 March 1964, DCL Collection, L.F.P.
[23] Lucas, Bud to Ruth Lucas, 1 April 1964, DCL Collection, L.F.P.
[24] Lucas, Bud to Ruth Lucas, 5 November 1964, DCL Collection, L.F.P..
[25] Lucas, Bud to Ruth Lucas, 1 February 1965, DCL Collection, L.F.P.
[26] Lucas, Bud to Ruth Lucas, 14 March 1964, DCL Collection, L.F.P.
[27] Lucas, Bud to Ruth Lucas, 26 April 1964, DCL Collection, L.F.P.
[28] Lucas, Bud to Ruth Lucas, 15 September 1964, DCL Collection, L.F.P.
[29] Lucas, Bud to Ruth Lucas, 10 October 1964, DCL Collection, L.F.P.
[30] Timothy Miller, *The 60s Communes: Hippies and Beyond* (Syracuse University Press, 2015), 56
[31] Lucas, Bud to Ruth Lucas, 24 January 1964, DCL Collection, L.F.P.
[32] Lucas, Bud to Ruth Lucas, 5 November 1964, DCL Collection, L.F.P.
[33] *See* Robert A. Caro, *Master of the Senate*, (New York: Knopf Doubleday, 2003)
[34] Lucas, Bud to Ruth Lucas, 25 November 1964, DCL Collection, L.F.P.. This UCLA project would appear to predate what is now generally accepted as "the first" computer dating service, dubbed "Operation Match", started in 1965 by students at Harvard.
[35] Kathleen Kinkade, *A Walden Two Experiment: The First Five Years of Twin Oaks Community* (New York: William Morrow & Co, 1974), 72
[36] Lucas, Bud to Ruth Lucas, 5 November 1964, DCL Collection, L.F.P.
[37] Lucas, Bud to Ruth Lucas, 8 December 1964, DCL Collection, L.F.P.
[38] Lucas, Bud to Ruth Lucas, 25 November 1964, DCL Collection, L.F.P.
[39] Lucas, Bud to Ruth Lucas, 8 December 1964, DCL Collection, L.F.P.
[40] Lucas, Bud to Ruth Lucas, 6 January 1965, DCL Collection, L.F.P.
[41] Lucas, Bud to Ruth Lucas, 1 February 1965, DCL Collection, L.F.P.
[42] Lucas, Frances to Ruth Lucas, 14 May 1965, DCL Collection, L.F.P.
[43] Lucas, Bud to Ruth Lucas, 18 June 1965, DCL Collection, L.F.P.
[44] Lucas, Bud to Ruth Lucas, 9 June 1965, DCL Collection, L.F.P.
[45] Lucas, Bud to Ruth Lucas, 9 June 1965, DCL Collection, L.F.P.
[46] Lucas, Bud to Ruth Lucas, 30 June 1965, DCL Collection, L.F.P.

[47] Lucas, Bud to Ruth Lucas, 4 September 1965, DCL Collection, L.F.P.
[48] Lucas, Bud to Ruth Lucas, 14 September 1965, DCL Collection, L.F.P.
[49] Lucas, Bud to Ruth Lucas, 18 September 1965, DCL Collection, L.F.P.
[50] Amanda Miller, "SDS Chapters 1962-1969", *Mapping American Social Movements Through the 20th Century*, University of Washington, https://depts.washington.edu/moves, accessed 3 September 2022
[51] Lucas, Bud to Ruth Lucas, 18 September 1965, DCL Collection, L.F.P.
[52] Lucas, Bud to Ruth Lucas, 12 November 1965, DCL Collection, L.F.P.
[53] Bud and his brothers would eventually buy the house from the other heirs for $8,000 cash plus 1,000 shares of R. J. Reynolds Tobacco Company stock, an increase over the highest previous offer of $57,000.
[54] Lucas, Eliza to Personal Diary, 4 February 1966, DCL Collection, L.F.P.
[55] Lucas, Eliza to Personal Diary, 5 February 1966, DCL Collection, L.F.P.
[56] Lucas, Eliza to Personal Diary, 16 February 1966, DCL Collection, L.F.P.
[57] Lucas, Bud to Ruth Lucas, 20 February 1966, DCL Collection, L.F.P.
[58] Lucas, Bud to Ruth Lucas, 5 May 1966, DCL Collection, L.F.P.
[59] Lucas, Bud to Ruth Lucas, 20 May 1966, DCL Collection, L.F.P.
[60] The date of 13 May 1965 comes from notes Ruth made on the back of an envelope containing one of Bud's letters: "Tues 12th all well, Wed. did not go Thurs 14th about 2pm still smoldering—bought sp. '35—built Mill 36 & 37."
[61] Lucas, Bud to Ruth Lucas, 23 September 1966, DCL Collection, L.F.P.
[62] Kinkade at 26
[63] Kinkade at 25
[64] Kinkade at 26
[65] Kinkade at 27
[66] Kinkade at 27
[67] Kinkade at 27
[68] Lucas, Bud to Ruth Lucas, 13 December 1966, DCL Collection, L.F.P.
[69] Lucas, Bud to Ruth Lucas, 17 October 1966, DCL Collection, L.F.P.
[70] Lucas, Bud to Ruth Lucas, 13 February 1966, DCL Collection, L.F.P.
[71] Lucas, Bud to Ruth Lucas, 6 January 1967, DCL Collection, L.F.P.
[72] Lucas, Bud to Ruth Lucas, 16 January 1967, DCL Collection, L.F.P.
[73] Lucas, Bud to Ruth Lucas, 21 March 1967, DCL Collection, L.F.P.
[74] Lucas, Bud to Ruth Lucas, 21 March 1967, DCL Collection, L.F.P.

Chapter 13. Leave your home behind you

[1] Lucas, Bud to Ruth Lucas, 20 June 1967, DCL Collection, L.F.P.
[2] Lucas, Bud to Eliza Lucas, 20 July 1967, DCL Collection, L.F.P.
[3] Lucas, Bud to Ruth Lucas, 7 October 1967, DCL Collection, L.F.P.
[4] Lucas, Bud to Ruth Lucas, 17 October 1967, DCL Collection, L.F.P.
[5] Kinkade at 28
[6] Lucas, Bud to Ruth Lucas, 21 October 1967, DCL Collection, L.F.P.
[7] Lucas, Bud to David Lucas, 18 May 1945, DCL Collection, L.F.P.

[8] Kinkade at 160
[9] Lucas, Bud to Ruth Lucas, 9 February 1968, DCL Collection, L.F.P.
[10] Lucas, Bud to Ruth Lucas, 6 July 1968, DCL Collection, L.F.P.
[11] Kinkade at 115
[12] Kathleen Kinkade, 1968. Our population explodes. *The Leaves of Twin Oaks*, (7), 1.
[13] "Communal Living Movement Gains in U.S.", *Alexandria Daily Town Talk*, 13 August 1969
[14] Kinkade at 30
[15] Kinkade at 113
[16] Kinkade at 240
[17] Kinkade at 240
[18] Kinkade at 241
[19] Kinkade at 241
[20] Kinkade at 240
[21] Kinkade at 238
[22] Tamara Jones, "The Other American Dream" (15 November 1998, *Washington Post*)
[23] Kinkade at 105
[24] Jones, note 22
[25] Kinkade at 134
[26] Kinkade at 134
[27] Kinkade at 113
[28] Kinkade at 114
[29] Kinkade at 145; Kathleen Kinkade, 1968. A baby in community. *The Leaves of Twin Oaks*, (7), 3.
[30] Lucas, Bud to Ruth Lucas, 20 September 1968, DCL Collection, L.F.P.
[31] Kinkade at 32
[32] Kathleen Kinkade, 1968. What about the people. *The Leaves of Twin Oaks*, (7), 8
[33] Lucas, Bud to Ruth Lucas, 20 September 1968, DCL Collection, L.F.P.
[34] Lucas, Bud to Ruth Lucas, 29 September 1968, DCL Collection, L.F.P.
[35] Lucas, Bud to Ruth Lucas, 25 October 1968, DCL Collection, L.F.P.
[36] Lucas, Bud to Ruth Lucas, 30 January 1969, DCL Collection, L.F.P.
[37] Lucas, Bud to Eliza Lucas, 29 January 1969, DCL Collection, L.F.P.
[38] Lucas, Bud to Ruth Lucas, 14 February 1969, DCL Collection, L.F.P.
[39] Lucas, Bud to Ruth Lucas, 28 February 1969, DCL Collection, L.F.P.
[40] Lucas, Bud to Ruth Lucas, 24 March 1969, DCL Collection, L.F.P.
[41] Lucas, Bud to Ruth Lucas, 29 March 1969, DCL Collection, L.F.P.
[42] 1978 Custody Litigation, DCL Collection, PDFs, L.F.P., 27
[43] Lucas, Bud to Ruth Lucas, 4 May 1069, DCL Collection, L.F.P.
[44] Lucas, Bud to Ruth Lucas, 29 March 1969, DCL Collection, L.F.P.
[45] Lucas, Bud to Eliza Lucas, 4 May 1969, DCL Collection, L.F.P.
[46] United Press International, "Vietnam War Cost to U.S. Estimated at $108 Billion", *Dallas Morning News*, 29 March 1973

[47] Lucas, Bud to Ruth Lucas, 29 March 1969, DCL Collection, L.F.P.
[48] Lucas, Bud to Ruth Lucas, 25 September 1969, DCL Collection, L.F.P.
[49] William Hinton, "Background Notes to Fanshen", *Monthly Review*, October 2003
[50] Lucas, Bud to Ruth Lucas, 27 July 1969, DCL Collection, L.F.P.
[51] Lucas, Bud to Ruth Lucas, 14 February 1969, DCL Collection, L.F.P.
[52] Lucas, Bud to Ruth Lucas, 14 May 1969, DCL Collection, L.F.P.
[53] Lucas, Bud to Ruth Lucas, 4 April 1969, DCL Collection, L.F.P.
[54] Lucas, Ruth to Eliza Lucas, 17 September 1969, DCL Collection, L.F.P.
[55] Lucas, Bud to Eliza Lucas, 25 September 1969, DCL Collection, L.F.P.
[56] Lucas, Bud to Eliza Lucas, 28 September 1969, DCL Collection, L.F.P.
[57] Lucas, Bud to Ruth Lucas, 12 October 1969, DCL Collection, L.F.P.
[58] Lucas, Bud to Ruth Lucas, 25 September 1969, DCL Collection, L.F.P.
[59] Lucas, Bud to Ruth Lucas, 21 November 1969, DCL Collection, L.F.P.
[60] Lucas, Bud to Eliza Lucas, 20 November 1969, DCL Collection, L.F.P.
[61] Lucas, Bud to Ruth Lucas, 20 December 1969, DCL Collection, L.F.P.
[62] Lucas, Bud to Ruth Lucas, 2 February 1970, DCL Collection, L.F.P.
[63] Lucas, Bud to Ruth Lucas, 8 February 1970, DCL Collection, L.F.P.
[64] Lucas, Bud to Ruth Lucas, 17 February 1970, DCL Collection, L.F.P.
[65] Lucas, Frances to Eliza Lucas, 4 March 1970, DCL Collection, L.F.P.
[66] Lucas, Bud to Ruth Lucas, 1 January 1962, DCL Collection, L.F.P.
[67] Lucas, Bud to Ruth Lucas, 17 February 1970, DCL Collection, L.F.P.
[68] Lucas, Bud to Ruth Lucas, 16 March 1970, DCL Collection, L.F.P.
[69] Lucas, Bud to Ruth Lucas, 17 February 1970, DCL Collection, L.F.P.
[70] Lucas, Bud to Ruth Lucas, 4 March 1970, DCL Collection, L.F.P.
[71] Lucas, Bud to Ruth Lucas, 16 March 1970, DCL Collection, L.F.P.
[72] Lucas, Bud to Ruth Lucas, 16 March 1970, DCL Collection, L.F.P.
[73] Lucas, Bud to Ruth Lucas, 4 March 1970, DCL Collection, L.F.P.
[74] Lucas, Frances to Eliza Lucas, 4 March 1970, DCL Collection, L.F.P.
[75] Lucas, Frances to Pamela Lucas, 18 April 1970, DCL Collection, L.F.P.
[76] Hewson to Ruth Lucas, 4 April 1970, DCL Collection, L.F.P.
[77] Lucas, Bud to Ruth Lucas, 4 April 1970, DCL Collection, L.F.P.
[78] Lucas, Bud to Ruth Lucas, 4 April 1970, DCL Collection, L.F.P.
[79] "Making History: Penland Weaving Institutes, 1929-1938", Hunter Library Digital Initiatives, *Western Carolina University*, accessed 26 March 2022
[80] Lucas, Bud to Ruth Lucas, 4 April 1970, DCL Collection, L.F.P.
[81] Lucas, Bud to Ruth Lucas, 21 April 1970, DCL Collection, L.F.P.
[82] Lucas, Bud to Ruth Lucas, 4 June 1970, DCL Collection, L.F.P.
[83] Lucas, Bud to Eliza Lucas, 15 October 1971, DCL Collection, L.F.P.
[84] Journal, 16 August 1979, DCL Collection, L.F.P.
[85] Lucas, Bud to Ruth Lucas, 6 July 1970, DCL Collection, L.F.P.
[86] Lucas, Bud to Ruth Lucas, 8 July 1970, DCL Collection, L.F.P.
[87] Lucas, Bud to Ruth Lucas, 24 December 1970, DCL Collection, L.F.P.
[88] Lucas, Bud to Eliza Lucas, 10 January 1971, DCL Collection, L.F.P.

[89] Lucas, Bud to Ruth Lucas, 1 February 1971, DCL Collection, L.F.P.
[90] Lucas, Bud to Ruth Lucas, 17 February 1971, DCL Collection, L.F.P.
[91] Lucas, Bud to Ruth Lucas, 25 September 1969, DCL Collection, L.F.P.
[92] Lucas, Bud to Ruth Lucas, 28 June 1971, DCL Collection, L.F.P.
[93] Lucas, Bud to Ruth Lucas, 11 October 1971, DCL Collection, L.F.P.
[94] Lucas, Bud to Ruth Lucas, 3 March 1971, DCL Collection, L.F.P.
[95] Lucas, Bud to Eliza Lucas, 24 March 1971, DCL Collection, L.F.P.
[96] Lucas, Bud to Ruth Lucas, 12 March 1973, DCL Collection, L.F.P.
[97] Lucas, Bud to Ruth Lucas, 29 March 1971, DCL Collection, L.F.P.
[98] Lucas, Bud to Ruth Lucas, 15 May 1971, DCL Collection, L.F.P.
[99] Lucas, Bud to Ruth Lucas, 26 September 1971, DCL Collection, L.F.P.
[100] Catherine Price, *Vitamania: Our Obsessive Quest for Nutritional Perfection* (New York: Penguin Books, 2015)
[101] Lucas, Bud to Ruth Lucas, 26 September 1971, DCL Collection, L.F.P.
[102] Lucas, Bud to Ruth Lucas, 18 September 1971, DCL Collection, L.F.P.
[103] Lucas, Bud to Ruth Lucas, 15 May 1971, DCL Collection, L.F.P.
[104] Lucas, Bud to Ruth Lucas, 29 November 1971, DCL Collection, L.F.P.
[105] Lucas, Bud to Ruth Lucas, 15 January 1972, DCL Collection, L.F.P.
[106] Lucas, Bud to Ruth Lucas, 8 March 1972, DCL Collection, L.F.P.
[107] Lucas at 5-6
[108] Lucas, Bud to Ruth Lucas, 14 April 1972, DCL Collection, L.F.P.
[109] Lucas, Bud to Ruth Lucas, 24 August 1972, DCL Collection, L.F.P.
[110] Lucas, Bud to Ruth Lucas, 10 September 1972, DCL Collection, L.F.P.
[111] Lucas, Bud to Ruth Lucas, 27 October 1972, DCL Collection, L.F.P.
[112] Lucas, Bud to Ruth Lucas, 10 September 1972, DCL Collection, L.F.P.
[113] Lucas, Bud to Ruth Lucas, 1 December 1972, DCL Collection, L.F.P.
[114] Lucas, Bud to Ruth Lucas, 21 December 1972, DCL Collection, L.F.P.
[115] Lucas, Bud to Ruth Lucas, 12 January 1973, DCL Collection, L.F.P.
[116] Lucas, Bud to Ruth Lucas, 12 February 1973, DCL Collection, L.F.P.
[117] Lucas, Bud to Ruth Lucas, 23 May 1973, DCL Collection, L.F.P.
[118] Lucas, Bud to Ruth Lucas, 11 June 1973, DCL Collection, L.F.P.
[119] Lucas, Bud to Ruth Lucas, 29 June 1973, DCL Collection, L.F.P.
[120] Lucas, Bud to Ruth Lucas, 30 July 1973, DCL Collection, L.F.P.
[121] Lucas, Bud to Ruth Lucas, 2 June 1975, DCL Collection, L.F.P.

Chapter 14. Stranger in a strange land

[1] Lucas, Bud to Ruth Lucas, 10 October 1976, DCL Collection, L.F.P.
[2] Lucas, David to "Misty", 30 March 2000, DCL Collection, Other Documents, L.F.P.
[3] 1978 Custody Litigation, DCL Collection, PDFs, L.F.P., 29
[4] 1978 Custody Litigation, DCL Collection, PDFs, L.F.P., 27
[5] Journal, 3 April 1978, DCL Collection, L.F.P.
[6] Journal, 8 April 1978, DCL Collection, L.F.P.
[7] Journal, 9 April 1978, DCL Collection, L.F.P.

[8] Journal, 16 April 1978, DCL Collection, L.F.P.
[9] Journal, 2 May 1978, DCL Collection, L.F.P.
[10] Journal, 12 July 1978, DCL Collection, L.F.P.
[11] Journal, 28 June 1978, DCL Collection, L.F.P.
[12] Journal, 26 July 1978, DCL Collection, L.F.P.
[13] Journal, 16 September 1978, DCL Collection, L.F.P.
[14] Journal, 24 September 1978, DCL Collection, L.F.P.
[15] Journal, 4 October 1978, DCL Collection, L.F.P.
[16] Journal, 6 October 1978, DCL Collection, L.F.P.
[17] Lucas, Ruth to Bud Lucas, 20 May 1979, DCL Collection, L.F.P.
[18] Journal, 18 November 1978, DCL Collection, L.F.P.
[19] Journal, 2 April 1979, DCL Collection, L.F.P.
[20] Journal, 15 April 1979, DCL Collection, L.F.P.
[21] Journal, 27 April 1979, DCL Collection, L.F.P.
[22] Journal, 3 May 1979, DCL Collection, L.F.P.
[23] Journal, 20 May 1979, DCL Collection, L.F.P.
[24] Journal, 21 May 1979, DCL Collection, L.F.P.
[25] Journal, 30 June 1979, DCL Collection, L.F.P.
[26] Journal, 6 August 1979, DCL Collection, L.F.P.
[27] Journal, 12 July 1979, DCL Collection, L.F.P.
[28] Journal, 14 August 1979, DCL Collection, L.F.P.
[29] Journal, 16 August 1979, DCL Collection, L.F.P.
[30] Journal, 26 August 1979, DCL Collection, L.F.P.
[31] Lucas, Ruth to Bud Lucas, 7 August 1979, DCL Collection, L.F.P.
[32] Journal, 21 January 1980, DCL Collection, L.F.P.
[33] Journal, 7 March 1980, DCL Collection, L.F.P.
[34] Journal, 18 April 1980, DCL Collection, L.F.P.
[35] Journal, 23 July 1980, DCL Collection, L.F.P.
[36] Journal, 2 February 1980, DCL Collection, L.F.P.
[37] Journal, 17 January 1981, DCL Collection, L.F.P.
[38] Journal, 12 June 1981, DCL Collection, L.F.P.
[39] 1978 Custody Litigation, DCL Collection, PDFs, L.F.P., 34-35
[40] 1978 Custody Litigation, DCL Collection, PDFs, L.F.P., 40
[41] 1978 Custody Litigation, DCL Collection, PDFs, L.F.P., 33
[42] 1978 Custody Litigation, DCL Collection, PDFs, L.F.P., 35
[43] 1978 Custody Litigation, DCL Collection, PDFs, L.F.P., 36
[44] 1978 Custody Litigation, DCL Collection, PDFs, L.F.P., 42-43
[45] 1978 Custody Litigation, DCL Collection, PDFs, L.F.P., 47
[46] Journal, 28 May 1982, DCL Collection, L.F.P.
[47] 1978 Custody Litigation, DCL Collection, PDFs, L.F.P., 43
[48] Journal, 31 May 1982, DCL Collection, L.F.P.

Chapter 15. New beginnings and new shoots

[1] Journal, 24 September 1982, DCL Collection, L.F.P.
[2] Lucas at 24
[3] See Lucas, Rod to Ruth Lucas, 19 May 1973, DCL Collection, L.F.P.
[4] Lucas, Bud to Ruth Lucas, 24 July 1986, DCL Collection, L.F.P.
[5] Lucas, Donya to Ruth Lucas, 26 June 1987, DCL Collection, L.F.P.
[6] Journal, 15 May 1990, DCL Collection, L.F.P.

Chapter 17. Looking backward

[1] Lucas, Bud to Ruth Lucas, 21 April 1972, DCL Collection, L.F.P.
[2] Miller at 58
[3] Brooks at 13-14
[4] Brooks at 115
[5] A. E. Housman, *A Shropshire Lad*, XIII, verses 1 and 2. The third to last line of the original reads, "But I *was* one and twenty."
[6] Lucas, Bud to Ruth Lucas, 25 May 1945, DCL Collection, L.F.P.

www.ingramcontent.com/pod-product-compliance
Lightning Source LLC
Chambersburg PA
CBHW030334010526
44119CB00025B/385